LANGUAGE OF THE GUN

LANGUAGE
OF THE GUN
YOUTH, CRIME, AND PUBLIC POLICY

BERNARD E. HARCOURT

The University of Chicago Press

Chicago and London

Bernard E. Harcourt is professor of law at the University of Chicago.
He is the author of *Illusion of Order: The False Promise of Broken
Windows Policing*, and the editor of and a contributor to *Guns, Crime,
and Punishment in America*.

The University of Chicago Press, Chicago 60637
The University of Chicago Press, Ltd., London
© 2006 by The University of Chicago
All rights reserved. Published 2006
Printed in the United States of America

15 14 13 12 11 10 09 08 07 06   1 2 3 4 5

ISBN: 0-226-31608-4 (cloth)
ISBN: 0-226-31609-2 (paper)

Library of Congress Cataloging-in-Publication Data

Harcourt, Bernard E., 1963–
   Language of the gun : youth, crime, and public policy /
Bernard E. Harcourt.
      p. cm.
   Includes bibliographical references and index.
   ISBN 0-226-31608-4 (cloth : alk. paper) —
   ISBN 0-226-31609-2 (pbk. : alk. paper)
   1. Juvenile delinquents—Arizona—Tucson—Attitudes.
2. Firearms—Social aspects. 3. Youth and violence. 4. Firearms and
crime. 5. Firearms ownership—United States. 6. Gun control—
United States. 7. Catalina Mountain School. 8. Social sciences—
Philosophy. I. Title.
   HV9105.A68H37 2006
   303.6′0835—dc22

                                                    2005016383

⊗ The paper used in this publication meets the minimum requirements of the American National Standard for Information Sciences—
Permanence of Paper for Printed Library Materials, ANSI Z39.48-1992.

For

Mia Ruyter

and our children,

Isadora and

Léonard

CONTENTS

"I have dirty hands—right up to my elbows. I've plunged them in blood, filth, and shit. Well what?" asks the party leader, Hoederer, in Jean-Paul Sartre's play *Les mains sales* (*Dirty Hands*). "Do you think you can govern innocently?"

There was a time, I confess, when I did. There was a time when I thought we could and should govern innocently—or, more precisely, *scientifically*. Much like Hugo Barine, the tragic figure in Sartre's play who is sent to assassinate the dirty politician, I believed we could study social phenomena empirically, identify causal pathways, and then draw the necessary legal and public policy inferences. I believed law and policy could be—more important, *should be*—governed by social science.

Barely twenty years old, Hugo carried a small pistol tucked away, his finger wrapped firmly around the trigger. He would give the Communist leader one last chance. One last opportunity to redeem himself, to change course, to stop compromising his principles. If that didn't work, Hugo would gun him down like a dog. Young, idealistic, and intellectual, Hugo was confident. He knew he was right. "Politics is a science," he exclaimed to his young bourgeois wife in a moment of exuberance. "In politics, you can prove that you're right and that others are just flat wrong."

Set in 1943, in a small Eastern European country occupied by the German army, *Les mains sales* was a play about a youth coming of age. Hugo did, in the end, use his pistol and kill Hoederer. But by the time he did, he was no longer sure why. Arrested and convicted, Hugo would spend several years in prison struggling day after day to figure out exactly what he had done. Ultimately, confronted with unimaginable political events, Hugo would revisit his youthful idealism and, in the process, infuse his act—the lethal use of his pistol—with new meaning.

Many years later, in the fall of 2000, far away, though also during a time of war—a war against drugs, a war against illegal immigration, a war against an epidemic of youth gun violence—I traveled to the Catalina Mountain School in the Sonoran desert of Arizona to speak with other youths. Youths who, like Hugo, had carried guns and sometimes used them. Youths who, like Hugo, were incarcerated. Youths who, like Hugo, were struggling to make sense of their gun possession and use.

My purpose: To explore the symbolic dimensions of guns and gun carrying among a group of incarcerated male youths in order to better understand and assess the laws and public policies in the United States addressing youths' possession of firearms. To learn from these youths what guns meant to them. To listen as they gave meaning to their acts of gun possession—or, in other cases, to their resistance to guns. To decipher their language of guns. To hear their stories of gun carrying. And, as I soon discovered, to experience firsthand their lust for high-powered semiautomatic weapons—for the 9-mm, the .45, the .38, the Tech-9, the Desert Eagle.

In surprising ways, my Catalina interviews and Jean-Paul Sartre's play became intertwined. This book, like *Les mains sales*, is about coming of age. It is about revisiting one's youthful idealism and, in the process, infusing acts with new meaning. In this book I advocate embracing the paradigm of dirty hands in the field of law and social science—a domain of human inquiry that is very foreign and resistant to the idea. I urge that we acknowledge and render transparent the ethical choices that are embedded in lawmaking and policy making. I advocate that we expose the hidden assumptions about human behavior that underlie our social science methods and that we openly evaluate these assumptions by assessing the price we pay when we decide to believe any one of them. Not, of course, that we lie or cheat or compromise our integrity. That is not the meaning of "dirty hands" that I embrace. What I urge, rather, is that we make explicit the behavioral assumptions that shape our laws and public policies in order to make our ethical choices open and clear.

"Politics is a science," Hugo exclaimed. It is precisely this idea, so commonly applied to law and social science, that we must resist. The very choice of methodological approaches that we take in social science research does not—and more important *cannot*—rest on a *scientific* decision. Methodological traditions in the human sciences—whether phenomenological, structuralist, or practice theory, to name but a few—are not themselves subject to scientific inquiry. The methodological approaches themselves are not falsifiable. There is generally some evidence to support each of the established methodological traditions, and as a result none of them can be *disproved* outright. Yet when it comes to their implications for law and public policy, each tends to lead in a different direction. In this sense the choice of methodological orientation in the field of law and social science is not *itself* a scientific choice. It is, rather, an ethical choice with important distributional consequences for society and the human subject.

This insight—this radical insight, I suggest—destabilizes the field of law and social science. It means that lawmakers and policy makers can no longer proceed in the traditional manner: *from* neutral social science, data collection, and empirical findings *to* lawmaking and public policy analysis. In the past, this was proper form. Researchers conducted an empirical study. They set forth their research methods. They laid out their data and empirical findings. And then they drew the necessary public policy conclusions. The logic was simple. The direction of inference was straightforward. Even the format of the research paper was set ahead of time. But all of that is in doubt if, as this insight suggests, the policy conclusions *themselves* are already shaped by hidden assumptions about human behavior that are *themselves* already embedded in the methodological orientation toward data collection and analysis. The choice of social science approaches and associated methods—whether statistical, ethnographic, survey research, or in-depth interviews—is itself a choice that shapes the orientation of law and public policy.

This insight, though, should not lead us to abandon the project of law and social science. On the contrary, it points to a new form of social inquiry. What it means is that we need to critically appraise the very methodological approaches that we use in the social sciences in order to assess their impact on our laws and public policies. To explore *what it costs* in terms of law and policy when we believe that any one of the methodological approaches is right. How is it that any one approach becomes accepted as truth? How do we come to adopt one particular method in a project of social inquiry? And at what cost? Once we know the answer to these questions, only then can we roll up our sleeves and get our hands dirty. Only then can we make *ethical* choices—*necessarily* ethical choices.

The insight, also, should not lead to empirical paralysis—to an inability to *do* empirical work, to *start* the empirical project. To be sure, the realization is daunting. If the insight is true—and true all the way down—then how can we even get started? Doesn't the very act of approaching an empirical object—a data set, a human subject, a practice—already carry with it assumptions about human behavior that will influence the direction of law and public policy analysis? How do we open our eyes to the empirical world and begin to work?

The answer is to give new meaning to the empirical act. To orient the empirical project specifically on the assumptions embedded in law and policy making. Rather than use the research to *draw* law and policy inferences, use the research to *expose* the assumptions about human behavior that are embedded in the methodological sensibilities and that, as a result, underlie the law and policy proposals. In other words, we must deploy the empirical project to promote transparency. Second, we need to design an empirical method that draws on multiple traditions and brings together qualitative *and* quantitative approaches: to develop a methodological sensibility that integrates the clinical *and* the actuarial, the in-depth interview *and* the multivariate statistical analysis.

My interviews of Catalina youths thus do not serve the traditional function or operate in proper form. They are not the basis on which I draw legal and public policy conclusions. In these pages, the tradition is turned on its head: instead of informing public policy, the Catalina interviews serve to explore, unveil, and dissect the assumptions we embrace when we espouse a particular law or policy. The interviews help answer the more fundamental question of law and public policy: Why do we believe what we do about youths' gun carrying, and at what cost do we believe it? The Catalina interviews also develop and employ an analytic method that integrates in-depth qualitative interviews, an experimental element of free association, map analysis, and a multivariate statistical approach to graphing relations between categorical variables that is called correspondence analysis. As a method of visually representing the associations between qualitative variables, correspondence analysis uses the logic of Pearson's chi-square statistic in computing distances for purposes of graphic representation. The goal of this integrated analytic method is, very precisely, to explore the language of guns among youths, to decipher the symbolic meaning of guns, to explore the relation between systems of meaning and youth gun policies *in order to* shed light on the assumptions about human behavior that shape the various legal and public policy options operating in the landscape of youths and guns.

In the process, this book seeks to reclaim empirical research from the tradition of law and social science: to appropriate it for a new project and give it a different direction. Here the empirical research—the Catalina interviews— acquires new significance. The analysis gives new meaning to the act of social research: no longer the basis of public policy, the research now unveils the hidden assumptions about human behavior that are embedded in law and public policy. This too resonates deeply with Sartre's play *Les mains sales*—a work that, at its core, struggles with the issue of assigning meaning to an act, a gesture, a homicide. Hugo, it turns out, was able to fire his pistol only when he found his young wife in the arms of the Communist leader, Hoederer. Did Hugo fire in a fit of jealousy, or did he fire out of political conviction? This question frames *Les mains sales* and is resolved only, if at all, by Hugo's subsequent acts—acts that attempt to reappropriate the earlier homicide and give it new meaning.

This book proceeds in three parts. Part 1 presents the Catalina interviews in their multiple dimensions. It explores, dissects, contextualizes, and models the language of guns among these youths. It graphically represents the language using mixed quantitative and qualitative methods, but it does not draw any legal or public policy inferences from the interviews. Part 2 then uses the Catalina interviews to unearth and explore the assumptions about human behavior that underlie the four principal methodological traditions in the human sciences: the phenomenological, the structuralist, the practice theoretic, and the performative traditions. As I interpret the Catalina interviews using these different approaches, the interviews themselves shed light on those fundamental assumptions. Part 3 turns to the legal and public policy alternatives concerning youths and guns. Here too the effort is to unearth—by means of the different theories of action the four methodologies embrace—the assumptions about human behavior that are embedded in the law and public policy proposals. Part 3 makes possible an evaluation of the price we pay when we adopt a particular methodological tradition. What are the concrete implications for law and policy? This, then, opens the door to ethical choice: it allows us—or rather it forces us—to get our hands dirty.

This argument, however, is not easy to accept, particularly among those of us who have dedicated so many years to methodological training, to scientific objectivity, to the discipline of the social sciences. Accepting it has taken me several years. So I invite you to take this book slowly, with an open mind and, perhaps, a generous touch. I urge you to quiet your impatience. I ask you to quell your immediate desire for proof. Take off your watch. Come breathe the pure air of the Catalina foothills. Come bask in the warmth of the desert. It is noontime. The sun is at its zenith. Let time stand still.

PART ONE

A SEMIOTIC OF THE GUN

1 CATALINA MOUNTAIN SCHOOL, TUCSON, ARIZONA

The Catalina Mountain School nestles in the shadow of the scenic Catalina Mountain foothills, approximately twelve miles north of Tucson, Arizona. The school is surrounded by the Sonoran desert. Tall saguaros, lanky ocotillos, agaves, palo verde, and low mesquite trees envelop the grounds. A little farther away, several sprawling suburban subdivisions, complete with mini shopping malls, have begun to crop up within three to five miles of the school.

The campus is well maintained and is attractive in its way. It has a sense of order. There are about ten buildings, including the administrative office and several cottages where the students live. The grounds are kept neat, with desert landscaping, and look like a summer camp. Picnic tables, paths, and the sounds of cactus wrens, grasshoppers, and the occasional roadrunner welcome the visitor. The air-conditioned lobby in the administration building provides welcome shelter from the beating sun.

Inside, the students are in uniform, wearing state-issued T-shirts and gray dungarees. They are escorted by security or teaching staff whenever they leave their cottages. Some "upper-level" students who have earned privileges for good behavior are allowed to walk unescorted on the premises, so long as they tell security where they are going. The perimeter of the school is demarcated by tall barbed-wire fencing. A security pickup truck continuously patrols the periphery, driving around and around outside the barbed-wire fence.

The Catalina Mountain School, owned and operated by the Arizona Department of Juvenile Corrections, is home to over 150 boys ranging from twelve to seventeen years old. These youths have repeatedly run afoul of the law, had been warned many times—slapped on the wrist, given probation, served a stint in reformatory—but apparently failed to heed the warnings.

"GLOCK, BERETTA, SMITH AND WESSON"

A confident young man, seventeen years old, enters the air-conditioned cinder-block administrative office turned interview room. He closes the door and seats himself in a plastic folding chair across the scarred conference table from me. I assign him his confidential number, CMS-66. I turn on a tape recorder. He says he is from the north side of Tucson, a more affluent part of town. He says he was taking predental classes at a community college before coming to Catalina and had earned twelve credit hours. He says he has been incarcerated here for about three months on a gun charge. He explains that he had been on intensive probation for assault and marijuana use and previously served time in juvenile detention for possession of a firearm—a Glock .40, a powerful and relatively expensive semiautomatic pistol.

I show CMS-66 three color pictures of handguns taken from articles in the *American Handgunner* magazine. The first gun is an HS 2000 full-sized 9-mm semiautomatic service pistol from I. M. Metal of Croatia. It is made of polymer that looks like black plastic, and it closely resembles a Glock or a SIG 9-mm. The second gun is a Para-Ordnance P-14 LDA. This is a full-sized .45-caliber semiautomatic pistol with a five-inch barrel and looks like a classic Beretta or Ruger .45 semiautomatic. The third gun is a Smith and Wesson .45 Colt CTG revolver—the traditional .45-caliber revolver.

CMS-66 looks at the pictures. He is not in any rush. He seems to be enjoying this. In a cool, nonchalant voice he says, pointing to each picture in turn as he speaks, "Glock, Beretta, Smith and Wesson" (CMS-66, 4).

CMS-66 knows his guns. The first picture of the HS 2000 9-mm pistol he says resembles the Glock .40 he used to carry. "Looks kind of like the gun I had . . . [I]t had the plastic thing, but mine had an extended clip for law enforcement and looked kind of like this. It didn't have this fishtail" (CMS-66, 5–6). The other guns he learned about from his father and his older friends. His dad collected guns. He had a Dan Wesson .357 revolver, a Smith and Wesson .44 revolver, and an SKS (Samozariadnyia Karabina Simonova) assault rifle. His dad, he tells me, taught him to respect guns. "He was really into safety courses. He . . . kept his guns locked up and kept 'em out of my hands. He never let me play with them. He said, when we went out shooting, he said 'You don't touch till I give it to you. If you realize it's loaded, don't point it toward anybody. Even if it's not loaded. You never know, you could slip and not think, it could cost a life. Never point it toward anybody. Never do anything like that'" (CMS-66, 6–7).

The way CMS-66 tells it, he received the Glock .40 for Christmas when he was fifteen years old. His best friend—who was about five years older—gave it to him. "He got it brand new in the box," CMS-66 says. "With two clips, one was the extended clip, and the real bad thing about the gun, he gave it to me with Teflon bullets. You know what those are? You know, armor-piercing . . . But I got rid of those and I gave them back. I don't plan on shooting anyone with a bulletproof vest. So he can keep them. That was his thing" (CMS-66, 11).

His friend's "thing" was the drug trade. CMS-66 started hanging out with the older teenager at about age thirteen, near the time when his father died. His friend was about eighteen then and was selling small amounts of cocaine. CMS-66 was being raised by his mother, and the older friend took CMS-66 under his wing and helped support them both. "He took care of me. He gave my mom money," CMS-66 explains. The source of the money, though, was drugs. CMS-66's friend had started selling crack and slowly progressed to larger amounts of powder cocaine. CMS-66 stuck with his older buddy and soon started getting to know other dealers. "You know, we're right next to the Mexican border, so you start meeting people who are, like, big drug cartel down in Mexico. And there's my friends, they were just getting really big . . . They were always taking me under their wing. 'We'll always take care of you.' 'You're like our little brother.' Like big brother types you know. I was always with these people. Whatever they did, I wanted to do. Whatever they were doing, I was doing" (CMS-66, 10).

The older friend encouraged CMS-66 to go to school and make a life for himself. "He bought me books all the time, and he'd pay for my books at school and pay for a couple of writing classes and a math class," he recalls. "He paid for them. He was always encouraging me" (CMS-66, 10). But it wasn't easy. "I didn't like working at Blackjack Pizza and all of that. So I'd hook a couple of people up, 'Hey do you need an ounce of coke to make into crack?' 'Yeah.' 'I can get it.' Raise the price a little bit, pocket a hundred bucks" (CMS-66, 10).

His friend gave him the Glock .40 for protection when they were hanging out together. Protection for CMS-66, in case things heated up, but also protection for his friends. An extra gun could always come in handy. "They were just, like, 'Hey, you're safer with it.' They all had guns, you know . . . I think they felt more safe if I had it, that's just one more person, you know, in case. You know, the main worry was . . . there's professional people who just rob drug dealers and that was the thing. They'll kick down your door. If there's seven of them and only a couple of his friends and me, just one more person with a piece makes a person safer" (CMS-66, 23).

CMS-66 claims he was careful with his gun. Safety was deeply ingrained in him, not only by his father but also by his friends. "I never played with it," CMS-66 stresses. "I was always real instilled with 'Don't play with it; it's not a toy, leave it under the seat in case you need it. Don't play with it, don't show it to people'" (CMS-66).

Armed with his Glock .40, CMS-66 began to live two lives. He had one life with his friends in the drug trade. They liked guns. They would carry. They needed to carry. When he was with this crowd, "all my friends were packing. Everybody's packing. If you're not packing, you're on the losing end, everybody has a piece there, you know" (CMS-66, 17). But he had a separate life at school, a life disconnected from drugs, guns, and the street. "School was always separate from everything that was going on in my life . . . [E]veryone was always saying, 'You're a really smart kid.' I was in gifted and talented. School was always something that I was doing no matter what, that always was more important, that always stayed aside from everything I was doing in my life" (CMS-66, 16). Two worlds. Two lives. In his own imagination, they were separate. "I kind of lived a double life. I was like this good kid in school, did his homework, then once I left school, I'd go hang out with these other people" (CMS-66, 16).

CMS-66 started community college at seventeen. His peers there were less impressed by guns. "One friend that I was getting a ride home from Pima [with], he seen me take [my gun] out of my waist and put it under the seat. He was just, 'Whatever man, just keep it away from me, man'" (CMS-66, 9). "He kinda acted different about it. He asked me about it, 'Why do you have it?' 'Just for protection.' I was kind of embarrassed as to the people I was hanging around with, as to the college community, you know . . . So I was always acting different around the college. I'd leave it in my car, try to leave it alone" (CMS-66, 23).

CMS-66 was on high-intensity probation when he got busted for the Glock .40. He had been adjudicated for assault at school at age thirteen, and later he tested positive for marijuana while on probation, which is how he ended up in the JIPS (Juvenile Intense Probation Services) program. He was almost sixteen when the police pulled him over while he was driving. They searched the car and found the Glock under his seat.

What does CMS-66 think about guns today?

> People need to understand that guns are dangerous, you know, people need to understand that they're a *very* dangerous thing. In the wrong hands, they're deadly. But you know, they're not a toy, and you know you shouldn't have them around, knowing your kids. Even myself, I'm still a child; I shouldn't be possessing guns. Maybe when I'm twenty-one, maybe taking a firearm safety course . . . I think it's good that there are strict laws to monitor who has guns and who doesn't. Even though they're not really enforced

that much, you know, a lot of people have guns who shouldn't. You know what I'm saying? There should be more laws to enforce exactly who has guns. (CMS-66, 5)

CMS-66 was arrested and incarcerated for possessing the Glock .40. He served his time for the handgun but now he is incarcerated again. A parole officer came to his house and found a shotgun in his room.

THE SEDUCTION OF GUNS

"Glock, Beretta, Smith and Wesson." CMS-66 is proud of his knowledge. He wants to impress me. He also wants to reassure me. He's had safety training; he knows how to handle guns. At the same time, he can hardly contain himself, he is so taken by the pictures of the guns. The fishtail, the extended clip, the plastic thing—these facets are sources of such intense fascination, curiosity, fixation, and *desire*.

I interviewed thirty youths at the Catalina school and, more than anything, was deeply struck by their fascination with guns, their attraction to firearms. The interviews revealed rich sensual, moral, and political-economic dimensions of guns and gun carrying among the youths. For them, guns have a powerful sensual, almost sexual, dimension.

I began all the interviews by displaying the three pictures of guns from the *American Handgunner*—the 9-mm, the .45-caliber semiautomatic, and the Colt .45 revolver—and offering a free-association prompt: "What are you thinking about?" A few of the youths expressed visceral opposition to them. Several conveyed their deep dislike for guns, calling them "dumb" (CMS-53, 5), "stupid" (CMS-69, 5), or "pussy shit" (CMS-4, 16). "Anybody can fight with a gun, anybody can pull a trigger," a seventeen-year-old European American youth contended. "It takes somebody, like a real man, to fight somebody" (CMS-53, 5).

But many more were filled with lust. For them the very sight of the handguns inspired a deep sense of awe and desire. They would fixate on the photos and, with slight laughter or giggling or quiet moaning, manifest a kind of lust for the guns. Many of the youths wanted to shoot the guns, or at least touch them. Most were hooked, deeply attracted to the pictures of guns. In response to three photographs and the simple free-association prompt ("What are you thinking about?") many youths answered that they just liked guns, pure and simple.

"They're cool. I want to play with them. I want to go out and shoot them" (CMS-4, 3). "Guns are nice. They just, I don't know, I just, I just like guns a lot"

(CMS-46, 5). "I would like to have one of these . . . I always want, I always like, I always like guns . . . Yeah, I always like to have one" (CMS-6, 6–7). "I want to go shoot them. I want to see how they handle" (CMS-3, 8). "They look tight. They look nice" (CMS-10, 3). "They're nice-looking guns" (CMS-17, 7). "I kind of like how they look. I just want to go shoot them" (CMS-43, 6). "Those are some tight guns. I like them. I like the way they look" (CMS-13, 5). "I love guns. Hell, yeah, I love guns. [I love] everything about a gun" (CMS-62, 9). "Those are some pretty tight guns" (CMS-16, 5). "I think they're cool. I like them. They're nice. Someday I want a gun collection" (CMS-25, 16). "[Smiling] It's just tight right there . . . I like it . . . It's just tight like the way it looks. The way you can shoot. Those can shoot, like, ten rounds, huh? But they get jammed a lot. I had one" (CMS-21, 8–9). "I'd say they look pretty tight . . . They look cool" (CMS-7, 5).

It is difficult to express in words the richness of emotions the pictures evoked in these youths. It is tempting to invoke psychoanalytic terms—notions of a deep drive for pleasure of the same magnitude and somehow connected to a sexual drive. CMS-10, a seventeen-year-old Mexican American gang member, recounted his experience with his favorite guns in these subliminal terms: "I had me two baby nines. I fell in love with those. They look beautiful to me. They were chrome, like, perfect size, they had some power to them. I was, like, damn, I really don't use them because I don't want to get them burned. Somebody's body to it. I have them at home on a shelf, I don't really use those. Those [are] just, like, I'm gonna keep those for a long time . . . They're, like, tight. They're just all chrome" (CMS-10, 35).

Guns can be deeply seductive objects of desire. They hold a surprisingly powerful and passionate grip over many youths. The intensity of the attraction in some cases is remarkable. As a sixteen-year-old Yaqui youth tried to make me understand, "I like guns. I like 'em. It just gives you a rush. Gives me a rush" (CMS-65, 22). "Everybody likes guns these days, dude," another youth said. "Hell, yeah. They're exciting. I mean what the hell. You feel powerful when you have a gun. You get respect" (CMS-62, 11). Similarly, the intensity and sexuality of their opposition to guns, for the few who are repelled by them, is striking. To them, guns are "pussy shit" (CMS-4, 16), they're for "pussies" and "wimps" (CMS-2, 6). Real men do not need guns.

At the same time, carrying a gun has a strong moral dimension to many youths. Most of those I interviewed associated guns with a form of aggressive, preemptive protection, and many felt self-righteous about the need for protection. They felt morally entitled in the much the same way that many adults speak of their right to carry arms in self-defense. A Mexican gang member, raised in Los Angeles, protested in indignant terms that when he and his gang peers were carrying guns for protection they wouldn't even think of not using them. "We don't choose not to [use guns] because it's either our life or their life" (CMS-10, 23). Another youth, seventeen years old, said, "It's either them shoot me and kill me and my family being all depressed and quiet or just try and protect myself . . . I'd rather have my life" (CMS-48, 27).

In other cases, youths invoked notions of "enemies" and conceptions of warfare. Guns, for them, were about getting back, seeking revenge in gang rivalries. A sixteen-year-old Yaqui gang member, who lived on the Pascua Yaqui reservation, told me: "I know when I have my gun, that's when I'm going after people. I'm not doing it to defend myself. I'm doing it because I want to kill somebody else. I want to shoot somebody else" (CMS-65, 19). For some youths, guns are all about "shooting at my enemy" (CMS-10, 5).

Youths' gun carrying also has an economic dimension. For many, handguns have important exchange value. They represent a commodity to be traded or sold for cash or drugs. A seventeen-year-old Mexican American youth reported: "We used to get in robbing houses that have a lot of guns, and trade 'em for pounds or ounces of cocaine or just sell them . . . Living close to the border, guns are very valuable to the drug dealers. If you know the right people, you can get good deals for a gun" (CMS-14, 7). Guns were a commodity to him, and he was making a market. A sixteen-year-old African American youth similarly associated guns with their exchange value. He had sold a number of guns in his short life on the streets. "That's what I had guns for. I sold them all the time" (CMS-31, 14). A seventeen-year-old Mexican American youth said, "I just have guns to sell them. Make some money off them. That's actually what they're for" (CMS-48, 8). For these youths, guns represent a special commodity that allows them to become self-reliant, to become entrepreneurs.

THE LANGUAGE OF GUNS

The Catalina interviews revealed a rich set of experiences with guns. The vast majority of the Catalina youths I interviewed—twenty-six, or 87 percent of them—had possessed guns at some point in their lives. And the firearms they carried were often high-caliber semiautomatic pistols. The 9-mm is, in the words of a seventeen-year-old Tucson youth, "the size of the moment" (CMS-43, 20). "It's just going to be more powerful," a seventeen-year-old student impatiently explained, "and it's kind of just gonna go pretty much right through you" (CMS-21, 26). Or, as a seventeen-year-old gang member stated, semiautomatics "look nicer," they're better "if you want to let off quick rounds," and "they'll just put a hole in somebody's ass" (CMS-16, 29, 6).

As a result of this rich set of experiences, I was able to decipher in the interviews a distinct language of guns with at least three registers—clusters of ways of talking about guns, connected groups of linguistic associations with guns. The first register I call the "action/protection" cluster. In this register the male youths associate guns with the need for protection and the desire to live a risky, dangerous, active life—to live in the fast lane. In this cluster, youths talk about the power of having or brandishing a gun, the risks of dying in a gun-fight, the fear of getting caught and going to jail. This cluster is tinged with desire, with a deep attraction to guns. Its linked associations reflect an "action" motif.

In this cluster, guns are perceived as dangerous yet attractive, necessary for aggressive, preemptive protection, powerful and power giving. Despite the fact that—or perhaps because—guns are perceived as instruments of death, the youths value them for their power, for their ability to control their immediate environment. Guns are attractive and eroticized because they confer control. "If somebody is doing something I don't like and I point a gun at them, they'll stop," one youth said (CMS-4, 17). Guns mean being able to get what you want, do as you please, and protect yourself. "If you're doing a drug deal, you want to have a gun to, like, 'Yeah, I'm strapped,'" another youth explained. "So I'm going to go in, and do this, and then I'm going to get out of there. And if they try and trick me and pull a gun, I have a gun. So, somebody is going to get shot, and hopefully it's not you" (CMS-2, 28). The different symbolic meanings in the action/protection cluster help give context to each other. The very idea of attraction is linked to the danger of guns. In this first cluster of meanings, it is the action, the danger, the death—the risk of being caught and sent to jail—that makes guns attractive and powerful.

A second register connects two associations: commodity and dislike. I refer to this as the "commodity/dislike" register. The close association of the two meanings again helps to give them context. Viewing guns as a commodity is more often associated with disliking guns than with attraction to them. This is reflected well in the comments of one seventeen-year-old Mexican American youth. "I don't like them," he volunteered. "They take a life. Why you gonna be taking a life for? Ain't no good." But he had guns. Why? "I just have guns to sell them. Make some money off them. That's actually what they're for . . . I sold them, just buy me my clothes or buy some jewelry or something . . . Just, like, Guess clothes, Tommy Hilfiger, and then jewelry . . . hats, glasses, stuff like that" (CMS-48, 8).

The Catalina interviews reveal a close association, above average, between the sentiment of dislike and treating guns for their exchange value. They suggest an intriguing feature about the way some of these youths think about gun possession—an entrepreneurial, free-market way. It may be, in fact, that it is precisely because they are not enamored of guns that they are willing to part with them and sell them. Or it may be that the commodification renders them less attractive. In either event, the emotion of dislike is closely associated with the economics of guns.

A third register connects the idea of guns as recreational equipment with the felt need to "respect" guns, as well as with conceptions of guns as tools for self-defense or for suicide. This cluster suggests an association between using a gun for hunting, target practice, or personal defense and treating guns with respect. I refer to this as the "recreation/respect" register. This association is reflected in individual comments like that of a seventeen-year-old European American youth who was brought up with guns and enjoys target practice with his family: "I respect [guns]," he emphasized. "I might carry one. But I won't go around telling everyone, 'Yeah, I got a gun. Let's go do something. Let's go shoot in the desert. Yeah, I can shoot better than you. Yeah, I'm a sharpshooter, yeah I can do this, I can shoot thirty yards away and still hit dead center.' I don't brag about that. I know I could do it, that's the end of it" (CMS-17, 28).

These registers capture the main clusters of associations that the youths make with guns. Interestingly, the clusters cohere in some contexts and fragment in others. One of the more dramatic findings from the interviews, for instance, is that the three registers line up neatly with different carrying statuses. Youths who carry guns frequently or constantly tend to talk about guns in an action/protection way. Youths who carry guns less frequently tend to talk about them in the recreation/respect register. And youths who carry them even less frequently, or who do not carry at all, tend to associate guns with the commodity/respect cluster. In other words, youths' viewing guns as dangerous *and* attractive coincides with higher reported carrying. It suggests that the element of danger and death is a positive attraction and an important element in gun carrying. While in more conventional thinking this connection might be associated with less carrying, among these youths at the Catalina Mountain School the danger of guns is more closely associated with gun possession. They go together and give meaning to each other. They do not necessarily *cause* each other: it is not that danger and attraction cause gun carrying or that gun carrying causes youths to claim that guns are dangerous and attractive. Rather, they go together, and their association helps us to interpret each one. Their association infuses each with meaning.

How the clusters coalesce, fragment, and regroup in various practice contexts says a lot about what they mean and how to interpret them. There is, for instance, a perceived need among at-risk youths for aggressive, preemptive protection—a perception that is strongest among those youths who are more likely to be carrying guns and participating in gang activities. The self-protection meaning is central to gun carrying, to gang membership, but is also important to youths who are incarcerated on gun infractions. It sticks to the youths who carry—in and out of the reform school. It holds on tight to the imagination of the most dangerous youths. It defines the youths who carry more and simultaneously gives an identity or meaning to the act of carrying guns.

In this sense, it is crucial to explore how the different discourses of guns are associated within different environments (gang membership or youth incarceration, for example) in order to analyze how the contexts give meaning to the discourses—and vice versa, how the discourses give meaning to contexts. This is the task in part 1 of the book. Chapter 2 describes the process of selecting the Catalina youths, interviewing them, coding the interviews, and graphically representing the interview findings. The chapter is somewhat technical, and some readers may wish to move ahead to chapter 3, which explores in more colorful detail the symbolic dimensions of guns among the Catalina youths. The chapter sets forth the nineteen primary meanings associated with guns and youths' gun carrying. Chapter 4 then examines how these primary meanings relate to each other—how the meanings cluster into groups of meaning that help inform the interpretation of the youths' responses. The chapter also presents the three principal registers of gun talk, which represent, in effect, the three primary and idealtypic clusters of meaning. Chapter 5 explores how these clusters coalesce and fragment in different practice contexts. Finally, chapter 6 offers a glimpse of the sensual, moral, and political dimensions of guns and gun carrying among the Catalina youths.

2

A ROAD MAP OF THE CATALINA INTERVIEWS

I went to the Catalina Mountain School to explore how this select group of incarcerated young males talk about guns, to discover what guns mean to them, to probe the symbolic and emotional dimensions of guns, to better understand youths' gun carrying. The goal of the interviews was, very precisely, to conduct a semiotic analysis of the gun: to explore the language of guns among youths, to analyze youths' voices in relation to gun experiences, to decipher the symbolic meaning of guns. I wanted to tap as directly as possible into their perceptions, beliefs, and practices surrounding guns. I wanted to get inside the structure of meanings that gives significance to firearms. It is, of course, never possible to enter another person's interpretive framework completely—the task itself is so highly problematic—but my goal was to understand the youths' language of guns and structure of meanings *as well as possible*. I wanted to focus microscopically on the gun, to chart all the webs of meaning, and to analyze how they relate.

SELECTING THE CATALINA YOUTHS

I chose the Catalina school because I wanted to speak with youths who had a lot of firsthand experience with guns. Research consistently reveals that male youths in detention acknowledge the highest level of gun carrying among school-aged youths.[1] A 1991 study by Joseph Sheley and James Wright (1995) of 835 male juveniles in correctional facilities in four states—California, Illinois, Louisiana, and New Jersey—found that 86 percent had owned at least one firearm at some point in their lives. Seventy-three percent of the inmates had owned three or more types of guns (1995, 40). A 1995 study of 42 male juvenile offenders detained at five facilities in metropolitan Atlanta found that 41 (97.6 percent) had owned handguns at some point in the past (Ash et al. 1996, 1755). A RAND study conducted in 1998, involving interviews with 34 youthful offenders aged sixteen and seventeen detained in the Los Angeles Juvenile Hall, revealed that 75 percent had been threatened with a gun at least once, and 66 percent had been shot at at least once (Goldberg and Schwabe 1999, 11, 12). In contrast, though still high, carrying rates among the regular high school population are much lower. For school-aged male youths generally, rates of gun carrying range from about 5 percent to 35 percent depending on the study, geography, and survey instrument (Page and Hammermeister 1997, 505–6). The high end comes from the 1991 study by Sheley and Wright (1995), which also surveyed 758 male students in ten inner-city high schools (1995, 40, 43).

Consistent with this research, the Catalina interviews revealed high rates of gun carrying. Although the vast majority of the Catalina youths (twenty-two of them, or 73 percent) were *not* incarcerated on gun-related offenses, twenty-six (87 percent) had possessed guns at some point in their lives. Twenty-three (77 percent) had carried one or more guns on their persons. And nineteen of the youths (63 percent) had what I would consider to be significant histories of gun possession and carrying. In other words, most of the Catalina youths had firsthand and in most cases extensive personal histories with firearms.

I also chose the Catalina school because I wanted to speak with those youths who are, in the public imagination, the "superpredators." These are youths who had violated social rules repeatedly, to the point of being sent to a correctional facility for a long time. But they are also youths who are going to return to their homes or home institutions, to their friends, and to their neighborhoods when they reach their majority. In other words, they are going to be reintegrated into society. The Catalina youths fit this description well. Each one of them had repeatedly run afoul of the law for second-tier crimes such as burglary, robbery, auto theft, drug possession and sale, firearm possession, criminal damage, running away, or curfew violations. Each one had been warned, some several times, but had failed to heed the warnings. These Catalina youths had not, however, been convicted of the most violent offenses, such as murder, for which they would automatically have been transferred to the adult system, treated as adults, and sentenced to terms extending into their majority. The youths at the Catalina Mountain School represent, in this sense, a certain stratum of high-risk youths: the "worst" juvenile offenders, who will be freed when they turn eighteen.

I decided to interview thirty Catalina youths. In order to conduct thirty interviews, I sought consent from the parents or guardians of seventy students out of the total population of 158 at the Catalina Mountain School. I sought consent for so many because there was high student turnover at the school and because I expected many parents or guardians to refuse. From my conversations with teaching, security, and administrative staff, it was clear that a significant number of students rotated in and out of the school. One of the teachers said that about five youths in his cottage of about twenty students (Crossroads) would be leaving the week I would begin my interviews. Moreover, on the first weekend that I went to the school to obtain parental consent, the parents of thirteen juveniles refused. In addition, some of the students listed as being at the school were in fact at a state mental health institution or otherwise unavailable.

I used systematic random sampling to select the seventy youths. My purpose was not, I should emphasize, to obtain a representative sample in order to generalize the empirical findings to youths in America, or to youths in Arizona or even in Tucson, or for that matter to the complete group of youths at the Catalina Mountain School. Thirty interviews is obviously not an adequate sample to generalize from—and it is important to keep that in mind throughout the research. But I did want to avoid selection bias as much as possible. I wanted to avoid choosing, for instance, only youths whose parents visited them or, even more conveniently, only wards of the state, youths with no parent. I wanted instead a random mix of youths at Catalina—a group that reflected the age, ethnic, and family diversity of the school.

To perform the systematic random sampling, I obtained from the administration an "alpha report"—an alphabetical list of all the juveniles detained at the school. The six-page report listed a total of 158 male youths. I selected a name on the list at random and then went through the list, highlighting every tenth name on the alpha report until I had seventy names. Whenever I reached the end of the list, I then counted to ten from there, scrolling back to the top of the list (without skipping names that had already been highlighted). I continued in this way, scrolling through the list four times until I had highlighted seventy names.

I then sought parental or guardian consent for those seventy youths in three ways. First, I tried to obtain consent from those parents who visited their sons at regular visitation times. Parents may visit on Saturdays from 8:00 to 11:00 a.m. and 12:30 to 3:30 p.m. and on Sundays from 8:00 to 11:00 a.m. I spoke with the selected parents as they signed in near the visiting area. I informed them of the nature of the project and of the confidentiality of the research and told them that participation was entirely voluntary and strictly confidential. Second, for the youths who were wards of the state, I contacted the youths' caseworkers at child protective services at the Arizona Department of Economic Security and sought approval directly from them. Third, I sent letters to the parents who did not visit and asked them individually for their consent. In these ways I was able to obtain thirty-one parental/guardian consents out of seventy, and I interviewed the first thirty juveniles for whom I had obtained consent.[2]

Parental consent, though, was only one small layer of the approvals necessary to conduct this research. Getting permission for this type of research has become today a trial by ordeal. Because the research involves interviewing youths from twelve to seventeen about matters that may give rise to criminal liability, I had to seek approvals all the way from the juveniles themselves, their parents, and the local correctional facility to the federal government in Washington, DC. For this research I had to obtain, among other things, site approval from the Arizona Department of Juvenile Corrections in Phoenix, Arizona (obtained on March 9, 2000), institutional review board approval from the University of Arizona Human Subjects Committee in Tucson, Arizona (obtained on May 23, 2000), as well as a Certificate of Confidentiality from the United States Department of Health and Human Services in Washington, DC (obtained on August 8, 2000). In addition, I of course had to get consent from the juveniles themselves. Each youth was informed of the nature of the project and of the confidentiality of the research. They were all advised that participation was entirely voluntary. No money was offered. Strict confidentiality was assured at the beginning of the interviews and repeatedly discussed during the interviews whenever any of the youths asked or seemed concerned. All the youths who were interviewed agreed to participate, and both they and their parents or guardians signed consent forms.

The age, family, demographic background, and criminal charges of the thirty Catalina youths I interviewed are detailed in table 2.1. As the table demonstrates, the youths ranged from fourteen to seventeen years of age. Four were wards of the state. The largest ethnicity was Hispanic: thirteen of the youths identified themselves as Hispanic, with some combination of Mexican, Mexican American, and Puerto Rican. Twelve of the youths identified themselves as Anglo and gave a variety of national origins. Three identified themselves by Native American tribe—two as members of the Pascua Yaqui tribe and one as Shoshone. And two said they were African American. The charges that ultimately brought them to the Catalina Mountain School ranged from auto theft, robbery, and burglary to parole violations for substance abuse and gun possession.

It is practically impossible today to get research access to youths, especially to talk about such risky topics as firearms, which could elicit incriminating admissions. This accounts in part for the limited number of interviews I was able to conduct. The original research design included three other sites. The first was the JIPS (Juvenile Intensive Probation Services) program, a high-intensity supervision program for juveniles on probation. The second and third were two public high schools, one in what would be considered the inner city area of Tucson and one in a wealthy neighborhood in the Catalina foothills. The original research design thus included 120 interviews. I was not able,

TABLE 2.1. *Age, family, demographic background,*
and criminal charges of the Catalina youths

ID	AGE	GUARDIAN	ETHNICITY (SELF-IDENTIFIED)	GRADE	CURRENT CHARGE
CMS-2	16	Mother and father	White (Irish, Italian)	9th	Burglary first degree of armed residence (including Mac-90, M-16)
CMS-3	16	Mother and stepfather	Hispanic, Puerto Rican, Spanish, Italian	GED	Intimidation, domestic violence, criminal damage, alcohol, runaway
CMS-4	17	Mother and father (military)	White (Italian, southern)	GED	Domestic violence, threatened intimidation
CMS-6	17	Mother and older sister	Mexican	10th	Drug use
CMS-7	17	Mother	White (German, Russian)	GED	High-speed chase, endangerment
CMS-8	17	Ward of the state	White (Irish)	GED	Grand theft auto (GTA)
CMS-10	17	Mother (never knew father)	Mexican (born in Mexico)	GED	Violation of probation (burglary, robbery, trespassing)
CMS-13	15	Mother and father (military)	Black	9th	Firearms, GTA, and burglary
CMS-14	17	Mother and father (ex-military)	Mexican American, Mexican, Italian, Native American	GED	Burglary, drugs, violation of JIPS
CMS-16	17	Mother	Mexican and one-fourth Pascua Yaqui	Drop-out	Car theft, possession of marijuana and crack cocaine
CMS-17	16	Mother; did not know father; has stepfather	White (English, German)	10th	Absconding on parole (car theft), runaway
CMS-21	14	Ward of the state	Mexican	8th	GTA, criminal damage, burglary, curfew, alcohol, lying to police
CMS-22	17	Father; mother also lives with him	Mexican American	Drop-out	Assault on corrections officer and on other inmates

(continued)

TABLE 2.1. *(continued)*

ID	AGE	GUARDIAN	ETHNICITY (SELF-IDENTIFIED)	GRADE	CURRENT CHARGE
CMS-23	16	Mother; father out of state	White (Italian)	9th	Absconding parole (burglary)
CMS-25	17	Mother	White (Scottish, German)	10th	Sexual misconduct with a minor
CMS-31	16	Mother and father	African American	11th	Violating probation (concealed weapon and never at home)
CMS-34	16	Mother and father	Mexican (born in Mexico)	9th	Stealing cars
CMS-37	15	Ward of state	Mexican and Native American (Shoshone)	9th	Assault, disorderly conduct, weapon (knife)
CMS-39	16	Mother and father	Hispanic, Puerto Rican, Mexican	GED	Gun possession
CMS-40	17	Ward of state	White (German, Scottish), [and a bit Native American]	GED	Absconding from placement and GTA
CMS-43	17	Grandparents; father deceased, mother out of state	White (Irish, German)	12th	Burglary
CMS-46	17	Mother and father	Hispanic	10th	Possession of marijuana and DUI
CMS-48	17	Mother and father, but father was in prison	Mexican American	9th	Absconding from placement
CMS-53	17	Mother; father deceased	White (Irish, Norwegian)	11th	Assault and weapons misconduct
CMS-54	16	Mother	Mexican American	7th	Theft of firearms
CMS-62	17	Mother and father	Mexican American	10th	Parole violation (illegal substances, alcohol and marijuana, violating curfew) on original charge of robbing liquor store
CMS-65	16	Mother and father	Pascua Yaqui	9th	Aggravated assault with deadly weapon
CMS-66	17	Mother; father deceased	White (Dutch, German)	Pima College	Possession of shotgun
CMS-69	16	Mother and father	White	9th	Burglary
CMS-70	15	Mother and father	Mexican	9th	Possession of deadly weapon

though, to get approval from the administrative office of the courts, which oversees the JIPS program, or from the other schools. The administrators at the Catalina Mountain School, in contrast, were eager to encourage research on juveniles and opened their doors to me.[3] This accounts in part for the number of interviews, but it is also what makes these Catalina interviews unique.

In addition to interviewing the Catalina youths, I also conducted formal, indepth interviews with over a dozen officers, administrators, and participants in the juvenile justice system in Tucson in order to get to know the institutions and practices that would be familiar to the youths. I interviewed, among others, Commissioners Karen Adam and Hector Campoy of the Pima County juvenile court in Tucson; Robert L. Tucker, superintendent of the Catalina Mountain School; Captain John Leavitt of the Tucson Police Department; Teresa Godoy, supervising attorney in the gang unit of the Pima County prosecutor's office; Clint Stinson, an attorney with the Pima County prosecutor's office at the juvenile court; Connie Corcoran, a probation officer at the Pima County juvenile court; Sergeant Kirk Simmons of the Tucson Police Department, who is in charge of the Gang Resistance Education and Training (GREAT) program; Officer Steve Huber, who is assigned to supervise students at the Magee Middle School in Tucson; and Special Agent Jim Molesa of the Drug Enforcement Agency, stationed in Tucson. I also conducted participant observation at the Pima County juvenile court, observed Officer Huber's GREAT class at Magee Middle School in Tucson, and attended the court-ordered Firearms Awareness Safety Training program in Tucson, for young gun offenders at the Pima County juvenile court.

INTERVIEWING THE CATALINA YOUTHS

Interviewing people about the symbolic meaning of an object is doubly complicated. Layers of meaning—the meanings of the questions and the meanings of the answers, the meanings of the answers and the meanings of the guns—are stacked on top of each other. Interviewing for meaning is in this sense an exercise not only in constructing meaning from a discourse but also in mining those meanings to infer and discover other meanings—here, the symbolic meaning of the gun. In order to address these concerns, I approached the thirty interviews in the tradition of interviewing as a form of discourse. From this perspective, the interview is not just a clinical set of stimuli and responses but is itself a search for meaning, where two parties are jointly constructing the meaning of the questions and answers, and where these meanings are themselves contextually grounded (see generally Mishler 1986, 52–65).

I began each interview with an experimental free-association prompt. After a few short questions concerning the youths' age, ethnicity, criminal record, and institutional history, I would show them three color pictures of handguns taken from articles in the November–December 2000 issue of the *American Handgunner* magazine. The three handguns, described earlier, were an HS 2000 full-sized 9-mm service pistol from I. M. Metal of Croatia, a .45-caliber Para-Ordnance P-14 LDA, and a Smith and Wesson .45 Colt CTG revolver (see figs. 2.1 to 2.3).

FIGURE 2.1. *Picture of an HS 2000 full-sized 9-mm service pistol from I. M. Metal of Croatia. Made of polymer that looks like black plastic. Closely resembles a Glock or a SIG 9-mm (Photo courtesy of* American Handgunner *magazine, November–December 2000, 60; www.americanhandgunner.com)*

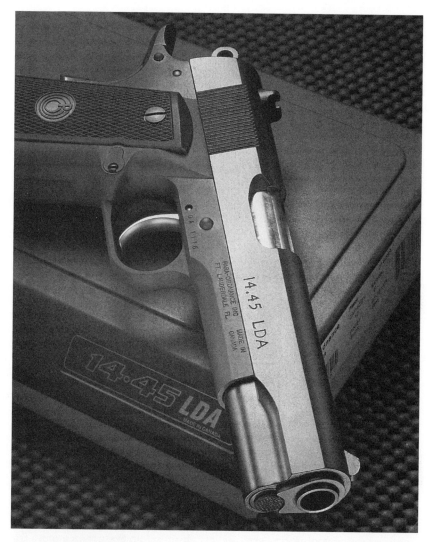

FIGURE 2.2. *Picture of a Para-Ordnance P-14 LDA. A full-sized .45-caliber pistol with a five-inch barrel (Photo courtesy of* American Handgunner *magazine, November–December 2000, 42)*

Before giving the Catalina youths much time to place the pictures within the interview context, I would ask each one, "What are you thinking of right now?" I would then follow up by further free-association prompts such as, "What are the first experiences these guns remind you of?" and "What do these guns make you think of?"

FIGURE 2.3. *Picture of a Smith and Wesson .45 Colt CTG revolver (Photo courtesy of* American Handgunner *magazine, November–December 2000, 68)*

By starting with free association and allowing the Catalina youths to tell stories about guns, the interviews focused more directly on the *youths'* associations—on the contexts within which they relate to guns and on the meanings they associate with them. The free-association approach offers better access to the youths' concerns, beliefs, desires, and fears than a more traditional approach (see generally Hollway and Jefferson 2000, 152, 36–37). Free association, of course, has its roots in psychoanalysis and is also closely linked to Gestalt theory (see Kris 1982; Hollway and Jefferson 2000, 36). My use of free association, however, is guided more by the idea of interviewing as discourse. By letting the interviewees lead the discussion through free association, the interviews more naturally focused on the webs of meaning that the youths associate with guns. In addition, by starting with free association, I hoped to avoid tainting the interviews with prior discussion of, for instance, their reasons to carry guns or their parents' views on firearms. Using photographs as an experimental device also helped mediate the discussion about meaning. Although an interview is never a natural setting, using pictures helped create a more concrete situation. It helped give life to our discussion. It made the guns slightly more real.

After the first free-association prompts, I would then ask a number of other questions about gun carrying, peer practices, and gun sources that also provide insights on the question of social meaning. I would ask the youths about their history of gun carrying and use, about situations where they or their friends had used guns, about sources of firearms, about policies intended to deter gun carrying, and about their contacts with the police. I asked them to tell me incidents involving guns that they had witnessed or heard about: situations where they or a friend had used a gun, or had not but wished they had. This part of the interviews was semistructured: the interviews followed a protocol in order to address similar sets of questions, but at times, to improve the flow of the conversation, I would modify the order of the questioning or probe different areas. Most questions were intentionally open-ended, and I used follow-up questions to probe the answers.

Throughout, I used a mixed interview technique that included not only direct open-ended questions but also comments intended to elicit additional information. I found it important to multiply approaches, given that meanings are so deeply ingrained, so far beneath the surface of consciousness. I therefore included interview by comment—such as expressing puzzlement or bewilderment at the youths' responses, replaying comments to elicit further elaboration, and making evaluative and other comments (see generally Snow, Zurcher, and Sjoberg 1982, 292–304).

The interviews were conducted during the two-week class recess at Catalina Mountain School in the fall of 2000. Conducting the interviews during this short period reduced possible contamination. Before the formal interview, I would ask each youth whether he had heard about the project, and although some said they had heard about it from their parents, only one said he had heard about it from a fellow student. On further probing, it was clear that he had not learned much about the research and had not been contaminated in any way by the little he had heard.

The interviews were conducted in a conference room in the school's administration building. The door to the room was closed during the interviews, creating a private atmosphere. Each student was informed of the purposes of the research, of the risks of participating in the interview, and of the confidentiality of the answers. Each student was asked for his consent to be interviewed and signed a written consent form. Each was also strenuously told about the importance of being truthful. After the long process of obtaining informed consent, the length of the interviews depended on how talkative the youths were. Most had a lot of experiences to share and were not shy. These interviews lasted about an hour and a half—a long time for an adolescent to stay focused on one topic. A small group of youths, however, were more taciturn and inhibited, and the shortest interview lasted forty-five minutes. On average, the interviews lasted one hour and ten minutes. Each of the Catalina youths was assigned a number ranging from CMS-1 to CMS-70, based on the earlier random sampling. During the interviews, their names were never used, and their identity was not revealed at any point. The interviews with the thirty youths were tape-recorded and later transcribed by two assistants.

CODING: MAP ANALYSIS

Identifying meanings is undoubtedly one of the greatest challenges that researchers face in a project like this one (see generally Emerson, Fretz, and Shaw 1995, 108–41). A common fallacy is to impose our own categories or outside categories on the subjects or to present completely static taxonomies. This is particularly tricky during coding. It is important to "pay close attention to how members themselves characterize and describe particular activities, events, and groups . . . [and to] listen closely to what members say in the course of their ordinary activities about what something 'was about' or what import an occurrence has for them" (Emerson, Fretz, and Shaw 1995, 114). The key is to try to figure out as well as we can how the subjects actually relate meanings to each other, how they classify meanings themselves, so as to get a better purchase on those categories and their relationships.

To address these concerns, I used a combination of open and focused coding. First, I used open coding to try to glean all the potential analytic meanings. At this first juncture, I was interested in meaning categories "less as a way to sort data than as a way to name, distinguish, and identify the conceptual import and significance of particular observations" (Emerson, Fretz, and Shaw 1995, 151). At this stage I coded a wide range of meanings. After identifying these categories, I then conducted more focused coding. At this second juncture, the idea was to use "fine-grained, line-by-line analysis of the [interviews]" in order to locate the meanings and determine their relationships (Emerson, Fretz, and Shaw 1995, 160).

A wide range of techniques are used in the social sciences for coding textual matter, the most popular being content analysis. Content analysis focuses on how frequently terms are used in a text or a set of texts. Basically, it simply counts the number of times a particular word, concept, or cluster of words is used in identifiable texts. By comparing the number of uses and their distribution, it offers insight into modes of discourse and the substance or content of texts (see generally Weber 1984; Fan 1988; Roberts 1989). The problem with content analysis is that it does not pick up on the relation between terms. It focuses exclusively on the particular concept identified and does not address the relations *between* concepts.

Another broad class of procedures, usually referred to as "map analysis," specifically addresses the relational aspect of concepts. Map analysis refers to a group of coding methods that includes cognitive mapping, relational analysis, and meaning analysis, among others. The focus of map analysis is on "networks consisting of connected concepts rather than counts of concepts" (Carley 1993, 78). It compares texts in terms of both concepts and the relation between concepts. Thus, "where content analysis typically focuses exclusively on concepts, map analysis focuses on concepts and the relationships between them and hence on the web of meaning contained within the text" (Carley 1993, 77–78). Map analysis can take a number of approaches toward relationships, focusing either on the proximity of concepts (for example, whether they are in the same sentence), on the linguistic relation between concepts (emphasizing the sequential story relationships), or on the meaning of the relationships (focusing on their conceptual nature). Under the third approach, the relationships can be categorized into different attributes of strength (the intensity of the relationship), sign (positive or negative relationship), direction (who or what is the subject, who or what is the object), and type (possession, friendship, etc.) (Carley 1993, 92–108).

As Kathleen Carley points out, a large number of choices need to be made when coding—choices about concepts, level of analysis, generality of concepts or relationships, and so forth. In this project I have opted for three related levels of meaning, which I have called primary, secondary, and tertiary. Primary meanings are the ones the youths have at the forefront of their imaginations and that they themselves seem to believe in and apply to guns. These are the meanings they volunteer when prompted through free association—when asked what they are thinking about when they look at the photos or what experiences the photos make them think of. These are the meanings they repeat or emphasize and seem most wedded to. I generally coded only free-association responses in this category unless another meaning that developed during the course of the interview was repeated and emphasized. Secondary meanings are meanings that the youths seem to believe in and are aware of but that they rattle off without much emphasis when pushed further on why they would carry or own a gun, or when prompted on the benefits of having a gun. They express these without much emphasis. They are cognizant of them, but no more. I generally coded these secondary meanings in the interview only after I had finished the free-association prompts. Rarely, I coded a meaning articulated during the free-association prompt as secondary if it was rattled off in a banal and unmeaningful way. Tertiary meanings are meanings the youths attribute to other people—to their parents, to their friends, to people in the street. So if they say, for instance, "My friends think guns are stupid," this would be coded as a tertiary meaning. The respondent is cognizant of the meaning and uses it but attributes it to someone else.

Because of the complexity of these relationships, and because of the need to reconstruct meaning fragments or to imply meaning, computerized techniques are less useful. As others have noted, computer programs are less powerful and accurate when the research is trying to extract information that is only implied in the text: "The search procedure to explicate implicit information has been one of the central problems faced by researchers in artificial intelligence who are interested in locating the deep structure or complete understanding of texts" (Carley 1993, 88). This work needs to be done manually. As a result, I personally did the coding by hand.[4]

CORRESPONDENCE ANALYSIS

I then used correspondence analysis to graphically represent and interpret the relationship between these primary meanings in different youth contexts. Correspondence analysis is a method of visually representing the associations between different categorical variables. Its primary goal is to "transform a table of numerical information into a graphical display, facilitating the interpretation of this information" (Greenacre 1994, 3; Weller and Romney 1990). It is not a method of testing a hypothesis, although it does draw on the logic of Pearson's chi-square statistic in computing distances for purposes of graphic representation. Correspondence analysis is most often used to portray data for visual inspection and analysis rather than to test statistical significance (see generally Blasius and Greenacre 1998).

Correspondence analysis is far more familiar to researchers in Europe and Japan than in the United States. It is referred to under various names and may be familiar to readers under another name, most commonly canonical analysis, principal components analysis of qualitative data, optimal scaling, multidimensional scaling, or, in French, *analyse factorielle des correspondences* or *analyse des données* (Weller and Romney 1990, 14). The reason there are so many terms for correspondence analysis is that the method was invented on several occasions in several countries. Although it was popularized in the early 1960s by Jean-Paul Benzécri in France under the name *analyse des données*, the algebraic formula underlying the method was developed as early as 1935 and independently redeveloped in the 1940s (see generally Greenacre and Blasius 1994, viii; Weller and Romney 1990, 14; van Meter et al. 1994).

Much of the contemporary impetus for correspondence analysis traces to Pierre Bourdieu and especially to his attempts to relate social and cultural realms—practical contexts and social meanings. This effort is most clearly reflected in his two seminal works, *Distinction: A Social Critique of the Judgement of Taste* ([1979] 1984) and *Homo Academicus* ([1984] 1988). Both of these texts are exemplary not only in relating the duality of practice and culture but also in utilizing correspondence analysis as a way to present the relationships. In *Distinction*, for example, Bourdieu explores the social dimension of judgments of taste by closely analyzing the relations between social and cultural space. Bourdieu's thesis is that social space—the structure of classes and class distinctions created by differences in education, employment, wealth, age, sex, and parental occupation, among others—shapes and is itself in part constituted by cultural space, the structure of preferences in music, painting, and the arts. To understand either, it is critical to explore both and especially to decipher how they relate to each other. It is in the shared space of social attributes and cultural preferences that we can begin to understand how socially structured relations of taste are formed.

Similarly, in *Homo Academicus*, Bourdieu explores the social field of the French academy and uses correspondence analysis to relate the various academic disciplines and the status of academicians to the upbringing, education, and socioeconomic background of academics and their parents (Bourdieu [1984] 1988, 42–50). By means of the graphic display of the relations between these variables, Bourdieu is able to represent, in a measured way, his interpretation of the social space of the French faculties. Bourdieu explains his interest in correspondence analysis this way:

> To account for the infinite diversity of practices in a way that is both unitary and specific, one has to break with *linear thinking*, which only recognizes the simple ordinal structures of direct determination, and endeavour to

reconstruct the networks of interrelated relationships which are present in each of the factors. The structural causality of a network of factors is quite irreducible to the cumulated effects of the set of linear relations, of different explanatory force, which the necessities of analysis oblige one to isolate, those which are established between the different factors, taken one by one, and the practice in question. (Bourdieu [1979] 1984, 107)

For these reasons, Bourdieu is a strong advocate of correspondence analysis. It is, in his words, a technique of data analysis "which 'thinks' in terms of relation, as I try to do precisely with the notion of field" (Bourdieu and Wacquant 1992, 96; see also Breiger 2000, 94; van Meter et al. 1994, 131–33).

There are two ways to understand correspondence analysis: geometric and algebraic. The geometric approach is easier to explain. In essence, correspondence analysis takes a contingency table of rows and columns—where rows (for example, persons) and columns (for example, meanings of guns) index different types of phenomena—and represents all rows and columns as points in a single "space" of some number of dimensions (often two). The location of each row is a function of the tendency for that item to have its own distribution across columns. Conversely, the location of each column-point in the "space" is a function of the tendency of that property to be manifested with differential likelihood by each of the row items. In this sense the underlying logic is that the rows "are" the columns and vice versa.

The mathematical computation is based on singular value decomposition, which is used to break down a rectangular matrix into a smaller number of common factors. In more technical terms, singular value decomposition "factors or decomposes a matrix into row and column structures together with the associated singular values, as a vehicle for the derivation and computation of metric scaling in a variety of forms" (Weller and Romney 1990, 15; see generally Blasius and Greenacre 1994, 53–78; Weller and Romney 1990, 17–26 and 55–70).

In simplified terms, from the geometric perspective, correspondence analysis can be described as a process in three parts. In the first step, it takes a contingency table (a two-by-two table of categorical variables) and norms the cell entries by row proportions and weights. In other words, it turns the row entries into percentages (row profiles) and then weights these by the relative mass of each row in relation to the total number of observations. This places all cells on a comparable metric in relation to each other. In step two, it plots these entries in multidimensional space using these weighted cell values to determine vector points for each row and column. When it does this, it does not use Euclidian distance but instead uses "chi-square distance." This makes sure that the multidimensional space reflects distances in relation to what one would expect if the contingency table had been completely random. In step three, it reduces the dimensionality to two dimensions. Using weighted least squares, it finds the plane that captures and explains as much of the multidimensional distribution as possible. It then produces a two-dimensional graph—a "correspondence map"—that visually represents the contingency table. If the two primary dimensions explain a lot of the variation, this two-dimensional graph may explain, say, 75 or 90 percent or more of the inertia—the spread of the vector points in multidimensional space (see generally Greenacre 1994, 8–17; Greenacre 1993).

We then have to interpret the correspondence map. There are various ways of doing so. One approach is to interpret the dimensions by associating with each dimension those row and column labels that seem most expressive of it. Pierre Bourdieu uses this first method (see, e.g., Bourdieu [1979] 1984, 260–64; Bourdieu [1984] 1988, 40–62). Another approach has to do with the angle and location of the points with respect to the center (or origin) of the graph. Leo Goodman has written extensively on this second method (see, e.g., Goodman 1996, 1997). In this project I employ the first method and focus primarily on how certain categories give meaning to the dimensions of the correspondence maps.

Correspondence analysis is not without its critics. Some argue that it is model-free or theory-free insofar as it does not test hypotheses. It is often criticized for being "merely descriptive" (Breiger 2000, 95, describing, but not endorsing, the criticisms; see generally van Meter et al. 1994, 134–35). Its proponents, however, claim this is a virtue. It is a method that lets the data speak without imposing any preconceptions. The guiding principle is that "the model must follow the data and not the reverse" (Greenacre and Blasius 1994, viii; van Meter et al. 1994, 134). Naturally, other statistical methods, such as log-linear modeling, can be used to complement correspondence analysis once hypotheses have been formulated.

The distinct advantages of correspondence analysis, then, are these: The method is relational and allows us to visualize the full structure or system of relationships. Instead of dealing with one variable and its effect on the variable to be explained, it represents the full gamut of variables and their interrelations. It also allows us to represent the duality of practice and culture. As Breiger explains, "A great deal of the popularity [of correspondence analysis] with structural analysts and practice theorists alike derives from its ability to portray two types of entity . . . in the 'same' space" (Breiger 2000, 99). Correspondence analysis is particularly appropriate to studying the duality of meanings and practices because it allows us to visually represent the web of meanings and practices. It holds constant routine associations and portrays only those that are "above average." It shows us how the categories are inter-related in different contexts.

3 SYMBOLIC DIMENSIONS AND PRIMARY MEANINGS

Primary meanings are the spontaneous, unfiltered first reactions, the immediate thought that comes to mind when a youth sees a gun. These are the primary meanings I am looking for—probing the thirty Catalina youths, experimenting with their immediate reactions, listening carefully to their words, watching their expressions. In order to get as close as possible, I use three pictures of guns—two semiautomatics and a classic revolver—and offer free-association prompts. "What are you thinking?" "What experiences do these guns remind you of?" "What do these guns make you think of?" The very first response, the immediate utterance, is what I consider the primary association. And the interviews reveal a wide range of primary meanings. As I openly code the interviews, I discover nineteen.

PROTECTION AND, SEPARATELY, SELF-DEFENSE

The most frequent association with guns is protection in an aggressive, preemptive manner. Under this rubric, guns are seen as a way to avoid being victimized in everyday encounters with other youths—to avoid getting "jumped," being "punked," or being "disrespected." Of the thirty youths interviewed, almost half, fourteen to be exact, mention "protection" as a primary association in discussing guns, and five of these repeatedly refer to "protection." This is, not surprisingly, very consistent with other research on juvenile gun possession.[5]

What is particularly interesting about the notion of "protection" that I identify—and code as "protection"—is how it differs from the more conventional meaning of self-defense—which I identify and code separately as "self-defense." The latter notion appears as a primary meaning in only three interviews. It signifies something very different: the need to have a gun to defend yourself against an armed intruder or robber in a conventional setting. Under the "self-defense" rubric, youths mention the need to have a gun if they own a nice house or car. A sixteen-year-old Anglo youth incarcerated at the school on a charge of burglary says, "If I had my own house I would [want a gun] . . . But I wouldn't carry it around with me. I'd leave it in the house" (CMS-69, 13). Another youth states that a lot of people use guns "in the right ways." When prompted he explains, "Mainly for protection against, if somebody's going to shoot you, of course you should have protection, protect yourself, like police do" (CMS-8, 8). Another sixteen-year-old looks at the picture of the Smith and Wesson .45 Colt revolver and—after saying that it is "nice looking"—indicates that he would "use this to protect your house, have it sitting under your mattress and stuff, easy to reach, just in case someone comes in" (CMS-17, 7). "I think [guns] come in handy, living in big cities like Tucson or Phoenix, you know, if you have a nice car and nice house," one youth tells me. "Maybe have a gun in your house or in your car, registered, or whatever you do to make it legal. Just for protection I guess for when somebody tries to rob you. Keep it locked up for the kids" (CMS-14, 8). These youths are referring to a more conventional, adult, or propertied rationale for owning a gun, for keeping a gun under your mattress. They are referring to a traditional notion of *passive* self-defense, of protection from a stereotypic intruder or burglar.

This is not, though, the notion of protection that dominates the interviews. Instead, many more of the youths speak about guns as offering protection from everyday encounters, from getting "jumped," "punked," or "disrespected"—a daily, constant threat. Carrying a gun and having a reputation for doing so helps prevent being victimized. As a fifteen-year-old African American youth who purchased a Ruger .22-caliber pistol from a friend for $150 recalls, "My momma always said that guns, they bring trouble automatically. I don't know. I guess it was true. But I still had to protect myself whether it did or not. *Trouble come automatically when you don't have a gun*" (CMS-13, 26).

Gun carrying is a *preemptive* measure against victimization. "Strap," which is the slang term most frequently used to refer to guns in the interviews, means "protection." A sixteen-year-old school dropout who carried all the time explains that "strap" refers to "the sheriff's holster." To call a gun a "strap" is to say that it's "just for protection." "Because," he says, "if out there you don't have a strap, you're going to get killed. Because fools shoot at you and you don't have a gun, what are you going to do? Are you just going to sit there and party? Hell, no. What are you going to do? You going to run? You're going to get shot in the back. That's pretty much why I had a gun" (CMS-2, 12).

In this sense, gun possession is often part of an identity youths try to project to avoid being victimized. CMS-16 is a good illustration. This seventeen-year-old Mexican Yaqui youth began carrying a gun when he was eight or nine, hanging out at the neighborhood park, which was an open drug market, and holding drugs for older dealers. He joined a gang very young and began carrying, he says, to protect himself from his peers. "When I was younger, I used to kick with those fools, and I was looking, 'There's a bad mother fucker right there. Look at that shit. Nobody fucks with that fool.' And in the movies, 'Man, that's a bad mother fucker.' And I just wanted to be a bad mother fucker . . . Like, nobody, nobody crosses him" (CMS-16, 35). He wanted to be a "bad mother fucker" precisely so that no one would mess with him, no one would punk him. And he needed to carry this identity at all times. He needed to carry it in a pre-emptive way, to ensure that he would not be harassed. "Fools just always trying to start shit with you," he explains. "Everybody always trying to, like, I don't know, kinda like trying to, like, punk you, or whatever . . . Like, tell you, or just punk you, like, 'Fool, you ain't this, you ain't that, blah, blah, blah . . .' And then, when you, probably especially when you're younger, that's when you got to fight back the most, because you got, once you start a reputation, you got to keep it, I guess. If you start off as being, getting punked and stuff, it's not good. Cause then everybody tries to punk you. And then if you, and then one day, somebody's punking you and you get tired of it, and you scrap them, then it's like, it's looked at as being forced into a fight. Like, you were forced to fight. Like, even though you beat him up, you, like, still fool you were forced to fight, you didn't fight that fool on your own . . . If you get a reputation for being forced to fight. That's a bad, that's a bad thing" (CMS-16, 35–36).

Protection, for many youths, turns precisely on this idea of not being harassed, intimidated, or "punked." The youths at Catalina offer a number of accounts of situations where they carried guns to protect themselves in this way. CMS-13, a fifteen-year-old African American gang member, carried guns constantly, in part because he likes them—"I like the way they look," he tells me, "just tight for you to have one of those guns for yourself" (CMS-13, 6)—but also for protection. He felt he needed to carry a gun "because there's, like, certain people I had problems with. I wasn't looking for problems, just people that I felt in danger, I guess. I'd go certain places and I'd get into it with certain people. Certain threats that don't feel right with you . . . Threats of other people having guns, threats of me getting shot at, stuff like that" (CMS-13, 13). So he carried a gun whenever he left his home. "If I went to clubs or whatever. Anywhere away from my house. I feel as if when I step out of my house I'm in danger of anything happening to me. So I would take it anywhere" (CMS-13, 16).

This notion of being punked is also closely tied to gang membership. One gang member who has seen a lot of action explains: "You earn your respect in a gang by not being a little punk. Don't get punked by other people" (CMS-10, 35). In fact, your willingness to fight back, to fend off being punked is often a symbol of being a true gang member. CMS-10 reports that young gang members are often tested by their own gang to make sure they are the kind of gang-banger who will stand up for the neighborhood. The gang will test the young member by sending an older gang member—an "OG"—whom the young member doesn't know. "So we send them to hit you up, about five of them, and you're by yourself . . . Tell you, 'Where you from, what gang you from?' And you tell them the neighborhood and they act like they gonna jump you and you go at it, then you know you got our respect. But if they hit you up and tell you 'Where you from?' and you see all these guys and you don't want to get jumped, you be, like, 'nowhere' and they'll fuck you up cause you not representing the neighborhood" (CMS-10, 35–36).

CMS-3, a gang member and drug dealer, carried a gun to protect himself primarily from other youths and friends who, he believed, wanted to steal his drugs. His carrying was intimately related to his criminal activity (drug dealing) and was done in an aggressive way. When asked how often he carried a gun, CMS-3 says, "Sometimes I would sleep with a gun. It just depends where I was at" (CMS-3, 29). If he was at home, he would not worry about carrying a gun. But when he was dealing drugs, he would always pack a gun for his own protection. "I remember, I was staying with this girl, I was on the run, I was in this apartment complex, and I was selling drugs and a lot of people there wanted to jump me for my drugs," he recalls. "There was a lot of friends that wanted me for my drugs. If I was just going to get a soda, I would carry a gun. And at the house I was at, there was a lot of dopies there too. A lot of drug addicts there. I remember if I was in the bathroom, I remember I would have my gun right there. You can't trust nobody" (CMS-3, 29).

CMS-39 is another gang member, sixteen years old, of Puerto Rican and Mexican descent, who started carrying guns when he was thirteen. He turned to carrying after being stabbed in the back in a gang-related incident. "It's just that I've got a lot of friends that have been shot by guns myself," he tells me. "When you are without [guns], you're, like, all you got is your hands. A lot of people aren't above that anymore, so they just rather shoot you and get it over with" (CMS-39, 5). In this sense, gun carrying is often closely associated with aggressive, confrontational, and sometimes delinquent behavior. The idea is that you have to be violent in order not to be the victim of violence, and that you often have to actively participate in the violence or even provoke it. In other words, the claim of self-protection is often intentionally associated with being involved in high-risk activities like gangs, drugs, or other crime. This may explain in part why most research shows that "weapon-carrying among youth appears to be more closely associated with criminal activity, delinquency, and aggressiveness than to purely defensive behavior" (Page and Hammermeister 1997, 506).

CMS-37, a fifteen-year-old ward of the state who had been cycled through at least a dozen group homes, states that he got a gun specifically to protect himself after an incident when he was fourteen. He and a friend who was a gang member were walking in a residential neighborhood in Tucson when two other youths walked up to them and asked, "Hey, fool, do you remember me?" The two then began shooting at CMS-37 and his friend. CMS-37 ran and was unhurt, but he promptly went to get himself a gun from another friend who was about eighteen. This older friend had several guns at his home and gave him a .45-caliber pistol to hold. CMS-37 subsequently bought several guns—including a 9-mm and a .22 pistol—from this same friend, who apparently had gotten his stash from his stepfather (CMS-37, 11–17).

Not surprisingly, for many of the youths, especially those who associate guns with protection, carrying a handgun makes them feel safer. They feel less anxious, less threatened. Guns make these youths feel "more calm" and "less paranoid" (CMS-13, 18). In their own words, "I feel more safe" (CMS-39, 17). And feeling safer, many of them believe, will mean that fewer people get hurt—that the risk of harm to themselves and others decreases.

"What do the guns make you think of?" "Just having them for, like, protection or, like, if someone shoots at me, of course if anything I'm going to shoot back" (CMS-21, 10). "I use them for protection" (CMS-70, 4). This notion of protection, in an aggressive, preemptive way, as a form of deterrence along the lines of "mutually assured destruction," is the association with guns most commonly held among these thirty youths. One youth, a sixteen-year-old gang member with a significant history of carrying, expressed the very logic of those policies. "For me the benefits are good but in a negative way. For me they're good cause if I don't have a gun and they have a gun, they're gonna pull it on me easier. But if I have a gun, and they have a gun, they're gonna kind of look out for their selves too cause they'll know that I have just as much power as they do with the gun. Cause I can shoot it just as fast. So they'll be, like, 'Oh,' but if I don't, I'm there helpless, so what could I do, hit 'em? If I have a gun I feel more safe. Most of the time, I feel safer" (CMS-39, 23).

DANGER AND, SEPARATELY, DEATH

Guns also symbolize danger to many youths—the danger of their going off by accident and hurting, or even killing, a young sibling or friend. Under this rubric, guns are associated with accidents, injuries, and mistakes that sometimes are fatal. Fourteen of the youths, in two cases repeatedly, associated guns with this notion, which I coded as "danger." One, a seventeen-year-old European youth of Irish descent, on being shown the photos, immediately thought of the time he accidentally grazed his toe with a .38. He used to take his guns apart and clean then and would try to do it blindfolded. "When I was about twelve. It barely grazed my toe. I got lucky. I've had guns go off in my house by accident. I've had my friend fire guns in the house by accident" (CMS-8, 7).

CMS-3, a sixteen-year-old Hispanic gang member with a long history of carrying guns, is very candid about this association when presented with the pictures of guns. He first laughs and says he wants "to go shoot them." When pushed further ("What else?"), he reflects and then says: "Guns sort of remind me of death . . . Whenever you see a gun there's always someone being shot at or something with the gun" (CMS-3, 8). The first experience the guns make him think of is precisely along these lines. "My freshman year [of high school]. We were at a kegger," he recalls. "We were getting drunk and, um, this guy was being stupid with this gun and he had a gun and he was trying to show off with it. He was just shooting around, fucking [around], he was being an idiot . . . We ended up having to beat him up because he was being stupid, like, he almost shot this girl. He was being real stupid, and he was real drunk . . . We just kicked his ass and took his gun . . . We didn't like try to pull a jack, we weren't trying to steal his gun. We were just getting pissed because he was being stupid" (CMS-3, 9).

In this sense, guns are often symbols of danger. Like CMS-3, several other youths say they like guns but express concern about the danger. "They look nice, but they're dangerous," says a sixteen-year-old Mexican youth (CMS-34, 4). "Like, they're, they look nice and everything. They can do powerful stuff, but, like, they're dangerous, cause I have two of my homeboys. One of my homeboys who shot his sister," he goes on. "He was just playing with it. He didn't know that, like, a bullet was there. He didn't have the clip but he didn't know a bullet was in there. He was playing with it and he shot her in the head" (CMS-34, 16).

CMS-53, a youth of Irish and Norwegian descent, has a similar reaction to the pictures: "Dangerous . . . You could get killed by them, get in trouble for them . . . A couple of my friends got shot . . . [M]y friend got in a fight with this other guy and he beat this guy up and he ran in his house and got a gun and starting shooting at our car when we were taking off" (CMS-53, 5). He immediately adds, free-association style, "There's guns in my house. My dad was a border patrol agent, and he had a bunch of guns" (CMS-53, 5). CMS-54, a

Mexican American youth, states: "Dangerous, I mean . . . they're not good for anybody, you know what I'm saying? Cause even, I don't know how to explain it, but if I could go back in time, I would never started getting into guns or any of that stuff" (CMS-54, 5). For CMS-46, a seventeen-year-old Hispanic youth who was raised around guns, guns are dangerous and need to be "respected" (CMS-46, 6).

It is worth noting that there are two senses of danger in play—one an idea of accidents and injuries, the second a more direct notion of "death." I coded the second "death" and found it in fewer interviews. About five youths talked about guns in this second sense. One youth, CMS-8, on being shown the photos, reacted with, "They're pretty deadly" (CMS-8, 6). Similarly, CMS-23, a sixteen-year-old who carried a .22, a .44, a .38, and a .45, first associates guns with "people getting killed," "drive by shootings," and the fact that guns "take someone's life" (CMS-23, 4–6). Under this second meaning, the idea is a direct connection to death. Guns are black; they are about dying. They smell of death.

ATTRACTION, DISLIKE, AND RESPECT

The youths articulate strong emotional responses to the pictures of the guns, many of them expressing desire and attraction or dislike and repulsion and some a respect for guns. I label these responses "attraction," "dislike," and "respect."

We've already heard the youths talk about attraction. "Guns are nice . . . I just, I just like guns a lot" (CMS-46, 5). This is a refrain, a recurring theme. Fifteen of the youths—half of them—reacted to the pictures of guns with immediate, spontaneous desire. I coded these as a primary association of "attraction." Several others responded with desire that was more muted but nevertheless identifiable. Here are representative excerpts of passages I coded as a primary association of "attraction," taken verbatim from the transcripts: "I want to go shoot them . . . Yeah, I want to see how they handle" (CMS-3, 8). "I would like to have one of these" (CMS-6, 6–7). "I'd say they look pretty tight. They look cool" (CMS-7, 5). "They look tight. They look nice" (CMS-10, 3). "Those are some tight guns. I like the guns on there" (CMS-13, 5). "Those are some pretty tight guns" (CMS-16, 5). "It's just tight right there. I like it. It's just tight, like, the way it looks" (CMS-21, 8). "Nice guns" (CMS-25, 7). "They look nice" (CMS-34, 4). "That's a wicked looking gun . . . [Laughter.] I just haven't seen guns in a long time" (CMS-37, 8–9). "I kinda like how they look. I just want to go shoot them" (CMS-43, 5). "I love guns. Hell, yeah, I love guns. [I love] everything about a gun" (CMS-62, 9).

Many of the interviews ended on the same note.

Q: Is there anything else maybe that you might want to tell me that I may
   have missed or anything you want to say?
CMS-62: Well, let's see. I just love guns.
Q: You just love guns?
CMS-62: Yeah. Hell, yeah. Yep. (End of interview with CMS-62, 47)

In addition to the fifteen youths who were attracted to guns in a primary, spontaneous way, several others expressed more muted, but nevertheless noticeable, desire. "I would like to have the .45 . . . I like them, truthfully" (CMS-40, 7–8). "They look, as in a term, they look cool to most people. But, not really . . . Well, they do. I mean, you can look at them mostly and just try to identify them" (CMS-8, 6).

A couple of youths expressed both attraction and repulsion. CMS-4, a seventeen-year-old Anglo youth, first reacted to the pictures of the guns with desire. "They're cool. I want to play with them . . . I want to go out and shoot them" (CMS-4, 3). But later in the interview he expressed contempt for guns. "In my opinion, I don't see people who carry guns as very macho or whatever you say. That's pussy shit. You pull the trigger, the gun does all the work. If you go scrap, you're gonna work, so you can say I beat that guy, but if you shoot him you can't say that" (CMS-4, 16). Similarly, CMS-48 at first gave a positive reaction: "Pretty nice guns . . . They're all right." But a few sentences later he said, "Seriously, I don't like guns." And a few minutes later he elaborated: "I don't like [guns because] they take a life. Why you gonna be taking a life for? Ain't no good" (CMS-48, 5–8).

Other youths simply dislike guns and respond to them with visceral disgust. Six of the youths did this—which I coded for the primary association of "dislike"—and a few others also expressed dislike. CMS-22, a seventeen-year-old Mexican American youth, is blunt. In response to the first prompt ("What do these pictures make you think of?"), he responds, "Pussies" (CMS-22, 7). "I don't like that stuff," he explains. "I think that's for punks" (CMS-22, 12). "I think it's for little girls. If you ain't man enough to scrap somebody, what's the use of you? Why you just gonna take somebody out and then go to prison? What you get out of it? Nothing. Your life's down the drain" (CMS-22, 14). He would much rather "scrap" the "old-fashioned" way—with his hands. If someone on the street pulls out a gun on him, he would usually tell them to put the gun down and scrap with his hands. "But most of the time people, they won't, they're afraid. That's why they use a gun. To me, at least, that's what I think. People use guns cause they're afraid to go out fighting. Afraid of getting beat up" (CMS-22, 7). Of course, CMS-22 realizes the risks of not carrying. Once another youth threw him some gang signs and he responded by inviting the guy to scrap mano a mano. The other guy turned around and unloaded a clip on him, shooting him twice. He pulled up his shirt and showed me the scars (CMS-22, 7–9). He wasn't joking.

CMS-53 similarly volunteers, "They're dumb. If you need them, they're good. If someone is trying to kill you or something. But I wouldn't shoot anybody or anything. I don't think they're worth it. I'd rather get in a fight with somebody than shoot somebody, personally . . . Anybody can fight with a gun, anybody can pull a trigger. It takes somebody, like a real man, to fight somebody. If you've got a problem, it's not worth shooting somebody over. I see people getting killed all the time over dumb things like drugs or money, or just arguments" (CMS-53, 5–6). "I never got into guns besides selling them, you know, trading them for drugs, never really got into . . . I don't like guns. Not really," says CMS-14 (6). "I think they're stupid unless you're hunting," CMS-69 says. "I don't really care for guns" (CMS-69, 5, 9).[6]

Part of what these youths dislike about guns is that they get in the way of "good" fights—fistfights, rumbles, playing with bats. Several of the youths talk about those other weapons—bats, knives, brass knuckles—as preferred. They praise the traditional fight. CMS-34, a sixteen-year-old Mexican youth, daydreams in our interview about fights without guns. "That's the fights I like," he says. "Like, when we're gonna go scrap. Sometimes some fools they're all scared to scrap and stuff. They start pulling guns. We had guns, one time, we had a gun, well, one of us had a gun, and we just left it in the car. And we said, 'What's up? Let's scrap.' If they pull a strap on us, we're gonna run back and get the straps and start shooting at them. But they didn't have guns, so we started fighting with them. That was nice" (CMS-34, 25). Other youths talk about liking bats better than guns. CMS-14, for instance, prefers bats "cause guns could kill somebody and that's murder. And serious in a small town. I don't want to kill anybody . . . I mean business needs to be taken care of. Like, if you scrap with somebody. But . . ." (CMS-14, 10). And others prefer knives. CMS-37, fifteen years old, says he would rather have knives or even bows and arrows. "I like 'em more . . . Silent . . . but deadly" (CMS-37, 22). In fact, CMS-37 had a knife fetish. He collected knives and blades, which is what got him in trouble in his group home and sent him to Catalina. Surprisingly, he was the only one who noticed there was a knife in one of the photographs of guns. His reaction was immediate, before I even had a chance to ask him a question.

> BH: All right. Let me show you some pictures of some handguns.
> CMS-37: That was the kind of knife that I got. That I got caught at school with.
> BH: Oh, really?
> CMS-37: One of those razor sharp . . . (CMS-37, 8).

The third important primary association is "respect." Four youths spoke strongly about guns as requiring "respect." "I like them," CMS-7 tells me, "but I respect them. I won't mistreat them or use them in the wrong way" (CMS-7, 6). "When I think gun, it's like power," he goes on. "But it's power that you can't neglect, you have to respect it" (CMS-7, 31). CMS-17, who was brought up with guns, says: "I respect them. I might carry one. But I won't go around telling everyone yeah, I got a gun" (CMS-17, 28).

You have to respect a gun, a seventeen-year-old Hispanic youth tells me. Respect means "being responsible and knowing that a gun ain't a toy, you know. And, like, as easy, it could take away someone's life, you know. Could take away your life, probably, and it's not a toy. I just, that's how I see the gun. A gun [can] potentially kill somebody, I mean" (CMS-46, 6). It is worth noting that this is from a youth who was adjudicated for possessing a .22 rifle and shooting within city limits and who wanted badly to buy a Ruger 9-mm (CMS-46, 15). CMS-66 was given a gun by his best friend, who also taught him to respect it. "I remember I shot it a few times till they taught me how to shoot it and how to take care of it, but I never played with it. I was always real instilled with, 'Don't play with it, it's not a toy, leave it under the seat for in case you need it. Don't play with it, don't show it to people'" (CMS-66, 6).

COMMODITY

To many youths, handguns have exchange value. They are a commodity to be traded or sold for cash or drugs. Seven of those I interviewed associated guns primarily with their cash value. CMS-14 is a good illustration. He is a seventeen-year-old Mexican American school dropout and a heavy user of drugs. He said in the interview that he didn't really like guns. He admitted he had fun shooting guns in the desert and even that guns made him feel "powerful." But his real interest in guns was trading them for drugs along the Mexican border, as described earlier. Guns were simply a commodity to him, something to trade for drugs or to sell. "Sell those and party and buy things, you know . . . Stereos, gold, help my family out, rent hotels, buy all kinds of beer, get all faded, live the fast life. Party hearty, all kinds of drugs, coke, cook all kinds of crack, sell it too, you know" (CMS-14, 7). This is the first experience the photographs of the guns brought to mind for CMS-14: "When I was four-teen, we broke into a house and a marine happened to live there, and we struck gold pretty much, shotguns, handguns, nines, .22s, .38s, I guess .45s, every-thing, man, but we had it. We just thought we should go blast someone, you know, we had our little urges and trigger events, when people get us mad when we're drunk, you know. I guess I tried to grow up too quick, you know. I was always hanging around with the older people. And just pretty much we struck gold. We had shotguns, rifles, we had it made. Just ended up getting pounds [of marijuana]" (CMS-14, 8).

Another youth, a sixteen-year-old high school dropout who passed his time dealing drugs, has a similar reaction to guns. Immediately on seeing the three guns, CMS-2 states: "This one [9-mm pistol] I would keep. These two [.45-caliber pistols] I would sell. I would keep that one [9-mm pistol] personally" (CMS-2, 3). "Forty-fives always sell, and that's what I did," he explains; sell the guns for drugs, and then deal the drugs (CMS-2, 4).

For CMS-31, a sixteen-year-old African American youth, guns were mostly a way to make money. He was, in fact, incarcerated at Catalina Mountain School on a probation violation stemming from an attempted gun sale. He needed money to go out, so he asked for some help from his seventeen-year-old cousin, who was a gang member. His cousin gave him a Glock .45 semiautomatic to sell. That cousin had about six other guns, including a 12-gauge sawed-off shotgun, a Tech-9, a couple of 9-mms, a .357, and a few others. His cousin had acquired these guns through a variety of sources: for instance, he traded crack for the Tech-9 and had an older friend buy a 9-mm at a gun show. CMS-31 hooked up with some guys at a park to sell the .45 Glock for $200, and that is when he was arrested (CMS-31, 6–9). On a previous occasion, when he was fourteen, CMS-31 and his friend stole a Smith and Wesson revolver from his friend's grandfather, who had a large gun collection. (Apparently, the grand-father "never knew it was missing" [CMS-31, 13].) They then sold the gun for $85. CMS-31 also got a chrome 9-mm from the same cousin and sold that one for $200 to the mother of a girl he used to go out with (CMS-31, 15–16).

CMS-48, a seventeen-year-old Mexican American youth, says, "I just have guns to sell them. Make some money off them. That's actually what they're for" (CMS-48, 8). For him, guns are about making money and buying clothes and jewelry—"Guess clothes, Tommy Hilfiger, and then jewelry . . . hats, glasses, stuff like that" (CMS-48, 8)—and to trade for drugs, too. He tells me how he would burglarize homes and often found lots of guns—a 9-mm, rifles, and once an Uzi. He traded the Uzi right away for three pounds of marijuana (CMS-48, 10).

"I used to sell guns, buy guns, trade guns," says CMS-10, a seventeen-year-old Mexican youth (CMS-10, 6). Another seventeen-year-old was given a .45 for beating up another guy, then traded it a week later for half a pound of marijuana. He then began selling guns for other people in exchange for drugs or money (CMS-22, 12–13). Another seventeen-year-old European American youth claims that he found several guns breaking into cars and that he would sell them as soon as he got his hands on them (CMS-43, 7). For these youths, guns were a commodity.

POWER

For others, guns are power. "When I think gun, it's like power. But it's power that you can't neglect, you have to respect it . . . [Power is] just something that almost everybody wants. Because to be powerful . . . it's better to be powerful than it is [to be] weak and submit. And for certain people that a gun gives them the power that they want" (CMS-7, 31). CMS-39, a sixteen-year-old Hispanic gang member, explains that guns "represent a lot when you hold them, a sense of power, relief, you know what I'm saying, security. When you are without it, you're, like, all you got is your hands. A lot of people aren't above that anymore, so they just rather shoot you and get it over with" (CMS-39, 5).

Ten out of the thirty youths mentioned power as a primary association with guns. To these youths, "power" means having control of a situation. CMS-6 says, "Like, you feel you're powerful with it, actually . . . That means that, like, if you have gun you can do whatever you want. Cause, like, you have it all. Cause you have a gun. You'll get your way cause you have a gun. That's the way I feel it sometimes, like if, like when I have a gun. I didn't actually try to use it, in a hard way" (CMS-6, 33). It means that "if somebody is doing something I don't like and I point a gun at them, they'll stop" (CMS-4, 17). It means being able to get what you want, do as you please, and protect yourself.

One youth in particular, CMS-16, made a point of emphasizing how guns can intimidate others. He is a seventeen-year-old Mexican gang member with an extensive history of gun ownership, possession, and carrying. He likes guns in part because they make him feel safe, but also because they intimidate others: "I like guns . . . I don't know. It's just a fun thing, I guess. Sometimes they make me feel safe, sometimes it's an intimidation on other people. Like, I can just pull a gun on somebody, if I point a gun at them, they're gonna get scared, stuff like that" (CMS-16, 23). He elaborates: "It's funny, like, you can just be talking to somebody, or, like, whatever, you could be doing whatever, and you just point a gun at somebody and they're ready to shit in their pants already. They're, like, 'Damn, what the fuck?' Or especially if you look mad, or if you, I don't know, it's weird. Or how easily people will give you something if you have a gun. It's funny" (CMS-16, 31).

Another youth described how others are scared or intimidated by guns, in a passage I coded as tertiary. "I seen people get scared before. Like my girlfriend, she went to my house, and she didn't know I had it. And then she gave me a hug and I was, like, 'hold on.' And I pulled it out, she got scared and she goes, 'What are you doing with that?' I was all, 'No, this is my friend's gun. I'm just holding it for him.' I hid it under the bed, under my mattress, under the bed. I had it in there. She was, like, 'You better get rid of it.' I was, like, 'No, no, I'm going to buy it.' She was, like, 'No!' She got mad. She told me, 'If you buy it, I ain't going out with you no more'" (CMS-6, 13). Her father had been killed by gunfire. "She hates guns. She told me she didn't want me to end up hurting somebody or have somebody shoot me" (CMS-6, 13).

The fear that guns can generate feeds this idea of power. CMS-7 recalls that when he carried a gun, "it made me feel pretty powerful." He admitted that it may even have changed the way he acted and says that when he was carrying, "I'd probably be more cocky" (CMS-7, 25). CMS-13, when he saw the pictures of the guns, immediately thought of "how much power they have over a lot of things" (CMS-13, 6). Another youth talks about "feeling powerful cause you have guns" (CMS-14, 7). "Hell, yeah, it's cool, raise hell, guns make you feel powerful." People act differently when you have a gun, especially if you are drunk. "They show more respect, [they're] a little more frightened, even older people" (CMS-14, 15, 18). To CMS-54, having a "bigger gun" meant that "I'll be a bigger person" (CMS-54, 4).

"The power, it's, like, you've got some power in your hand" (CMS-40, 9). "Everybody likes guns these days, dude," another youth tells me. "Hell, yeah. They're exciting. I mean what the hell. You feel powerful when you have a gun. You get respect" (CMS-62, 11).

JAIL

"It's too much time to fuck with guns" (CMS-4, 4). CMS-4 is one of four youths who had never possessed a gun and the only youth who had never fired one. From his interview, it was apparent that he had made the conventional calculation that the costs of carrying outweigh the possible benefits. He wants a gun to protect himself and his family. "I just want to protect my family," he says. "From stupid-ass kids around here, think they are hard and break into the house, do drive-by's or something, stray bullet hits my baby sister, and that'd be it. That kind of stuff, I wouldn't be able to handle. I'd go get a gun and blow 'em away" (CMS-4, 15–16). And he thinks guns are cool. "They're cool. I want to play with them." "I want to go out and shoot them" (CMS-4, 4–5). But he perceives the risk of incarceration—as well as the danger of guns—as simply too big. "It's kind of hard. It's a loser situation to be caught with a gun. You get time." Plus there is too great a risk of accidents. "I've got a two-year-old sister, a four-month-old sister, a thirteen-year-old sister, and an eleven-year-old brother. That's around the age that they like to play with that kind of stuff. Maybe if they were more mature" (CMS-4, 16). In the end, he has decided not to have a gun. "Not even worth it then" (CMS-4, 16).

This sentiment—that guns are liable to land you in jail—was shared by eleven youths, each of whom associated guns primarily with getting caught and doing time. Guns, pretty simply, can "put you in jail" (CMS-46, 5). I coded these primary associations as "jail." To CMS-2, guns are what "got me here now" (9). He doesn't want to have guns in his house when he is older because he wants to have children, and he does not want them to end up like him. A sixteen-year-old African American youth is incarcerated on a gun possession charge, and the picture of a gun makes him think of "when I got caught with it." "I was about to sell one of them, me and my friend," he says. "And we met a couple of my friends at the park, and somehow I guess the neighbors seen one of them. And they called the police. And the police came up, we got patted down and everything. Got caught with them" (CMS-31, 5). What does he think about guns today? In his words, "You can get a lot of money off of them. You can get in a lot of trouble with them too" (CMS-31, 17).

CMS-6 carried a chrome .25 semiautomatic around for about two months when he was sixteen. A friend was going to sell it to him for $60, but he had only $40, so his friend told him to hold the gun until he came up with the money. He was happy to have the gun, particularly to show it off. "Trying to show off," he says. "Trying to show people that I was better than everybody" (CMS-6, 13–14). But even when he was carrying it around, he was worried about getting caught, "cause I was scared, and I didn't want, I didn't want to get in trouble with it. So I didn't really want to have the cops get me in trouble for the gun. So I was, like, you know, just telling my friends, 'Hey look, check this out.' 'Oh, that's a nice gun. Are you going to let me use it?' 'No,'

I was, like, 'No, I ain't gonna let you use my gun. I just bought it.' They're, like, 'Yeah?' I was, like, 'Yeah.' 'It's my gun'" (CMS-6, 14). Ultimately he gave it back to his friend out of fear of getting caught. "I gave it back to him. I seen him and I told him, I told him that I didn't want my mom to know that I had a gun in the house, cause she would probably call the police on me if she knew. She didn't want me to be around guns and stuff. So I told him, I called him and I told him, 'Hey, man. If you want to come pick up your gun, it's here any-time.' And I got in trouble with the police. And they took me to juvenile. I didn't have the [gun]; thank God I didn't have the gun on me that day" (CMS-6, 9).

Another youth, a seventeen-year-old who had carried a .22 when he was twelve years old, ultimately decided to get rid of his pistol "because I was get-ting into so much trouble with the law already that if I . . . was going to keep carrying it, that if I shot somebody or something, I would get into more shit with the law. So . . . I gave it back to my friend" (CMS-25, 14). He had been car-rying it to school and putting it in his locker. In his interview, he suggested sev-eral times that on occasion the fear of going to jail had prevented him from using the gun. "When I had it in my locker at school, . . . like, some kids would mess with me and stuff, I would think about going to my locker and getting it. Then I'd always heard about the rumors, like, you can get in, like, deep shit and go to jail for bringing a gun to school, so I decided not to, because I didn't want to get locked up" (CMS-25, 16). Later in the interview he repeats this: "When I was at school. Like, I had it in my locker and the kids were messing with me. I could have walked to my locker, pulled out the gun, and capped them, just because I hated them. But I didn't because I thought of the consequences" (CMS-25, 24).

CMS-37, a fifteen-year-old Mexican Shoshone youth who had grown up in group homes, was given a .45 pistol by a friend to hold. The gun was "dirty"—it had been used in criminal activity. CMS-37 did not carry it on his person, "cause I was afraid I'd get caught" (CMS-37, 16). He understood that if he had been caught with the gun he might be prosecuted for other people's offenses. He was fourteen at the time.

For others, fear of going to jail plays an important, though less primary, role in their lives. A seventeen-year-old with a significant history of gun carrying volunteers that he once froze up in a gunfight because he was afraid of going to prison. "I just froze up, and I was just 'Oh, man, please, God, please don't make me use this. I don't want to go to prison, really'" (CMS-66, 26). CMS-34, a gang member, says that he doesn't carry guns on his person anymore because "now I'm in the system. I get sent to adult. So I'm an adult now . . . So, I can't mess up no more. Cause if I do, I'll go to prison, and that's not what I want" (CMS-34, 23). CMS-16, who had a significant history of gun carrying, drug dealing, gang membership, and gun dealing, says that his peers are carrying less now because they fear getting caught.

This is not to suggest that all youths are worried about serving time. On the contrary, a good number say they simply disregard the risk of incarceration for carrying a firearm. In their universe, the risk of death at the hands of rivals or other peers greatly outweighs the disadvantages of being sent to juvenile detention for carrying a gun. Fear of death or bodily injury far outweighs the prospect of spending months or even years in a secure facility. A sixteen-year-old European American youth who carried a .38 for several months while he was on the run from his family explains the trade-off in these terms: "If I get caught and I go to jail, I'll still be alive. If I didn't have a gun, and someone held a gun to me, and say I was going to be a slave or die, it's, like, there goes my life. And I had nothing to protect me for it" (CMS-17, 47). Similarly, a fifteen-year-old states that he really didn't care about getting caught by the police when he was carrying. "I'd care, but I just didn't want to take the chance of getting shot" (CMS-70, 15).

RECREATION AND, SEPARATELY, FUN

A number of youths immediately associate guns with hunting, target practice, shooting in the desert, or other recreational gun use. Youths often reminisce about hunting trips with their fathers and families or about going out to the desert and shooting at cacti or cans. Eleven of the youths associated guns primarily with recreation—and I coded these responses as "recreation."

CMS-8, a youth of Irish descent, sees the pictures of guns and immediately thinks of "just going out and shooting sometimes." "When I was like nine years old was the first time I went shooting. We tried almost every gun there was. It was with my mom's boyfriend: 20-gauges, 12-gauges, 14-gauges, 16-gauges, elephant gun, 9-mms, .45s, .44 Desert Eagles, Berettas, SKSs, Tech-9s, Tech-11s, .22s, .22 full auto, total .25s . . . My mom's boyfriend collects them. He collects them all the time" (CMS-8, 7). The right way to use a gun, he says, is for hunting or self-defense. His association with guns is this idea of going out and shooting for recreation.

CMS-17, sixteen years old, also reacts positively to the pictures of the guns. "They're nice-looking guns," he states. "Something to put on the wall, take out maybe every weekend and just practice shooting." When asked what the guns made him think of, he responds, "They bring back memories going up in the mountains shooting . . . I went up to the mountains, a lot of shooting ranges over there. We would go out in the mountains shooting and stuff. In Oklahoma we went out shooting, in Texas. I've been around guns all my life . . . Used to know how to use them, how to clean them, break them apart, put them back together, load them, rebuild them, fix them, take care of them" (CMS-17, 7–8). He would go shooting every weekend with his father—"shooting skeet, target, and stuff"—and also went hunting with his father three times. For him, guns are "a tool for you to go out hunting to survive with" (CMS-17, 9).

"I just want to go shoot them," says CMS-43, who is seventeen. "I would like to, just, to shoot them at cans and stuff . . . Like out to the desert" (CMS-43, 6). "I just, I just like guns a lot . . . Just cause, in New Mexico, ever since I was raised, I used to go hunting a lot with my dad," states another seventeen-year-old (CMS-46, 5). "I think they're stupid unless you're hunting," says another youth (CMS-69, 5). For these youths, the guns just remind them of hunting, or target practicing, or shooting in the desert. "Just target practicing with my brothers" (CMS-7, 5). "Shooting out in the desert or whatever" (CMS-14, 6). "Shooting with Grandpa" (CMS-70, 6).

For most of these youths, guns were also associated with having fun—the recreation of guns being something they enjoy. For one in particular, the immediate reaction is utterly unmediated. Guns just make him think of "fun"—here I coded his response separately and primarily as "fun" in addition to recreation, since the guns also reminded him of hunting with his uncle (CMS-62, 7). But for many others the recreational association is closely tied to having fun in a more muted way, which led me not to code them primarily as fun. CMS-16, for instance, has fun shooting guns because of the kick. "I like when, like, when they shoot, like, the kick. I like to shoot guns" (CMS-16, 23). CMS-40, an upper-level student, has mixed emotions about guns but finds them to be fun. "I like them, truthfully. They're dangerous . . . [I like them because of] the power; it's, like, you've got some power in your hand and, you know, I think they're just fun, you know, to go out and have a good time appropriately" (CMS-40, 9).

Many youths like the way guns handle. They like the feeling of shooting a gun. They like the action of the gun. CMS-37, for instance, says that he likes "the way they look" and "the action that they have" (CMS-37, 21). CMS-40 likes their mechanism, the way they are made, the way they work, the way the powder works. He compares them to a plane or a car (CMS-40, 11). CMS-46, who has been around guns since he was a small child, likes "just shooting and feeling the gun . . . just feeling it, and shooting it, the sound of it." "It just makes me feel, like, kind of excited. Like in having fun, having a good time. Shooting at targets. Seeing if, I don't know, just trying to, you know, like, get good at it, where you could shoot at targets, and you know, just practice" (CMS-46, 8–9).

Other youths want to collect guns. "Someday I want a gun collection," CMS-25 tells me. "I think that I like collecting . . . When I do, I'm going to collect old guns and stuff like, like back in, I guess, the western time. I guess. Or really nice guns. And everything. It's like, they're just cool" (CMS-25, 16, 31). "I like collecting guns more. More than using them," says another seventeen-year-old. "I only like them for collector's items; that's it. I like a lot of old-fashioned guns. But that's it . . . Just the way they looked, you know. How they worked, like the pellet kind of guns where they used to put the balls in there and the powder. Well, first the powder, and then the balls, they shove it down in there. It's just interesting to me" (CMS-40, 7, 17). The notion of guns as recreation is, in sum, closely tied to the idea of having fun.

ACTION

The action motif—living in the fast lane, shooting at others and getting shot at, carrying guns, confronting others, taking risks—is a recurring theme in the interviews. CMS-34, a Mexican member of the Brown Pride youth gang, is asked, "Do these make you think of any experiences you've had?" He immediately responds, "Getting shot at."

> I was, like, down Sixth, like, the railroad. Some guys were talking stuff to us, to my friend, and I was in the other car. And then he just pulled out a weapon . . . He pulled out one of those [AK-47s] and he shot my homeboy and killed him. Shot him in the throat. And my other two homeboys ran and then they started shooting at them, and hit my homeboy in the arm and then in the leg. And then that's when we came and then I had my .45. I mean I had my nine, the Glock, and I started shooting at them. And they shot back . . . We're from the South, they're from the West. So something happened, but that guy, he was all messed up, so he shot at my homeboys and killed them . . . We were in a Blazer, we're, like, five. I only had my nine, my homeboy had two .45s, and my other homeboy had a .357, I forgot. And we started shooting at them. And I remember two, I heard that two of them died. But one of us died too. (CMS-34, 5–6)

For eight youths, the pictures of the guns immediately triggered memories of shoot-outs, of getting shot at, of street life *with guns*. Later in the interviews

I would ask each youth about gun incidents, and I heard many stories like this. But for these eight youths—youths I coded "action"—the stories came out without any prompting. These are the things that guns immediately make them think of.

> Getting shot at . . . I was coming from a friend's house and he's a gang member . . . On the North Side. Right there at River and . . . First, I think it was . . . We were walking from a friend's house. And he was gonna go to my house. And these kids were, like, "Hey, remember me . . ." And then they just started blasting at me and my friend . . . My friend just looked back, and right when we looked back all of a sudden. BOOM. We just heard shots . . . Like the whole round, I think. (CMS-37, 9–12)

> Reminds you of the streets . . . Just that I had the same type of gun before. I been shot at with the same type of gun . . . It's just cause my neighborhood, people don't like my neighborhood, cause, you know, they're rivals. They always shoot up my neighborhood . . . Just that I've a lot of friends that have been shot by guns myself and since. (CMS-39, 4–5)

> People getting killed . . . I was [in] an apartment with some friends and another group of guys come on us with guns . . . My friends pulled out their guns . . . Cops pulled up. They . . . I don't know where they were. They just—we heard the sirens . . . And everybody just started running. (CMS-23, 4)

> Shootings . . . We were cruising down Sixth Avenue and some fool started shooting. There was a big gunfight . . . They were shooting at each other. Los Betos. You know where Los Betos is? I just saw little fools shooting at each other. Like four against three other dudes. Just shooting at each other. Bullets flying everywhere. (CMS-62, 7–8)

> Makes me, like, when I was sitting on the outs at a party and some fool got crazy and I shot. Boom. Boom. I was at a party and I had a 9-mm . . . Like this one fool, he got mad . . . He tried to start a fight with me and I got mad and I was drunk. And so I got up and he went to his car. I thought he was going to pull out a gun so I shot his car. Boom. I hit the door and I shot again and I don't know where it hit because I took off running. Then he pulled out a gun and ba-da-da-da-da. And I turned around . . . I dunno [what kind of gun it was]. I was gone. (CMS-2, 5–6)

For these youths, guns are action.

KILLING AND, SEPARATELY, REVENGE

Even more raw, for some youths guns are specifically about killing people they hate or seeking revenge in moments of anger. CMS-25 was an angry youth. The sight of guns made him think of "killing people." "Killing people. I wish I had a gun right now . . . Kill the people I hated . . . People make fun of me because of my sexual orientation. They make fun of me because of who I am. They make fun of me, of other things, and I hate them for that. So I'd rather kill them than put up with their bullshit" (CMS-25, 7–8). When asked what it was about guns that he thought was cool, he responded, in a flat tone, "You can kill people with them. If you really wanted to" (CMS-25, 16).

CMS-3, a sixteen-year-old gang member and drug dealer, also associates guns with killing, which for him is intimately associated with gang rivalries. He explains that gang rivals just shoot at each other to kill. I asked him to elaborate.

> CMS-3: Well, if you're a Blood and I'm a Crip, you're my rival. I don't like you, you don't like me, just from the start.
> BH: Right. But do you want to kill me?
> CMS-3: Yeah. I want your ass dead.
> BH: It's that bad.
> CMS-3: That's just the way it is. I don't like you one bit. You could be the coolest fucking person there is, I mean. You could be, who knows, if I had a sister, you could be my sister's husband or something. But that's just the way it is.
> BH: OK.
> CMS-3: You could save my life maybe sometime.
> BH: What if a rival saved your life? You'd still want to get rid of them?
> CMS-3: I'd just let them go that time. (CMS-3, 21–22)

When CMS-65, a sixteen-year-old Yaqui gang member, looked at the pictures, they made him think of "murder" and "killing people" (CMS-65, 13–14). For him, guns are for killing people, *not* for protection. "I don't carry around a gun for protection. Like if I'm going to carry around a gun, I'm going to go do something with it. But I don't carry, like, 'Oh, they're going to shoot me.' Like I should pull out my gun too. If they catch me sleeping, like I'm walking by myself and I don't have my gun, and if they want to kill me, they're going to kill me. But I know when I have my gun, that's when I'm going after people. I'm not doing it to defend myself. I'm doing it because I want to kill somebody else. I want to shoot somebody else" (CMS-65, 19).

In a similar vein, the first experience with guns that comes to mind for a seventeen-year-old gangbanger born in Mexico is "shooting at people, in my neighborhood . . . in LA" (CMS-10, 4). He first started gangbanging when he was twelve and living in Los Angeles. When he thinks about guns, what he thinks about is "shooting at my enemy" (CMS-10, 5).

As many of these comments attest, the notion of "killing" is often closely related to the idea of revenge. CMS-25, an angry youth mentioned earlier, weaves ideas of killing with ideas of taking revenge on youths who have made fun of him—who have taunted him, ridiculed him, and mocked him, especially for his sexuality. In his case I also coded his associations as primarily related to "revenge." Others spoke about revenge in this way. CMS-4, a seventeen-year-old white youth who had never fired or carried a handgun, was very protective of his four-month-old sister and the rest of his family. Though he never had a gun, he wanted one "to protect my family" (CMS-4, 16). When asked if there was a situation where he would want a gun, he mentioned the risk of his baby sister's being hit by a stray bullet and dying. "That kind of stuff I wouldn't be able to handle, I'd go get a gun and blow 'em away" (CMS-4, 16). Guns for him symbolize a way to get revenge, to express anger and sadness.

BELONGING

Other youths associate guns with being a part of something, with belonging—being a gang member, or having friends, or covering for others. Five youths spoke about guns in this manner. CMS-21 is a good example. He is a fourteen-year-old Mexican American who is a ward of the state. He talks a lot about guns but has never owned one. Instead, he held guns for other people, mostly for his home gang members. Once he held a Desert Eagle for a friend for three months. "He gave it to me," he says. "Just told me to hold it. I never really had a gun of mine. People just told me to hold them . . . Like they had bodies on it or something. They'll be, like, 'Hold this shit. Hide this shit.' Good enough" (CMS-21, 9). And so he did, he held guns for three peers. Many times it was for just a day or even just an hour—if they were on the run. "I used to hold probably like, maybe . . . for only three people. Only three different people. But the, I would hold different guns . . . I would go out in like the desert . . . And kind of like bury it under some bushes. I would never bring it to my house, though, cause of the fact that my mom would probably throw it out or call the cops or something" (CMS-21, 22).

CMS-66, an Anglo youth, talks about guns in a way that also combines carrying and belonging. Carrying a gun—and carrying *someone's* gun in particular—means being a part of a group. It means having a bond, being close, sharing something important. CMS-66 was given his gun by a mentor of sorts. "It was given me to by an older friend of mine," he explains. " 'Hey, if you need this, have this, in case anything happens,' cause I hung around with really the wrong crowd. They were really heavy hitters in the drug community. 'So if you hang around with us, you just might need this, so take this. But be careful with it, don't play around with it' " (CMS-66, 6). The giving of the gun was part of becoming a member of the group. CMS-16 became part of the neighborhood precisely by holding people's guns—and drugs. He describes how when he was in grade school,

> I lived on the North Side, on First and Grant, and that park right there, Mansfield Park. And I used to go to that park, like every morning. And all the older fools and shit, they were all, like, they were all, they were all ballers, they used to all sell crack and shit, and sell dope. And they were all in gangs, they all had straps. They all had guns. I don't know, I used to always see their guns. I used to hold guns for them and that's when I started selling dope for them. So then, though, and it was like a cover-up, well if the cops ever came, I would go down and swing. But I used to hold the guns and stuff.
>
> I would hold, like, a strap. They wouldn't have big straps. They would have, like, small straps, like brownies. They had little .38s or little .25s, and I would hold those. And then, there would be, like, I would hold their dope. And then, like, when somebody wanted some dope, they would go talk to them. And they would leave. And they would tell me that they wanted whatever, two or three, whatever rocks. So I would go there, they would count the money out for me, and then I would give them their dope and then I would go. Give them their money and that was it. (CMS-16, 6–8)

It was in this way that he became first a trusted member of the community and then a drug dealer and gun carrier himself. But the carrying at first was a way of belonging to the group.

CMS-16, a sixteen-year-old Mexican youth, got his gun as part of becoming a gang member. "I came from Mexico when I was ten. And I was in none of that stuff. I was just a little kid," he says. "We live on the South, and, like, there was a lot of gangs. I started going to school and I started getting involved with the gangs and stuff . . . They used to take guns to school and stuff . . . Then, they told [asked] me if I wanted a gun. I said 'Yeah, OK.' They gave me a little .25" (CMS-34, 7, 9).

SHOWING OFF, SUICIDE, AND TOOLS

There were a few other meanings that occurred less frequently. I have discussed some of these already—revenge and fun—and will turn now to the final three associations I coded: showing off, suicide, and the gun as a tool.

For some of the youths, guns are primarily associated with showing off. Approximately six admitted that they associate their own gun carrying with trying to impress other people and looking cool. CMS-6, a seventeen-year-old who likes guns a lot, carried a .25-caliber semiautomatic pistol "just to try to show off with it. You know, 'I got a gun' and stuff" (CMS-6, 9). "I just try to show off," he explains, "cause, like, a lot of kids, I don't know, had guns, and you know, it's just, like, 'Yeah, it's tight, you got a gun,' you know" (CMS-6, 13).

Showing off is also, of course, intertwined with other meanings, such as power and also revenge. So, for instance, CMS-6 mentions several meanings in the same breath when he discusses showing off with guns: "I guess, trying to show off, trying to show people that I was kind of powerful, that I had a gun too. That if anybody would try to do anything I would hurt them with a gun" (CMS-6, 27). He says that he would carry a gun "probably to get back at the people who probably hurt me in my life. Get back at them in some way. Or scared. Try to scare them" (CMS-6, 30). This is why he would carry a gun: "Just to have, to try to get, sometimes to get, if I seen the people that hurt me before, try to get them back somehow. Or just try to show off with the gun. To show them that I'm powerful, that I have a gun. If they would try to do anything, I would just shoot them. Or just, but, if you're gonna have a gun for hunting, you gotta have a gun to hunt" (CMS-6, 31). Similarly, CMS-54 carried a gun simply to look cool. "To look harder, or to look like all the, you know, someone mean and stuff, you know" (CMS-54, 23). Other youths also mention showing off their guns. CMS-21, a fourteen-year-old, for example, brought a .22 pistol to school just to impress his friend and prove to him that he had the gun (CMS-21, 23).

For some, the pictures of guns immediately trigger memories of friends who have committed suicide or even of times when they thought of committing suicide themselves. CMS-40 was one of those youths. He had stolen a car and found a 9-mm in it. He kept the gun overnight and was contemplating suicide. He eventually returned the gun to its owner the next day—he had stolen the car from someone he knew—but he was marked by the experience. For him, guns trigger thoughts of suicide (CMS-40, 5). Several others, when presented with the pictures of guns, immediately think of friends who committed suicide. A seventeen-year-old European American recalls, "My friend killed himself with a 12-gauge . . . It was when we were walking in the door, he shot himself. Couldn't stop him" (CMS-8, 7). "One of my other homeboys shot him-self. I had a nine too, it was his dad's. It was my friend's dad's, and I stole it from him. But I only had it for, like, two days. And my friend, he was all messed up and his girlfriend left him, or something, I don't know what happened. He went to the room and got it, went to his room and shot himself in the head. It was some stuff, crazy stuff" (CMS-34, 16). Finally, for one youth, guns are just a "tool." CMS-17 spent a lot of time target shooting with his father and had been around guns all his life. For him, guns are "a tool": a tool "for life. For hunting. It's just that you see everyday tools and that's why we have it here with us . . . It's your protection, it's a tool for you to go out hunting to survive with . . . I put it in a category with a sledgehammer, crowbar . . . a grinder, and stuff" (CMS-17, 9).

Overall, these three final meanings are too closely associated with one or two individuals, and therefore their contextual nature is overly determined by the characteristics of those individuals. For this reason I avoid discussing these associations in much of the subsequent analysis.

Table 3.1 summarizes the nineteen primary meanings. To get a preliminary idea of the relative importance of each primary meaning, I performed focused coding of the interviews and selected the top primary meanings given by each youth. Some of the youths made as many as eight primary associations that I was able to code; others made fewer, and one made only one such association. The mean of coded primary associations was almost five—4.66 to be exact. Consistent with the sampling scheme, I selected the top five primary meanings given by each youth, yielding 150 observations. In those cases where there were originally fewer than five meanings coded, I counted the top meanings as many times as necessary in order to reach five. The point of this exercise is to avoid having certain youths influence the findings more than the others. Over-all, this method was consistent with the sampling scheme (individual youths were sampled randomly), and it equalized each one's contribution to the over-all picture of gun associations. In this way each youth contributed five obser-vations to the data set. Table 3.2 lists, in descending order, the frequency with which the various primary associations were observed.

TABLE 3.1. *The primary meanings of guns to the Catalina youths*

LABEL	DEFINITIONS AND ASSOCIATED EXPRESSIONS
Action	Guns are about living in the fast lane, being an adventurer, shooting and getting shot
Attraction	Guns are tight; guns are cool; I like guns; I love guns
Belonging	Guns are about feeling like you belong to something, to a group; people ask you to hold their gun for them, making you feel that you are in with them
Commodity	Guns are a commercial object that you sell or trade for money, cash, or favors
Danger	Guns are dangerous; you do not want to have them around when you have kids because they might shoot themselves by accident, or you could shoot someone by accident; you could even shoot yourself by accident
Death	Guns are about death and dying
Dislike	Guns are for weaklings; real men do not need guns, they fight with their hands; I don't like guns
Fun	Guns are just a lot of fun; they are fun to shoot; they feel good when you handle them
Jail	Guns can get you in a lot of trouble with the law; you can get caught and go to jail
Killing	Guns are for killing people; for going out and shooting at people
Power	Guns are powerful; you feel powerful when you have a gun; other people are intimidated when you have a gun
Protection	Guns are necessary to protect yourself from other youths; you need to carry a gun so that other youths don't mess with you, don't punk you
Recreation	Guns are for hunting or for target practice; for shooting at cans; for shooting at cacti
Respect	Guns are something you need to treat with respect; you need to respect a gun
Revenge	Guns are to seek revenge for past injustices; to get back at people for what they did to you
Self-defense	Guns are for protection to deter a home invasion or theft of your car; you keep a gun under your mattress in case a burglar comes in the house
Showing off	Guns are for showing off to other youths and making yourself seem cool and with it
Suicide	Guns are for committing suicide
Tool	Guns are a tool, like a hammer, a screwdriver, a saw; they are just an instrument like other instruments

TABLE 3.2. *Frequency of primary meanings of guns among the Catalina youths*

LABEL	FREQUENCY
Protection	20
Danger	17
Attraction	15
Commodity	13
Power	12
Dislike	11
Jail	11
Recreation	11
Action	8
Killing	7
Belonging	5
Death	5
Respect	4
Self-defense	3
Showing off	2
Suicide	2
Tool	2
Fun	1
Revenge	1
Total	150

THREE CLUSTERS OF PRIMARY MEANINGS

For most of the youths at Catalina, guns have not a single primary association but multiple ones. Guns may represent protection *and* power, fun *and* death. CMS-4, for instance, speaks not only of protection but also of power, of accidental shootings, *and* of getting caught and spending time incarcerated (CMS-4, 16–17). For CMS-13, in rapid succession, guns are about power, protection, *and* looks (CMS-13, 6). These associations are fluid and shifting. They bleed into each other. They combine in pairs or triplets to form fields of meaning. CMS-40 offers a good illustration: "I like them, truthfully. They're dangerous . . . The power, it's, like, you've got some power in your hand and, you know, I think they're just fun, you know, to go out and have a good time appropriately . . . So, truthfully, I don't, I don't think, as long as they're, I think a lot of guns should be made for protection only and not for abusing, or they can be used for entertainment, you know. And, like, the fastest draw or something, you know, or who can aim the best. But I don't think they should really be used to, to hurt people. I don't like killing. I don't like a lot of violence" (CMS-40, 9).

The various associations feed on each other. They help to define each other. A meaning achieves a particular identity, takes on a certain valence, in relation to other associations. Danger combined with death means something different than does danger combined with fun. Once we identify and isolate the primary meanings, it becomes crucial to explore the relationships between them, for it is precisely these relationships that help us understand how the associations fit together.

The goal, then, is to map the observed primary meanings in relation to each other. This can be accomplished by using correspondence analysis, a method of visually representing the relations between variables—here, between the different meanings or between meanings and practices. As discussed in chapter 2, correspondence analysis offers a method of portraying data for visual inspection and analysis. It allows us to visually represent two different structures—the structure of primary meanings and a practice structure such as gang membership—on the same graph and thereby to visually represent the relationships not only within each structure but between the two. It thus "allows both the social and the cultural dimensions to be plotted within the same measurement space" (Mohr 1998, 362).

THREE CLUSTERS OF PRIMARY MEANINGS

A simple correspondence analysis of the primary meanings of guns reveals three major clusters of interrelated meanings. This simple analysis visually maps the nineteen-by-thirty contingency table that consists of the frequency table made up of columns that represent the nineteen primary meanings of guns observed and of rows that represent the thirty individual respondents. The three major clusters of meanings indicate higher than average associations between any two primary meanings.

The first and most important cluster of associations I label the "action/ protection cluster." In this cluster are the following meanings (ranked by frequency): protection, danger, attraction, power, jail, action, belonging, death, showing off, and fun. These associations are linked insofar as they seem to revolve around the "action" motif. In this cluster, guns are perceived as dangerous yet attractive, necessary for aggressive, preemptive protection, powerful and power giving. They are both dangerous and likely to land you in jail and also associated with death. They confer power and membership. And they are useful for showing off. Despite the fact that guns are perceived here as instruments of death—or perhaps because of it—the youths value them for their power, for their ability to control their immediate environment, and for their appeal.

The symbolic meanings in the action/protection cluster help give context to each other. Guns in this cluster are more likely to be viewed as attractive, but the very idea of attraction is defined by the proximity to these other associations. It is an attraction linked to the danger of guns. It is an attraction to power and action, not so much to the gun as a tool for hunting or as a commodity to obtain other valued goods. It is the action, the danger, the death, the risk of being caught and sent to jail that makes guns attractive and powerful in this first cluster of meanings. And protection is also defined by its associated meanings. The notion of aggressive, preemptive carrying gets its meaning from the close association with action and belonging.

A second cluster connects two meanings: commodity and dislike. I call this the "commodity/dislike" cluster. This is a robust cluster associated with several respondents (about six). The close association of the two meanings helps to give them context. Viewing guns as a commodity is more often associated with

TABLE 4.1. *The three clusters of primary meanings of guns*

CLUSTER	ASSOCIATED MEANINGS
Action/protection	Protection, danger, attraction, power, jail, action, belonging, death, showing off, and fun
Commodity/dislike	Commodity and dislike
Recreation/respect	Recreation, respect, self-defense, suicide, and tool

disliking guns. This is reflected well in the earlier comments of several of the youths, who interlaced rejection of guns with treating them as a commodity. Recall the seventeen-year-old Mexican American who volunteered, "I don't like them" but who had guns just "to sell them. Make some money off them. That's actually what they're for" (CMS-48, 8). What the correspondence map reveals is that there is a close association, above average, between this sentiment of dislike and treating guns for their exchange value. It reveals an intriguing feature about the way some of these youths think about gun possession.

A third cluster connects a group of meanings, including (again ranked by frequency) recreation, respect, self-defense, suicide, and tool. This cluster is closely associated with a few respondents and suggests an association between using a gun for hunting, target practice, or self-defense and treating guns with respect. I refer to this as the "recreation/respect" cluster. It suggests that those youths who think about guns in terms of recreation are more likely also to treat guns with respect. The correspondence map reveals an above-average association between recreation and respect.[7]

The three clusters can be identified on the correspondence map that is reproduced in figure 4.1, obtained using the application SAS, Release 8.1. One can see the first and most important cluster of associations—the "action/protection" cluster—at the left of Dimension 1. The second cluster—"commodity/dislike"—is in the lower right quadrant of the map, on the bottom of Dimension 2 and to the right of Dimension 1. The third cluster is in the upper right quadrant of the map and connects a group of meanings, including recreation, respect, self-defense, suicide, and tool. It will be useful to keep these clusters in mind as we place these associations within the context of youths' gun carrying and other activities. They are summarized in table 4.1.

IDENTIFYING THREE IDEALTYPES

It may be useful to think of these three clusters of symbolic meaning as archetypes, and it may be especially helpful to imagine youths who draw on

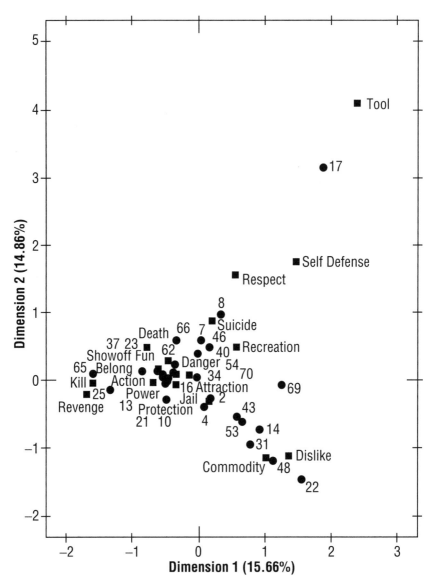

FIGURE 4.1. *Simple correspondence analysis of primary meanings of guns*

particular archetypes as in some sense representing a Weberian idealtype. Though they are rarely expressed in their pure form, the three major archetypes represent the poles that define the space of youths' gun carrying. To give the archetypes more definite shape, I offer three of the Catalina youths as idealtypes. Their names, of course, are fictitious. But their stories are real, based on the interviews—or at least as real as the youths' self-construction, self-understanding, and self-imagination. I begin with the action/protection idealtype, whom I call Jesús.

Action/Protection

Jesús is a seventeen-year-old Mexican American—"Mexican and White," he explains (CMS-16, 4). He was raised by his mother, who is Mexican and part Yaqui. He never met his father and does not know his father's ethnic background. He was raised on Palo Verde on the south side of Tucson—the tough side, closer to the Mexican border.

When Jesús was about eight years old and in grade school, he lived in central Tucson and would hang out in Mansfield Park every morning before going to school. He met a bunch of older males who were into drugs. They sold crack. They were mostly in gangs and carried guns. Being young and adventurous, he started to hold their guns, and then he started selling dope for them. He was their cover. If a cop came by, he would go down and play on the swings.

> I used to go there in the beginning, in the mornings, just to catch, like, the bus, and then I would go to school. And, like, after school, most of the time, I would just come home. I would change my clothes and just go to the park . . . This kid, they had a recreation center that I used to just tell my mom I was going to the rec center. Just go there and kick with all the older fools . . . Like, seventeen. Like my age, now. Some of them were older, like nineteen, twenty . . . And all the older fools and shit, they were all like, they were all, they were all ballers, they used to all sell crack and shit, and sell dope. And they were all in gangs, they all had straps. They all had guns. I don't know, I used to always see their guns. I used to hold guns for them and that's when I started selling dope for them. So then, though, and it was like a cover-up, well if the cops ever came, I would go down and swing. But I used to hold the guns and stuff. (CMS-16, 8, 6)

Soon Jesús began holding all kinds of guns and drugs. "They would have, like, small straps, like brownies. They had little .38s or little .25s, and I would hold those. And then there would be, like, I would hold their dope" (CMS-16, 8). A year or two later, Jesús started selling dope for himself. One of the older guys in the neighborhood "asked me why I was selling dope for those guys when I could just be selling dope for myself and make my own money. And that's when I started selling dope for myself and then he told me just to hold [a gun]" (CMS-16, 9).

First Jesús borrowed the gun, a small .25-caliber handgun. A little later he got his own gun, a .38-caliber pistol. He was about eleven. He kept the gun at his "homey's" house, right near the park, and began to develop a little routine. "I would come back off the bus, I would walk home, change my clothes, tell my mom I was going to the park, or that I was going to my homey's house, I would leave, go to my friend's house, get my gun, and go to these little, like, projects, right, and go to this Chinese fool's house and get my dope. And then I was just kicking in the alley" (CMS-16, 10).

He started carrying his .38 everywhere he went—"Most of the time, I would carry it at my waist, or at the small of my back" (CMS-16, 11). At about that time, Jesús started "kicking" with a local gang—hanging out, doing things. "I just wanted to be with the hood or something. I kinda wanted people to look at me as like, 'Man, that fool is from, he's from Palo Verde Blood. That fool's crazy. Don't even talk to, don't even fuck with that fool.' That's how I wanted it to be . . . So nobody would, I don't know, so I would have a reputation, I guess, . . . of being a bad motherfucker" (CMS-16, 35).

Jesús was "jumped in"—initiated—at thirteen. He's South Palo Verde Blood. He has seen a lot of action. He's been shot at. He's been in gunfights. And he's got lots of tattoos to prove it. On his hands, he has two Ss for "South Side," his gang, South Palo Verde Blood. He has his nickname or street name tattooed on this hand. He describes the tattoos to me as he displays them:

> That's just an upside-down cross. And then I got three dots right there, and my crazy life, or whatever, Mi Vida Loca. And FTW, Fuck This World. And then that used to be my mom's name, but I don't know, it got messed up over time . . . I got four dots on my finger, that's for the raza, for the race . . . Just like, it's for the race, like, for Mexican. And then, right here, . . . that's my cousin, that's his name . . . That's me. And . . . those two are like my best homeys . . . They're like my best friends. They'll go with me for anything . . . And then, I got three dots right there, Mi Vida Loca. (CMS-16, 24–25)

Jesús tells a story of when his homeys were not there for him—a time they told him to go talk shit at these guys from another neighborhood:

They just, they like instigated it, kind of, for me to go over there and talk shit to them . . . Cause when you're younger, when you're younger and shit, you gotta represent more, I guess. You gotta put in work to show that you're whatever, that you'll represent the hood, even no matter what the conditions. And then, when I went over there, they punked out on me, I guess. Cause I went over there and I was just telling them, I was all, "You motherfuckers aren't shit. You guys are just a bunch of craz." And I was just telling them, I was all, "You ricketts ain't gonna do nothing." . . . And then they pulled guns on me and I—they pulled a big gun, they pulled a 12-gauge, or I don't know what kind, it was a gauge, it was a shotgun, and then. I was thinking that these other people that were here had my back. And I had a gun, but if I'd have reached for it, I'd have got smoked. I'm thinking these guys over here have my back, and then I just heard them all getting in their car and they left. They left me there . . . And then, when they did that shit, I shut up. I shut up, but then, I thought those other fools had my back, and then when they bounced, I don't know, it was weird . . . They told me to leave. I left! I left quick. (CMS-16, 30–32)

These days Jesús is an OG—that's "old gang member" or "original gang member," depending on whom you talk to. He is more laid back. He is willing to hang out with gangsters from other gangs. He is less interested in starting trouble:

When I was younger, I was just, I thought I had to live up, kinda to a standard, of the hood or whatever . . . [W]hen I was out this time, everybody, I don't know, they always wanted to see me do something, like, cause I don't know, I guess people, cause I was locked up for, I've been locked up for, I was locked up for a long time before I went back to the hood, for like, a while, a few years. And then, when I went back, everybody was like, "Oh, shit, you're so and so, yeah, I heard about you. Blah, blah, blah . . ." Yeah. That's nice. And everybody, they wanted me to like, they wanted to see me do something, or like they wanted to see somebody start shit with me. So like I can do something.

And I don't know, it wasn't that way for me when I was out this time. I was chilled. I was, like, kicked back. I was just drinking a lot. I still got, I was still getting guns and all that, but I didn't always want to go out and do something. And everybody was always telling me, like, "Well, yeah, we hear that, you know, that you're down for this or whatever. What's up, let's go." "Yeah, I'm down for it, dog, but I used to do that when I was younger. Go ahead and

do it." "Oh, you're not going to come?" "No, I'm not going to go." But sometimes I just find myself just telling them that I'll do it, telling them, like,
"Yeah, you're down to go do this." "What's up, let's go put in work then." Or
the younger fools, I don't know, cause, I, I don't know, it's weird. Like the
younger fools, I'm not old or nothing, but like the younger fools that are
growing up they want to be from the hood and stuff, I find myself telling
them what the older fools used to tell me. Like, "Oh, you think, you think
you're down for the hood? You think, you think you're a Blood, you think
you're a dog? Look at that boy, that fool's wearing all blue, right there. Look
at that shit. See him? Go run up on that fool. Fool, you ain't, go run up on
that fool, you ain't from the hood. Go ahead. Go stab that fool, go ahead,
you got a knife, you think you're bad, go stab him." And then they go do it.
I don't know. (CMS-16, 36–37)

Jesús wants to go to college and then join the Marines. Right now, he's
incarcerated. Jesús started getting in trouble with the law when he was nine,
charged with throwing rocks, criminal damage. He was frequently put on probation but would not check in with his officer, or would not be at home, and
was caught in violation of probation. Jesús dropped out of school in sixth
grade. He was charged with assault with an aggravated weapon—"I beat
somebody up with a stick and a bat"—and then for stealing a tractor and running into some cars and knocking down part of a house. He was placed in
Adobe, a detention facility, and was released on probation. He was arrested
again for car theft, possession of marijuana, and possession of a deadly narcotic, crack, and that's what brought him to the Catalina Mountain School.

Still today, Jesús likes the sight of the guns. "Those are some pretty tight
guns, that one and that one," he says, referring to the two semiautomatics.
"Yeah. Revolvers are better for other stuff, but the semis look nicer . . . Like if
you want to get away with a murder or something . . . [With revolvers the] bullets stay in the chamber . . . [Semis are better] just for look, really. Just for look,
if you want to let off quick rounds" (CMS-16, 5–6). "I like guns," he explains.
"It's just a fun thing, I guess. Sometimes they make me feel safe, sometimes it's
an intimidation on other people. Like, I can just pull a gun on somebody, if
I point a gun at them, they're gonna get scared, stuff like that . . . I like when,
like, when they shoot, like, to the kick. I like to shoot guns" (CMS-16, 23). Jesús
was never caught with a gun, though, or charged with a gun offense. When he
was out, he never thought of the police catching him. "I don't think, I never
think like, the police are gonna catch me . . . I know they'll catch me sooner or

later, but I don't think that 'tonight, I'm gonna get caught.' Or I shouldn't have this gun because I think I might get caught. Because I just think that's kind of like jinxing myself" (CMS-16, 47).

Commodity/Dislike

Yusuf is a sixteen-year-old African American from the southeast side of town, a sprawling part of Tucson where low-income subdivisions are encroaching on the desert. He wants to go to Pima College and would like to become a rapper. He likes music. For the time being, though, he too is incarcerated at Catalina.

Yusuf was not raised with guns. His parents did not have guns, and they do not like them. The first time Yusuf held a gun was when he was about thirteen. A cousin of his "was trying to sell one of his 12-gauges." "It wasn't loaded or anything," he explains. "I held it" (CMS-31, 20–21). When he was fourteen, Yusuf was arrested for possession of a Glock .45-caliber semiautomatic handgun that he had gotten from his cousin. His cousin, who was seventeen, was a gang member and had six or seven guns. "He had a sawed-off 12-gauge, a Tech-9, and he had this one little, little, and I don't know what it is . . . He had a couple of 9-mms. Like a .357, and some other ones I can't name . . . He got the Tech-9 off of this one person that smokes crack. And he gave him some crack, and he gave him the Tech-9 . . . He bought a 9-mm from this gun show by my house. Well, he didn't, he got somebody to do it" (CMS-31, 6–7).

Yusuf told his cousin he needed some cash. "Like, I told him I needed some money. And, like, cause my mom, she didn't have none. And I needed it to go out, like, me and my friend —— were gonna go out, and [he] knew somebody that wanted to buy a gun. And I said, 'What, could I get [a gun] and go get some money?' And he was, like, 'Yeah'" (CMS-31, 8).

Yusuf got the Glock .45 from his cousin, and he and his friend went to a park to sell the gun for $200.

Well my friend, ——, he said he knew about somebody who wanted to buy a gun. And he called them. They said, "Yeah, we're looking for one." So we went and met them at the park . . . Then, like, somehow, I guess one of the neighbors or somebody, seen. Cause the cops just, like, rolled up . . . Like, we didn't hear no one until we're about to, like we turned around, and all of a sudden, they were just, like, there . . . Like, one came from behind. Like, we seen one walking up, and then we started walking away. But then, a lady came behind me and she, like, started patting me down . . . And then she grabbed her gun and told us to get on the ground. (CMS-31, 8–9)

Yusuf had sold a few guns before. His friend—the same friend—stole a Smith and Wesson six-shot revolver from his own grandfather: "Cause his grandpa has a gun collection. He never knew it was missing" (CMS-31, 13). The gun looked like an old western gun—"a six-shooter type of gun" with a ten-inch barrel. They had it for about two weeks and were able to sell it to one of his friend's friends for $85. Both he and his friend were fourteen at the time. Yusuf had also gotten a chrome 9-mm from his cousin and sold that one for $200. He sold it to the mother of a girlfriend. "I used to go out with her daughter," he explains. The mother told Yusuf she needed a gun, and Yusuf hooked her up. That particular gun, Yusuf had for only a short time. "The chrome nine, I had that one for only, for like only, like two days or a day. Cause I got it and then the next day and gave it to her" (CMS-31, 16).

Yusuf also had found a 9-mm in a paper bag in an alley behind his home. Someone had been stashing it there. He called it his "Russian nine." "I found a Russian nine. It was like a Russian model, something like that. I found one of those . . . where I used to live, on —— and ——, it was like in an alley. It was in a plastic—not a plastic, a paper—bag, along with bullets and all that. It looked like somebody was stashing it or something" (CMS-31, 5). The gun was wet, and it was rusting.

Yusuf carried his "Russian nine" sometimes. "Not all the time, like I was afraid to carry it," he explains. "Cause all I do is go to school or go, like, you know, like, go to school or something. Like I wouldn't carry it like, to go to school or to my friend's house . . . Cause it's a gun. It's not like I'm gonna have to use it at school or nothing . . . Like, if I was going to party, for protection, I might want to take it . . . Just in case I need it . . . Just in case something happened" (CMS-31, 12). Mostly Yusuf just carries "to get rid of them and stuff." He took the Russian nine to a party once to sell it. "The clip was empty because the first time I took it to a party was to show one of my friends. Cause she was probably gonna buy it." A few times he carried it "just to try to be cool or something." On those occasions, "I didn't show it to people that wanted to buy it, I showed it to people I knew. I showed it to two or three people" (CMS-31, 17). But in the end he lost the Russian nine before he could sell it. "I don't know what happened to it," he explains. "Like, it just, I don't know. It just, like, got lost or something . . . It was behind my bed . . . I think I took it somewhere or something . . . Like, I remember having it last, but, like, I don't remember what happened to it" (CMS-31, 11–12).

Yusuf is not a gang member, though some of his friends are. Yusuf fired all his guns except the .45 "out in the desert and stuff." But he has never seen any real gun action. "I never was, I never, like, I never, sorry, never been around nobody who shot at somebody, or I never shot at nobody either. I've just, like, been around them. And I've shot them, like, like shooting bottles and stuff . . . I know people who said they've fired at people, but I've never been around or witnessed it" (CMS-31, 24). Yusuf does, however, recall a time when he wished he had pulled out a gun. It was when he was about to sell the .45:

> I just got the Glock .45 and me and my friend —— went over to a park. Like, some people just, like, stopped and were staring at us . . . They were going by and we were looking, like they just drove by. And then they stopped and turned around and came back. We were, like, "What are you looking at?" I was, like, "Yo." I told them, "I'm looking at you." And then they just said nothing. They were just sitting there. We were just standing there, and then they just left . . . At the end, when we were walking to the park, we were, like, talking and wishing we had pulled it out. (CMS-31, 25)

Whenever he carried a gun on his person, he feared getting caught. "It was always in the back of my head, you know, that the police could be there. But I was just thinking, 'Fuckin' hurry up and get it to her.'" Why did he do it anyway? "Because the thought of having the money was stronger, like greed and everything," he says (CMS-31, 29). Yusuf also sold crack and marijuana.

Yusuf has been at the Catalina Mountain School for three months so far. He was placed on probation in the JIPS program for possession of the Glock .45, but he violated probation by failing to be home when his probation officer came to see him. Before that, Yusuf had a record for assault and shoplifting. The first time he got in trouble was the shoplifting charge, when he was eight years old. When he was thirteen, he was adjudicated for assault—"I threw a basketball at a teacher" (CMS-31, 3)—and was placed on probation.

What does Yusuf think of guns? "You can get a lot of money off of them . . . You can get in a lot of trouble with them too" (CMS-31, 17). As for his friends, what do they think about guns? "You can get money off of them" (CMS-31, 19).

Recreation/Respect

Marc is a sixteen-year-old Anglo youth who has been living with his family on the east side of Tucson since he was twelve—more or less. He has spent a lot of the last two years in detention, and before that he spent a fair amount of time on the run.

Marc was born in Colorado and lived there the first year of his life. His mother divorced his father and remarried a man in the air force, so Marc moved a lot as a youth and lived in Texas, Germany, and Oklahoma.

This is his second time at the Catalina Mountain School. The first time, he spent nine months in detention for car theft. He was fourteen at the time. He was released on parole but ran away from home. He was sent to Eagle Point, another detention facility, for ten months and just recently got sent back to the Catalina Mountain School. He had a long record of adjudications before the car theft—mostly running away, destruction of property, breaking windows, assault. The first time he got in trouble was for assaulting his mother when he was thirteen.

Marc started shooting guns at a young age. His stepfather collects guns—handguns, rifles, and shotguns. He has fifteen or sixteen—or at least he had that many when Marc last saw them. "He gots a .38 special, a Colt .45, and I know he gots a .22. I always thought he had a .357, I'm not really sure. He never brings them all out . . . He used to keep them under our water bed. There's a little cabinet on the bottom. He built a door for it, put a lock on it. He used to keep them under there, but now he gots a gun safe and keeps them in the gun safe. Except for the .38, he keeps it on the bed and stuff. In case" (CMS-17, 12).

The first time Marc handled a gun was when he was five years old and got his first lesson:

> We were shooting mesquite and I was just standing around. He just picked me up off there and said this is a gun. This and that. Lecturing me about it. He sat down and he loaded it off a buck shot with the heavy one, not much gunpowder in it. So, and we, he held me back and I put my finger on the trigger. And he held the gun . . . He pulled the trigger. It slammed into my shoulder even though I was holding it tight. But he stopped me, but still, it hurt. From there, I will always respect a gun. (CMS-17, 29)

In Germany, Marc went shooting three times—once with a deer rifle, once with a 12-gauge, and then once with a .22-caliber handgun—all at the shooting range of the air force base. After that he did not handle guns regularly until he was about nine years old, when he was in Oklahoma.

> First, my dad, when he got there, locked up all his guns, cleaned them once a week. And just keep them, cause there's more moisture out there, so they get rusty quicker and stuff. And then he met some friends out there. They went hunting. And one morning I woke up early in the morning. I just woke

up, had to use the restroom, walked out in the kitchen, it was 1:30 . . . He walked out there. He said, "You got up. Do you want to go hunting with me this morning?" I had nothing better to do, so I said, "Yeah, why not?" I got dressed. He left a note telling Mom that I went with him. And he grabbed, usually I only seen him take out a 12-gauge, he brought out . . . a .20-gauge, which is not as strong, and it was pump action. It was real, it wasn't stiff. That's the best way I could put it. It was all sawed down where you pump it up, pull the trigger at the same time. And he didn't have a plug in so it held seven shots. He got that one out and he handed that one to me. He said, "Load it; if you can load it, that one's yours." . . . It was mine . . . from then on. And then, at first, I took it to my room and put it on my gun rack in my room. My granddad gave me one for my BB guns, and I took the top BB gun off, and put that one up there. My brother got jealous. My dad caught him taking it out one day. He just came in my room and picked it up, fixing to take it out with his friends. My dad took it away from him, I guess. He got a whipping for it. And then my dad told me what happened. I was, like, all right. And ever since my dad has held it. (CMS-17, 30–31)

After that, Marc started going shooting every weekend. "The main gun I would use, everybody was always using the pump action. The short 12-gauge that was made before the law was passed, with a weird handle and stuff. But the one I always used was a single-shot 12-gauge . . . Cause when we're shooting skeet, if I got, say I got more than one shot, I'll be real lenient, like everyone else, waste three or four shots trying to hit one skeet. I'll aim to fire one shot and I'll hit it" (CMS-17, 32). He went target shooting every weekend and went hunting about three times with his stepfather.

For Marc, the sight of guns "brings back memories [of] going up in the mountains shooting . . . I went up to the mountains, a lot of shooting ranges over there. We would go out in the mountains and shooting and stuff. In Oklahoma we went out shooting, in Texas. I've been around guns all my life . . . Used to know how to use them, how to clean them, break them apart, put them back together, load them, rebuild them, fix them, take care of them" (CMS-17, 7–8).

Marc used to be called Dead-Eye by his family and friends. It started when he was about nine years old, living in Oklahoma. He was at a picnic with his stepdad, a couple of his stepdad's friends, his brother, mother, and other family members. The adults had brought some guns for target practice and some dirt bikes. They had a "German special," as he calls it—a .22-caliber semiautomatic, "1909 special," "one of the first semiautomatics ever made." "We were all out just shooting with a .22. We were just target practicing to see who could shoot the targets with a .22. And everybody was missing. And I just walked up there with one shot and I made it dead center. That with just pulling the gun up and shot it. I did that three times in a row. Everybody started calling me Dead-Eye" (CMS-17, 8).

To Marc, guns are a tool. "I think they're a tool . . . For life. For hunting. For protection. It's just that you see everyday tools, and that's why we have it here with us. It's in the Constitution, the right to bear arms because of protection, like your dog for protection. It's your protection, it's a tool for you to go out hunting to survive with . . . I put it in a category with a sledgehammer, crowbar, . . . a grinder, and stuff" (CMS-17, 9).

Unfortunately, the meaning of guns has changed today, Marc says. Today, "it means death . . . Now if you look at it, everybody is carrying a gun to go out just to kill somebody. Before, people were killing with guns mainly because back then they didn't have cars, they had horses. If the horse wouldn't walk, or you fell off, you had a gun there to kill the horse and save your life. It was there to save your life from a certain animal. You had a gun there to feed your family and yourself, have a gun there cause just in case someone does break into your house and try killing you. It was an everyday tool back then and nobody looked down upon it. But now, you walk around carrying a gun and some people are afraid of you, cause they try to hold it on people, rob people with guns and stuff . . . People are misusing it now" (CMS-17, 10).

Marc has never had any gun possession charges. But he did carry a gun for a while when he was on the run. When this happened, he felt he needed a gun. "For protection. For just in case someone else pulled a gun on me, I have a fair chance" (CMS-17, 12). He carried a .38. "The serial number was filed off and everything else. I got it at a pawn shop . . . I had a fake ID" (CMS-17, 13–14). He was thirteen years old, accompanied by a nineteen-year-old friend:

We went, like, around. Cause he's the one who brought up the idea of me hitchhiking, buy yourself a gun. So we went walking around looking. He was looking at the big guns, like Colt .45, .357, and shit, more the big guns. And I was looking for a small one, something I can carry and won't get caught with it real quick. I picked out a .38 . . . I went up to the counter. I set it down. He looked at me, asked for ID. I showed him my ID. He said, "All right." He said, "That is $35." I paid him $35 and $5 for a box of shells . . . [Then] I went to Wal-Mart and bought a cleaning kit. We went out in the desert. We fired it. It was all messed up. I unloaded it, took it apart, cleaned it, put it back together. Tried it again, and it worked better, and that's it. (CMS-17, 15)

Marc carried the gun on his ankle and was on the lam for three months. "I went up to New York. Got there for, stayed there for a week. I met up with some friends there. Went down to Texas. I looked up my real dad. That's the first time I met him. And from there, I came back to Tucson" (CMS-17, 34). "I never pulled it out, I only, when I showered and stuff, I took it and set it in the bathroom where it was easy to reach just in case anything happened. When I slept, I took it off and put it under my pillow in the holster, that's it" (CMS-17, 35).

He respects guns. "I respect them. I might carry one. But I won't go around telling everyone, 'Yeah, I got a gun. Let's go do something. Let's go shoot in the desert. Yeah, I can shoot better than you. Yeah, I'm a sharpshooter, yeah, I can do this, I can shoot thirty yards away and still hit dead center.' I don't brag about that. I know I could do it, that's the end of it" (CMS-17, 28). He gets this from his stepfather. "[My stepdad] respects them," he explains. "Doesn't mistreat them. Doesn't go around bragging about guns. Doesn't destroy it; shoot it and put it away. He cleans it, takes care of them, oils them, keeps them in oiled rags, makes sure they are cared for and locked away in a gun cabinet" (CMS-17, 12). He also gets this from his mentor, Tom. Tom's an MP at Davis Monthan Air Force Base in Tucson. Marc knew him in Germany, and they hooked up again when Marc came to Tucson. He carries a Glock .40 and an M-16 rifle every day. "He shows that he respects them. But he likes them. He likes, he likes going out after his work's done, going to shoot his M-16. And his Glock .40. Cleans them, talks about them, brags about his guns and how he shoots, but he won't become stupid with them . . . He brags about how he keeps it clean, how they're always around, how he carries them, he become one with the gun, because he sleeps with them and everything. Eats with them, they're always there by his side, easy to grab" (CMS-17, 28).

Although Marc knew he shouldn't be carrying a gun when he was on the lam, he nevertheless concluded that he had to carry. The cost-benefit analysis was simple: "If I get caught and I go to jail, I'll still be alive. If I didn't have a gun, and someone held a gun to me, and say I was going to be a slave or die, it's, like, there goes my life. And I had nothing to protect me for it" (CMS-17, 47).

When he's older Marc wants to be an MP and then, after four years, an OCI (Operations Intelligence Officer, he explains to me), and then enter the CIA. For now he's at Catalina, finishing off his term for absconding from parole.

Of course, few of the youths that I have interviewed fit squarely into one or the other of these idealtypes. Many straddle different categories, combining different associations, moving between archetypes. CMS-66, you may recall, shares aspects of each of these idealtypes. He expresses, like Marc, a certain respect for guns, a respect his late father taught him. And like Jesús, he feels a strong need for self-protection, particularly when he is hanging out with his drug-dealing friends. His interview—like so many others—reflects genuine hybridity.

PLACING THE CLUSTERS IN PRACTICE CONTEXTS

My purpose has not been to exoticize my young informants—Jesús, Yusuf, Marc, CMS-66, and the other Catalina youths. Nor, for that matter, has it been to fetishize semiautomatic handguns, though I inevitably have. It is hard to reproduce these youths' words and voices—their slang, their grammar, their cadence—without appearing voyeuristic, without rendering them exotic and other. They are *so* young—fourteen, fifteen, sixteen, seventeen. And so fascinated, so thrilled, so excited by the mere sight of guns. The intensity of their reactions to the guns is remarkable. As a sixteen-year-old Yaqui youth tries to make me understand, "I like guns. I like 'em. It just gives you a rush. Gives me a rush" (CMS-65, 22).

One of the most striking aspects of the interviews is precisely this—how deeply seductive guns are to these youths, how passionate they feel about them. Guns are objects of desire, fascination, and lust—or deep repulsion—for practically all of them. They are powerful objects and exercise a remarkably strong grip on the youths: slick, metallic, well-engineered instruments; seductive companions; things to sleep with, to care for, to play with, to put in your pants; awesome, powerful, and desirable pieces of metal. And—to continue in this psychoanalytic vein—the deep attraction of guns is often combined with, and sometimes overshadowed by, their destructive potential. For some youths handguns evoke death, danger, and destruction, and the recognition, the fear, of their destructive potential feeds their desire. For some it overshadows their desire. For some it extinguishes it.

CONTEXTS AND MEANING

At the same time, context, situation, and environment shape the way youths interact with guns. Most of the youths live—when they are free—in a parallel universe of marginality. They use cocaine, acid, crystal meth, "rochas" (as they call the date rape drug), and marijuana. They sell drugs on the side. They break into homes, steal and sell guns, regularly carry firearms, claim a neighborhood, hang out with gangsters, tag, "jack" cars and other youths. Many of their behaviors—and certainly most of the central activities that organize their daily lives—are considered illegal or quasi-legal and are far out-side the mainstream in America. One way for many of the youths to make it—to avoid being "punked" or "jumped," to avoid being victimized, especially during their *own* criminal escapades—is to carry a gun and be willing to use it: to pull it out, to threaten others, to shoot.

Much of the gun possession I encountered, in fact, began passively, pur-portedly from a perceived need for self-protection in a hostile and dangerous world of criminality. This too is consistent with most research. A study con-ducted in 1995 of sixty-two incarcerated juvenile offenders in metropolitan Atlanta, Georgia, found that more than half of those who possessed guns received their first gun passively, without any specific plan. "Forty-two percent were given their first gun by a peer, an older youth, or a relative, often with the admonition that they needed it for protection. Five percent found their first gun; an additional 5% acquired their first gun by chance during a burglary or robbery" (Ash et al. 1996, 1756). A sixteen-year-old gang member told me, "We were robbing houses a lot, we were jacking cars, stealing cars, and he just told me, he said, he gave me a gun out of his backpack; he said, 'Here'; he gave it to me. We were going to rob a house, and he told me, 'If somebody's in there,' he said, 'just use this'" (CMS-3, 10). A sixteen-year-old Mexican youth stated, "My homeboy . . . has a lot of guns. He had that one, he just told me, 'Here, buddy, you can watch your back,' whatever. I said, 'Cool'" (CMS-34, 9). He started car-rying.

During the interviews, the youths' stories became increasingly familiar to me. They mentioned similar histories of how they started carrying. They offered recurring contexts where gun action occurs. They alluded to similar situations when guns are carried. The interviews revealed patterns of related meanings and recurring contexts. There is, for instance, the situation of youths staring at each other—what they call "dogging"—and then starting to verbally abuse each other or "talk shit." There is the repeated context of youths at a party competing for a girl's attention, or gang encounters in which symbols get flashed in a ritualized way that leads to gunfire. These recurring contexts and situations form the backdrop, the medium, for the language of guns.

One recurring scenario is when youths "get dogged" and "talk shit." "Talk-ing shit" has a cadence to it. It has a timing. There is a certain back and forth. As one youth explains, it goes something like this: "What the fuck?" "What, bitch?" "I ain't no bitch." "I got your bitch." "You're a pussy." "No, you're a bitch." "I'm gonna kick your ass." Soon enough the talking escalates, and someone pulls out a gun. According to CMS-8, "talking shit" happens all the time—"left and right." Three or four times out of ten, it turns into a fistfight or someone draws a gun or a knife. It turns into a real gunfight or knife fight when someone disrespects someone else's neighborhood. Most of the time it is gang related, and sometimes it is race related. Sometimes "people do it for the stupidity" (CMS-8, 30–31).

CMS-34 is a sixteen-year-old Mexican gang member. Here is his account of dogging and talking shit. "What does it sound like?" I ask. "You never know. Like, you're looking at them. And they're, like, 'What the fuck? What are you looking at?' And I be, like, 'What?' And started talking shit like they started saying, 'Where are you from?' Started saying what gang they're in. If they're not from the same gang, then they just start fighting" (CMS-34, 25). CMS-62 recounts a situation where he almost shot some other youths. "They were from Phoenix, and they were saying fuck Tucson, this and that. Fuck this hood. Fuck that hood. I'm, like, you know what, fuck you, motherfucker" (CMS-62, 20). Ultimately he ended up just pistol-whipping them. The spark for the violence, though, was talking shit and disrespecting a neighborhood—or, here, the city of Tucson.

Another youth, CMS-14, also tells me how these encounters unfold. It starts with staring. "They passed us, they were dogging us. They were looking at us," he explains. This triggers a response. "We came out with bats; we thought we were going to have a little rumble." But things escalated one step further. "The person that was sitting in the back got out of the car real quick and then just boom, boom, shot a couple of times." Which ended the encounter. "We jumped in the car and we turned on the car and booked, and that's about it." Until another day: "And we ended up chasing them down later on in the future. They just kept running driving in circles in the complex." Until today: "So, then I ended up here" (CMS-14, 21).

In many ways these encounters trigger associations of self-protection, laced with fun, danger, death, action, power. They recall the action/protection cluster. There seems to be a close association between gun carrying, displays of weapons, and the perceived need to defend yourself. The idea of getting dogged is all about getting punked. It requires a certain response, or else it will bring on more disrespect. It has a lot to do with reputations as well.

CMS-3, a gang member and drug dealer, explains a little bit about reputations. According to him, there are three types of people. First, there are "wimps." "That's what we were saying, like, there's wimps, you know, like I said, if you are going to pull out a gun and you have no balls to pull out a gun, you better use it. Cause people they use it just to flash around just to show and intimidate you"—those people are the wimps. Then there are people who are "stupid." "Someone who's stupid. There's a stupid reputation . . . Suppose I go out and shoot shit for the fuck of it. I said, like at that party one time, a guy was just shooting, for the hell of it." And then there are "dangerous" people. "There's just people that don't care. There's people just shoot you because you piss them off" (CMS-3, 33). These reputations are closely connected to getting punked, or dissed, or messed with.

GUN CARRYING AS CONTEXT

The Catalina interviews reveal a close association between the action/protection cluster and carrying, and suggest the importance of exploring the interaction between meaning and context. One such context is gun carrying itself. How do the meanings of guns cluster in relation to the youths' history of gun carrying?

To determine carrying status, I ask each youth during the interviews to trace his history of gun possession and gun carrying. I discovered that there were certain identifiable categories of gun carrying. I coded each youth based on his history of gun carrying, using the categories listed in table 5.1.

A correspondence analysis of the social meanings by the gun carrying category from table 5.1 produces the correspondence map in figure 5.1. This map is extremely revealing. First, notice that the action/protection cluster (with the possible exception of "jail") remains tightly knit along dimension 1 and is by

TABLE 5.1. *Categories of carrying status*

LABEL	DEFINITION
NOCARRY	The youth has either never handled, shot, possessed, or played with a gun or has handled, shot, possessed, or played with a gun, but has never carried a gun around on his person.
ONECARRY	The youth carried only one gun on one occasion for more than a day; however, it could have been for three days or for three months or more. What matters is that the youth did it with only one gun on one occasion.
MULTICARRY	The youth carried two (or more) guns on his person for a period of more than a day on more than one occasion. This category captures youths who have carried guns on multiple occasions but who do not carry guns all the time.
CONSTANT	The youth carries a gun at all times. The youth tries always to be armed.

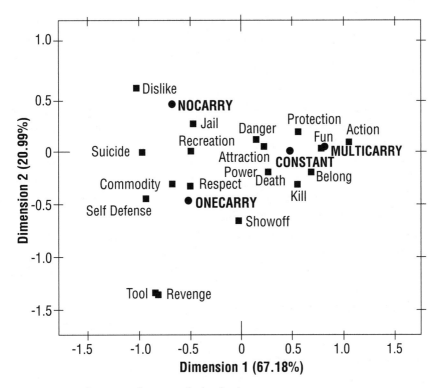

FIGURE 5.1. *Correspondence analysis of primary meanings of guns by carrying status*

itself on the right-hand side of the map. The cluster has stuck together. At the same time, the recreation/respect grouping and the jail variable are clustered together on practically the same point along dimension 1; and the commodity/dislike cluster is grouped to the left of recreation/respect, again on dimension 1. Both of these clusters are now on the left side of the map at the opposite extreme from the action/protection cluster.

The first dimension of the map reflects a spectrum from, at one extreme, the more active meanings (action, kill, protection) on the right side to, at the other extreme, more reactive or passive meanings (commodity, self-defense) on the left side. Dimension 1 spans the spectrum of the clusters noticed earlier: from action/protection, to recreation/respect, to commodity/dislike. In this sense dimension 1 ranges from attraction to guns on the right side, through respect, to dislike on the left side. This dimension is highly explanatory and accounts for about 67 percent of the inertia in the map.

What is equally remarkable is that dimension 1 also has a clean interpretation in terms of the carrying status of the youths. The high carrying statuses—MULTICARRY and CONSTANT—are on the right side of the map, whereas the low carrying statuses—NOCARRY and ONECARRY—are on the left side. The correspondence map reveals clearly that the action/protection meanings on the right side are associated with higher carrying statuses. Youths who carry guns on multiple occasions or who constantly carry guns are thinking about guns in more of an action/protection way than their cohorts who have carried only once or have never carried. In other words, the action-type meanings are more highly associated with carrying guns. In contrast, those youths who think about guns as a commodity or as recreation are more likely not to have much of a carrying history. The commodity/dislike cluster is in fact the farthest along the spectrum of low carrying. The recreation/respect cluster is on the low carrying side but closer to the middle of the map. It is fascinating how the map reveals strong associations between the clusters of meaning and different carrying statuses.

Dimension 2 is less easy to interpret. The most distinct meanings at the top include dislike, NOCARRY, jail, and protection; on the bottom, they include self-defense, ONECARRY, commodity, respect, and kill (excluding the meanings that are observed too infrequently). This distinction might reflect a spectrum from diffuse meanings (at the top) to more pointed and instrumental meanings (at the bottom). From this perspective, it is interesting that the more diffuse meanings are more closely associated with youths who have never carried, whereas the more pointed meanings are associated with youths who have carried on one occasion. In any event, dimension 2 accounts for only 21 percent of the inertia in the map, in contrast to dimension 1, which accounts for 67 percent, so it makes sense to remain focused on dimension 1.

GANG MEMBERSHIP AS CONTEXT

Gang rivalry is often woven into "talking shit" but just as easily can lead to gun violence on its own. Animosity and rivalry between gangs is routinely a spark for gunfights. CMS-65, a sixteen-year-old Yaqui gang member who is at Catalina Mountain School on a charge of aggravated assault with a deadly weapon, offers a chilling example. He and his three friends were on the reservation, looking for a rival, "to shoot him. To kill him" (CMS-65, 4). Why? I ask. "Because he's my rival" (CMS-65, 4). "Because he was my rival and I don't like him" (CMS-65, 6).

CMS-65 describes what happened next. "My rival came out of his house with a gun. It was like a little .22 that came out. Just started talking shit." "You fools come around here," his rival said, "You're going to get smoked, motherfucker . . ." "And I said 'Fuck you, motherfucker. What are you going to do with that strap, fool? You ain't going to do shit. You gonna start talking shit.' And I seen him. He was walking . . . He had his strap down. And I had my strap already. And I seen him raising his gun. And that's when I was, like, 'Pow.' That's when I shot" (CMS-65, 7). As CMS-65 shot at his rival, his gun jammed. His rival was shooting back at him. CMS-65 took off and was arrested about five minutes later in his friend's house nearby.

Here is another relatively typical gang incident. CMS-62 is seventeen years old, Mexican American, and has a long history of gun possession, gang membership, and drug dealing.

> I was in my hood, and I was walking. I had a royal blue rag hanging down my pocket . . . And I was walking through the park going to my homeboy's house through the alley . . . And some fools just rolled up. They're some Bloods. They started talking shit. And they were looking for my homey. Me and my homey, well, I'm, like, what the fuck. They started talking shit to me. "Fuck you." "Fuck your homey, motherfucker." What the fuck, and he was in my hood. And I'm, like, "Fuck you, you punk ass motherfucker." I was just talking shit. Running my mouth. Back and forth, you know. And they were, like, five of them in their car. There were two girls in there. They were a group of them in that car. They were all slammed up on fucking flammable. Fucking red everywhere. And I guess I started saying, "Wuz up, Blood?" This and that. "Motherfucker, I ain't your Blood, fool." "Wuz up, cuz?" "This is my fucking hood," I was telling them and everything, and I just started walking away because I knew one of those fools was going to pull out a strap. But I knew who they were. They always carry guns. I thought they were going to pull out a gun, but they didn't. So I just started walking away. I was, like, "If I catch you motherfuckers sleeping in my hood, we'll tango." And that fool was, like, "Fuck you." "Fuck your hood." And then drove off. If I had a gun that time, I would have shot at him. I would have shot. I would have shot at him. (CMS-62, 21–22)

Another gang member, CMS-13, recalls a time he was shot at by rivals:

> All of us were talking shit to them, but they started because they just cruised up on the side, dogging us and shit, blowing the horn. We didn't know who

the hell they were. And then they were, "Oh, yeah, that's that one guy" or whatever. They just started talking shit. Then we tried to pass them, and they kept speeding up and shit, and I know the guy laid down in the back and started shooting at us. Four or three shots. All together like six went off, but three or four hit the car. (CMS-13, 29)

As these stories indicate well, gangs and gang membership are an important context for carrying guns. Again, correspondence analysis can help us visualize this association more rigorously. Reviewing the interviews, I coded each youth for his affiliation with gangs. Youths were grouped within the three possible categories listed in table 5.2, depending on whether they claimed a gang, or denied gang membership but had friends and associates as gang members, or claimed to have no association whatever with gangs. I then ran a correspondence analysis of the social meanings of guns in relation to gang affiliation and obtained the correspondence map reproduced in figure 5.2.

The correspondence map is, again, very telling, especially the similarity with figure 5.1. Here again the action/protection cluster is neatly grouped on one end of dimension 1—again, with the exception of jail—whereas the recreation/respect and commodity/dislike clusters are grouped on the other end of the axis. The first dimension also reflects a clear spectrum of gang affiliation, from nongang youths at one end, through youths who are not themselves gang members but have friends in gangs in the middle, to gangbangers on the other extreme.

Like figure 5.1, the correspondence map reveals a close association between the meaning clusters and the gang statuses. The action/protection cluster is more highly associated with gang membership—with actually being a gang member. The meanings are clustered on the same side of the map as the GANG-STER status (left). In this map, however, the recreation/respect cluster is more closely associated with the lowest gang affiliation value—NONGANG—and the

TABLE 5.2. *Categories of gang status*

LABEL	DEFINITION
NONGANG	Youth is not a member of a street gang and does not affiliate with gang members
GANGASSOC	Youth is not a member of a gang but does have friends or associates who are gang members
GANGSTER	Youth is a member of a street gang

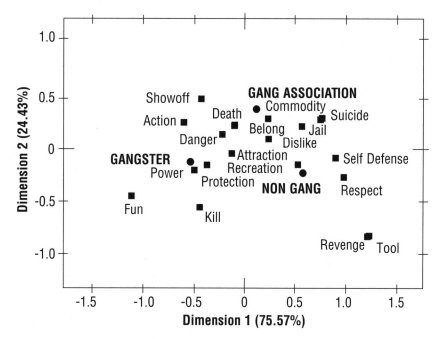

FIGURE 5.2. *Correspondence analysis of primary
meanings of guns by gang status*

commodity/dislike cluster is to the left and is more closely associated with
some affiliation with gang members—GANGASSOC.

These similarities and subtle differences between figures 5.1 and 5.2 are
striking. Given the centrality of the first dimension to both of these correspondence maps, and the fact that they reflect parallel meanings along the context
variables—gun carrying and gang affiliation—it may be useful to compare the
two along dimension 1. One way to get at this comparison would be to place
dimension 1 from figure 5.1 and dimension 1 from figure 5.2 next to each other
and see how the social meanings compare in terms of their relative locations.
This is illustrated in figure 5.3.[8]

The comparison confirms a number of significant points. First, the
action/protection cluster remains grouped in both contexts. Although
the ordering and associations of proximity differ slightly, by and large the
action/protection cluster sticks together. The commodity/dislike cluster also
sticks together but has moved from being at the extreme of dimension 1 in figure 5.1 to being more in the middle of dimension 1 in figure 5.2. In other words,
whereas commodity/dislike is highly associated with low gun carrying, in the

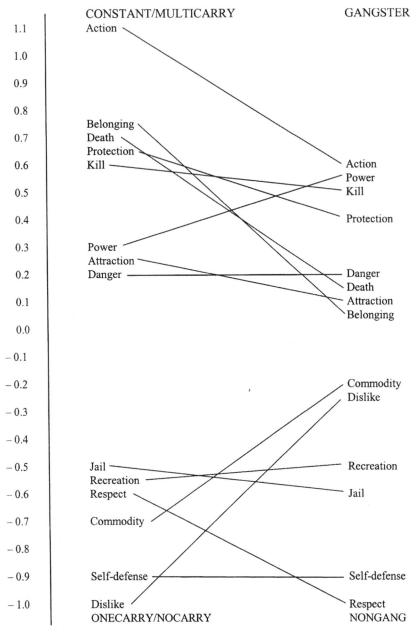

FIGURE 5.3. *Comparison of dimension 1 from figures 5.1 (left column) and 5.2 (right column)*

gang context it is associated with having friends in gangs. This might suggest that youths who trade in guns and are not overly attracted by guns are more likely to not carry guns on their persons and to not belong to a gang but are more likely to have friends in gangs. This may explain how they get the guns to sell, or how they know people to sell guns to. Gangs are often a source of guns and a venue for selling guns, which would explain why youths who have friends in gangs may be more involved in gun transactions. The recreation/respect cluster, on the other hand, has split up somewhat in the gang context. Respect for guns is now somewhat more distant from recreation and is at the extreme on the nongang dimension. It is fascinating that the action/protection cluster, in contrast, has remained robust, being grouped in both contexts. It suggests a real association of this cluster of meanings along both carrying and gang membership dimensions.

Another way to represent the comparison between figures 5.1 and 5.2 is to create a two-dimensional graph, using dimension 1 of figure 5.1 as the x-axis and dimension 1 of figure 5.2 as the y-axis. This reveals—and again confirms—the earlier conclusions. The graph is reproduced in figure 5.4.

Figure 5.4 reveals two dominant clusters of meanings in the contexts of gun carrying and gangs: in the upper right corner, the action/protection cluster and in the lower left corner, the commodity/dislike and recreation/respect clusters. There is no question, from this graph, that there is a close association between the action/protection cluster and the type of behaviors that policy makers are most concerned with: gun carrying among youths and gang membership.

DRUG SELLING AS CONTEXT

Youths who sell drugs also often feel the need to carry firearms. Recall what CMS-3, a gang member and a drug dealer, says: "I was staying with this girl, I was on the run, I was in this apartment complex, and I was selling drugs, and a lot of people there wanted to jump me for my drugs. There was a lot of friends that wanted me for my drugs. If I was just going to get a soda, I would carry a gun. And at the house I was at, there was a lot of dopies there too. A lot of drug addicts there. I remember if I was in the bathroom, I remember I would have my gun right there. You can't trust nobody" (CMS-3, 29).

CMS-2, a sixteen-year-old Anglo youth from the northwest suburbs of Tucson, dropped out of school and began dealing drugs in his suburban neighborhood. Because of his dealing, he carried a gun constantly and had an extensive history of possession and carrying. In fact, he is at Catalina for burglarizing a home where he thought he would find guns. "Someone told me that I could

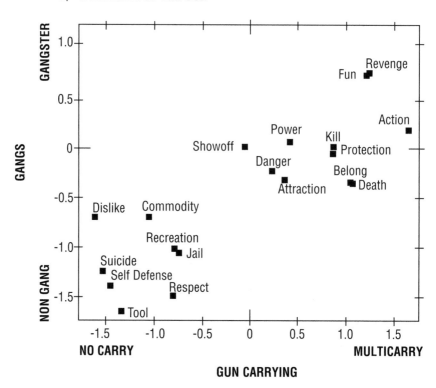

FIGURE 5.4. *Graph of dimension 1 from figures 5.1 (x-axis) and 5.2 (y-axis)*

find a house where I can find a lot of guns, and I went in and I stole, like, six-teen guns and left," he tells me (CMS-2, 1). He was caught about a month later with some of the guns from the burglary, including "a Mac-90, which is a big gun. A very big gun. An M-16, a street sweeper, and just a bunch of shotguns" (CMS-2, 36).

Since he dropped out of school, he spent most of his time dealing and "partying." "Partying on Mondays, Tuesdays, and Wednesdays. And just during the week when everybody was in school I would be kicking it during the day. Doing nothing. Selling . . . I was selling a little bit of marijuana and a little bit of coke and a little bit of acid, but not much. I wasn't a big-time drug dealer" (CMS-2, 39). He carried a 9-mm regularly. In fact, before his arrest, he would carry it "all the time. All day. If I'm sleeping . . . say I'm sleeping on the couch at my homey's house. I put in under the couch and when I wake up, put it in my pants" (CMS-2, 38).

The reason: drugs. In that business, you need to be armed. When you're dealing, he explains, "selling coke or something and the guy just takes your coke and he starts walking away, like. Little kid get out of here. And he's little, like someone my size, shhhh. Give me my shit. And you better give him your money . . . That's when I need a gun. It's when they need to overrule somebody. They need that power over somebody. Or when someone gots enough power to be shooting at them, they need that to go back. That's when most people need guns" (CMS-2, 23). As another youth says, "I used to do a lot of drugs, and there's, like, little problems. I'd be, like, I gotta have a gun or something. Just, like, a couple of times. Seriously, I don't like guns . . . Not much . . . But when I use them, I use them" (CMS-48, 6).

In order to get at this drug dimension, I coded the youths into three categories—those who had never sold drugs (NODRUGSALE), those who had sold drugs on occasion (DRUGSELLER), and those who sold drugs regularly (DRUGDEALER). I then ran a correspondence analysis on the primary meanings by drug context, which gave me the correspondence map shown in figure 5.5.

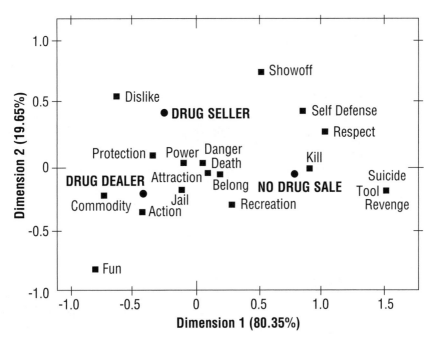

FIGURE 5.5. *Correspondence analysis of the primary meanings of guns by drug status*

The correspondence map is, again, fascinating. Notice that dimension 1 maintains some commonality with figures 5.1 and 5.2, insofar as the three clusters of meaning are still distinct. The far left side of dimension 1 is defined by the commodity/dislike cluster. Not surprisingly, that side of dimension 1 also maps on neatly to the DRUGDEALER end of the spectrum. Dimension 1 ranges neatly, again, along the context variable from DRUGDEALER on the far left, to DRUGSELLER, to NODRUGSALE on the far right.

The action/protection cluster is to the right of the commodity/dislike cluster and is still relatively united, though a little more scattered. Action and protection are the farthest on the left, the most closely associated with dealing drugs. Recreation and respect have separated somewhat. Respect seems to practically define the right end of dimension 1, which is most closely associated with not selling drugs. In this map, the kill meaning is more separate from the action/protection cluster, far to the right, more likely to be associated with not selling drugs.

Again, the shifts and movements of meaning can be best represented by comparing dimension 1 from figure 5.1 with dimension 1 from figure 5.5, which I reproduce in figure 5.6.

INCARCERATION AS CONTEXT

How do the social meanings of guns relate in the context of specific public policies? Among these youths, one public policy is clearly identifiable: incarceration. Several of the youths are incarcerated on gun charges, and others have previously been incarcerated for firearms possession. Is it possible to distinguish the youths by their history of gun incarcerations in order to explore how the policy of incarcerating youths affects the meanings they associate with guns?

To explore public policy as context, I obtained from each youth his history of detentions and incarcerations. I then coded the youths based on whether they are now incarcerated on a gun charge (GUNCHARGE), whether they have previously been incarcerated on a firearms violation but now are not (PRIOR), or whether they have never before been and are not now detained on a gun violation (NOCHARGE). These categories are described in table 5.3. A correspondence analysis of the social meanings of guns by the incarceration status of the youths produces the map in figure 5.7.

This map has several intriguing features. First, there has been an important and significant destabilization of the action/protection cluster. In contrast to figures 5.1 and 5.2, the action/protection cluster has exploded and is now

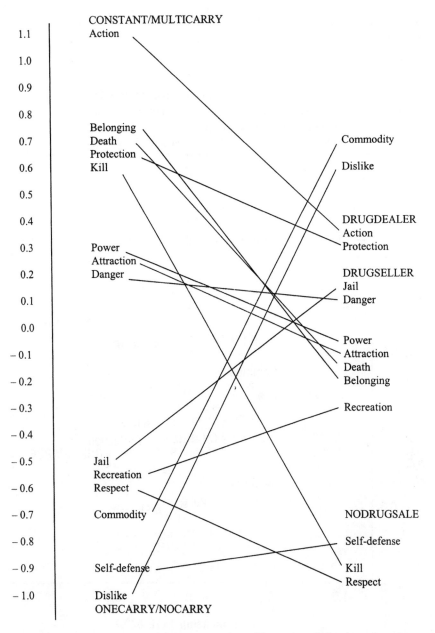

FIGURE 5.6. *Comparison of dimension 1 from figures 5.1 (left column) and 5.5 (right column)*

TABLE 5.3. *Categories of youth status for prior incarceration on firearms charges*

LABEL	DEFINITION
NOCHARGE	Youth has never been detained on a firearms violation
PRIOR	Youth has been previously incarcerated on a gun charge but is not now detained on a firearms violation
GUNCHARGE	Youth is now at Catalina Mountain School on a gun charge

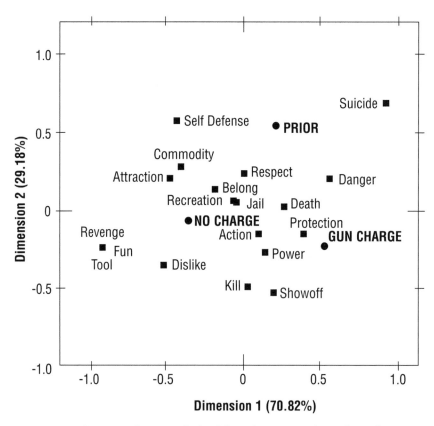

FIGURE 5.7. *Correspondence analysis of the primary meanings of guns by gun charge status*

distributed across the entire dimension 1. Danger and protection define the right side of dimension 1, whereas attraction and belonging now define the left side. Both attraction and belonging are now set apart, pushed out past respect and past recreation. In fact, danger has become the defining meaning in what could now be called the danger/protection cluster, a cluster that also includes death and power and is at the extreme right of the dimension. In contrast to the action/protection cluster, both the commodity/dislike cluster and the recreation/respect cluster continue to hang together. The recreation/respect meanings have moved closer to the center of the map, whereas the commodity/dislike cluster remains on the far left, defining the dimension.

At the same time, the gun charge variable—the contextual variable—is neatly aligned along dimension 1. Youths who are now incarcerated on gun charges are on the far right of the dimension. Those who are not now incarcerated on a firearms offense but previously have been are also on the right side, though slightly to the left along dimension 1. And those who have never been charged with a firearms offense are on the left of the dimension. In other words, dimension 1 forms a perfect spectrum for the contextual variable associated with the public policy of incarcerating gun offenders.

There are a number of other interesting aspects to the map in figure 5.7. Attraction and dislike are now clustered on the left side of dimension 1 and are associated with NOCHARGE. This suggests that the more emotional, visceral responses are somehow more closely associated with youths who have not experienced gun detentions. Danger, which was previously clustered near attraction in figure 5.1, is now more closely associated with death and protection, as well as GUNCHARGE. This suggests that the new danger/protection cluster—which is closely associated with being incarcerated on a gun charge—is no longer as attractive as it is in the context of gun carrying. The protection meaning, though, remains robustly located at the right of the dimension, again, as in figures 5.1 and 5.2, helping to define the dimension.

The best way to visualize the shifted meanings in these different contexts is to compare the locations of the social meanings on dimension 1 from figure 5.1 to figure 5.7—to place them next to each other and graph their relations, as I have done in figure 5.8. The comparison underscores the movement. It demonstrates how the action/protection cluster has been ripped apart and how attraction and belonging in particular are no longer part of the grouping. It confirms the shift of the recreation/respect cluster to the center, and it also reveals how robust the protection, death, and power meanings remain.

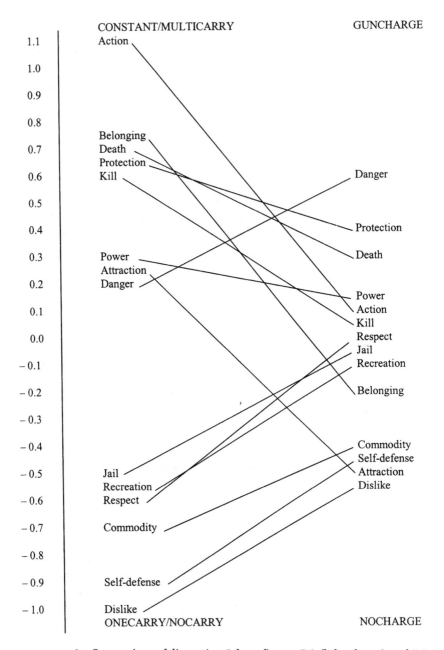

FIGURE 5.8. *Comparison of dimension 1 from figures 5.1 (left column) and 5.7 (right column)*

The comparison of figures 5.1 and 5.7 reveals that certain social meanings, particularly the action/protection cluster, relate very differently to each other depending on the contextual variables. When meanings are placed in the context of gun detentions, there is a significant shift in the attraction and belonging variables and a recontextualization of the notion of protection and of danger.

RACE AND OTHER CONTEXTS

There are other recurring circumstance where guns and certain meanings of gun possession predominate. Alcohol, for instance, is frequently associated with reckless gun possession and gunfights. As CMS-2 explains, "That's mostly when people use guns when they are all drunk or something about gangs or a drug deal goes wrong" (CMS-2, 23). There is also a strong correlation between gun violence and certain locations where youths feel they need to take a gun. So, for instance, CMS-3, a gangbanger, tells me it is important to carry a gun "when you're going to a party or something. A party that you don't know about . . . When you're going to someone else's hood. When you're going out of your neighborhood, out of your hood, I mean. You don't know what to expect" (CMS-3, 17; see also CMS-37, 19).

Another recurring practice among male youths is fighting over women. CMS-2, who was always carrying a firearm, preferably a 9-mm, recounted a story about going to a party with a "homegirl." She was "just a friend," he explained. This other guy, an older gang member, became angry when he saw them hanging out "because he thought he was with her." He was "roached out on pills." Here's what happened next: "He tried to start a fight with me, and I got mad and I was drunk. And so I got up, and he went to his car. I thought he was going to pull out a gun, so I shot his car. Boom. I hit the door, and I shot again, and I don't know where it hit because I took off running. Then he pulled out a gun and ba-da-da-da-da . . . I dunno [what type of gun he had]. I was gone" (CMS-2, 6).

CMS-46 also tells how, at a party, a friend got into a fight "over some girl" and exchanged gunfire (CMS-46, 30). In that case the other guy was "messing around with his girlfriend . . . Having sex with her, doing other things behind his back, and [he] had found out about it" (CMS-46, 31).

Another youth, CMS-14, tells this story:

Over in our neighborhood. And it was three houses partying right next to each other. One big yard thing. They had their own yards, but they got along, I guess. They'd met each other, I guess. All them three houses were involved. We were invited by some girls and this and that. What happened from what I understand is some guy was trying to mess with some girl that was his girlfriend, and he was drunk; they ended up with somebody slashing tires and then, "Yeah, you motherfuck, you mess with my girl," and I just remember he popped out this shotgun . . . And next thing you know, boom! Kneecap. He shot him in the knee. (CMS-14, 25–26)

The combinations can be lethal. CMS-48 talks about using cocaine at a party and getting into a fight over a girl. "This dude started talking shit . . . I got mad at him cause I was all hyped up, you know, coked out, or something. I think I was tweaked out. But really, I was up for a couple of days and I didn't give a shit, you know. I don't know, just drugs give you a different attitude, too. So I was just about to pull it out, and I was, like, in my head, 'What am I going to do that for?'" (CMS-48, 23). He stopped himself and didn't take out the gun. Many times, that would lead to a gun threat or use. As CMS-53 explained, "Alcohol and kids with guns don't mix at all" (CMS-53, 19).

One final, potentially significant dimension relates to race and ethnicity. How do the primary meanings coalesce and fragment along racial and ethnic lines? Are there clusters of meaning by racial or ethnic identity? Are there racially identifiable ways of interpreting the language of guns?

To address these questions, during the interviews I obtained detailed demographic background information from each youth. The racial and ethnic composition of my interviewees—which reflects well the overall racial and ethnic composition of the Catalina students as a whole—is summarized in table 5.4. The correspondence map that I ran based on this demographic information is reproduced in figure 5.9.

Note that the three individual meaning clusters remain relatively intact on the correspondence map along dimension 1, recreation being close to respect,

TABLE 5.4. *Catalina youths by race/ethnicity*

RACE/ETHNICITY	FREQUENCY
Hispanic	13
Anglo	12
Native American (incl. mixed)	3
African American	2

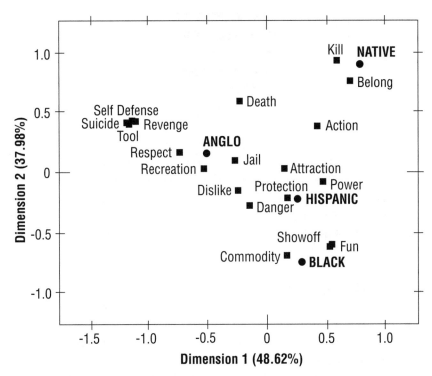

FIGURE 5.9. *Correspondence analysis of the primary meanings of guns by race/ethnicity*

commodity being close to dislike, and the action/protection cluster staying somewhat united. In contrast to earlier maps, the commodity/dislike cluster is now interspersed in the action/protection cluster. Although there are too few African Americans or Native Americans to draw reliable conclusions about those two groups, dimension 1 is neatly aligned by the two dominant race/ethnicity groups, with the Anglo majority on the left of dimension 1 and the Hispanic cluster on the right. Along dimension 1, then, the recreation/respect cluster is more closely associated with Anglo youths, the action/protection cluster with Hispanic youths.

THE SENSUAL, MORAL, AND POLITICAL DIMENSIONS OF GUNS

The focus on particular gun contexts and situations—carrying, gang membership, drugs, and incarceration, to name a few—demonstrates some fluidity in the meaning structures of youths' talk about guns. It is useful at this point to pan the lens out from the concrete contexts to explore some larger and recurring dimensions that permeate and cut across the different registers—what I refer to as the sensual, the moral, and the political dimensions of the language of guns.

THE SENSUAL DIMENSION

The interviews reflect how deeply seductive guns are to the youths at Catalina. To many, they are sensual objects. They have a sleek feel. A kick. They bring together metal, power, oil, and thrust. Let's start here, then, with the sensuality of guns.

"I like big guns," a seventeen-year-old gangbanger explains, "but I don't like carrying them with me. When I do carry a gun I want to carry, like, a good-sized one. The Ruger ain't even that big, it's, like, fat, about sixteen bullets, big bullets, and that would blow a hole through your chest" (CMS-10, 20).

"I like to reload bullet shells," another youth tells me (CMS-46, 17).

Another likes the way guns work. The gunpowder. "It's just, it's just weird. I don't know how to describe them. They're just, they're really, I think they're just . . . the way they make them, make them work, work on them, and how the powder in it actually works, you know" (CMS-40, 13).

Guns hold a surprisingly powerful and passionate grip over these youths regardless of which cluster they find themselves in. The intensity of the attraction, in some cases, is hard to communicate in words. One seventeen-year-old Anglo youth explains: "When you go to shoot a gun, you get butterflies in your stomach. You get nervous unless you do it quick. Like on stand-offs, when stand-offs happen. No one is gonna shoot until, the longer they wait, the more butterflies they get in the stomach. The more worried they get. They feel like vomiting. They think, 'Oh, God. I'm getting weak. I can't do this.' If you talk to them awhile, they get worried and they can't pull the trigger" (CMS-8, 32–33).

Gun violence can be exhilarating. Here are a few stories recounted by a seventeen-year-old gang member (CMS-10, 32). He's Mexican—"Pure Mexican; I'm straight Mexican, that's all I am"—and he moved to Tucson from Los Angeles. You can feel the excitement, you can hear the thrill in his stories:

> In LA . . . some guys came by and they just drove by, a drive-by, started shooting at us . . . Rivals, I don't know, didn't see them. We got in the car and chased them . . . They were using a Mac-10, somebody had a handgun, but I couldn't see what kind it was. It was small like a .25. We got in the car and started chasing them. There were about five people in their car. Three or four [in ours]. We got in, started chasing them. For a while we were chasing them, and finally they just ended up going to a dead end. When they got off, they started running and shooting at us, and we just started unloading. After we got them we just left . . . We seen blood and left . . . We went back to my house where we were at, just tell my boys. Later on, about 12:00, we went back to see what happened. There were still cops and all kinds of things. (CMS-10, 22–23)

> One time, we were at a park and I had a gun on me, in my pocket. Some guys came tripping, talking shit and then my boys were, like, "What the fuck." They started going and talking. Then I had a gun on me. They started talking. I told them, "What's your problem? What you want?" My boys said, "Nah, stay out of this" and all. I said "Fuck that." Then he goes, "What you want, problems too?" I said, "Whatever, you call it, what you want?" Then he took off his shirt, so I took off my shirt. I gave my gun to my friend, and they seen it and they just backed up. I said, "I ain't gonna use it, come on," and we just got in a fight . . . At first he didn't want to fight me because of the gun. But then I gave it to my friend, and he was, like, he didn't want to fight me. But after I hit him, he had no choice but to fight. (CMS-10, 24)

CMS-10 lives at the limit, at the very edge of life. And to him it is exhilarating. Deeply sensual—bloody, hot, passionate. Scary. Threatening. Defining. Guns have a grip on these youths.

THE MORAL DIMENSION

There is also a strong moral dimension to guns. Many of the youths feel self-righteous about the need for self-protection. A Mexican gang member raised in Los Angeles explains in indignant terms that when he and his gang peers are carrying guns for protection, they wouldn't even think of not using them. "If it's for safety, they're gonna use it. We don't choose not to because it's either our life or their life. So if it's a choice like that, we're, like, we're gonna use it, not hesitate to use it. But I never been in that kind of situation where we don't use it. If it's for our safety and we don't use it, I never been in that kind of situation" (CMS-10, 23). Another youth, a seventeen-year-old, says, "It's either them shoot me and kill me, and my family being all depressed and quiet or just try and protect myself . . . I'd rather have my life" (CMS-48, 27). Another states, "Because I got shot at that one night on Speedway. I was totally unprotected and I could have gotten killed that night, and I don't want that to happen again. I'm either taking them with me or just preventing that from happening by shooting back at them" (CMS-13, 33).

In other cases youths invoke notions of "enemies" and moral conceptions of "warfare." Guns, for them, are about getting back, seeking revenge in gang rivalries. A sixteen-year-old Yaqui gang member explains: "I know when I have my gun, that's when I'm going after people. I'm not doing it to defend myself. I'm doing it because I want to kill somebody else. I want to shoot somebody else" (CMS-65, 19). For these youths, guns are all about "shooting at my enemy" (CMS-10, 5). The notion of "enemy" carries enormous moral weight. Guns are a way of evening a deadly score. "By killing somebody," one gang member tells me, "you can earn a lot of respect. Cause a lot of my homeys died, and if the homeys see somebody get killed, be like something to get that for. Go to the funeral, tell them I'm gonna get them for you. Get them, that's for my homey, man" (CMS-10, 36).

Other notions of moral entitlement permeate the interviews. One youth, a fifteen-year-old African American gang member, feels morally entitled to guns simply because they are made. If they weren't supposed to be used, he protests, they shouldn't be produced. "Certain guns I think are for protection and they're just tight to have. Just tight for you to have one of those guns for your-self," he states. "It's good to have one. There's no problem with having one coming from me . . . Because you should be able to know what you want. *And if it's a problem to have one, then they shouldn't be made.* People do make it a problem to have them, but they still make them" (CMS-13, 6). This same youth also expressed a sense of entitlement to guns because the police are armed. "Some people carry guns just because the police do. Some people carry guns because police shoot at people. They think they have the right to shoot back. They do, I think, have reason to protect themselves. They gonna protect their self by saying you can't protect your own? Don't make no sense. Shouldn't go that way" (CMS-13, 26).

Guns and gun carrying, in this sense, have their own attraction beyond their merely instrumental value. Like other criminal objects and behavior, they are more than just a means to achieve material benefit. They may express moral judgment, moral condemnation, or self-righteousness.

In his brilliant essay "Crime as Social Control," Donald Black emphasizes that "much crime is moralistic and involves the pursuit of justice. It is a mode of conflict management, possibly a form of punishment, even capital punishment. Viewed in relation to law, it is self-help" (1983, 34). Most homicides, Black argues, are themselves reactions to conduct that the perpetrator perceives as deviant—whether during a fight, in self-defense, or because of provocation such as adultery, disloyalty, or affronts to honor. Similarly, most conduct classified as assault, and many acts classified as burglaries, thefts, and robberies, can also be understood as punishment or as an expression of a grievance. "In New York City," Black writes, "where over one-third of the people arrested for robbery are acquainted with their victims, the crime often arises from a quarrel over money" (1983, 37). Vandalism is also often a form of social control and may result from the victim's violating local norms or calling the police to intervene in social conflicts. Other crimes as well, including sexual assault, may often have moral elements. Black quotes a passage from Eldridge Cleaver's 1968 *Soul on Ice*, where Cleaver described his selection of white women victims: "It delighted me that I was defying and trampling upon the white man's law, upon his system of values, and that I was defiling his women—and this point, I believe, was the most satisfying to me because I was very resentful over the historical fact of how the white man has used the black woman. I felt I was getting revenge" (Black 1983, 38, quoting Cleaver). These offenses, Black observes, are "intended as a punishment or other expression of disapproval, whether applied reflectively or impulsively, with coolness or in the heat of passion. Some [are] an effort to achieve compensation, or restitution, for a harm that has been done" (1983, 35–36).

Jack Katz, in his seminal *Seductions of Crime*, similarly highlights the moral and sensual dimensions of crime that are reflected in the Catalina interviews. As Katz emphasizes, there are "positive, often wonderful attractions within the lived experience of criminality" (1988, 3). These sensual dimensions are too often sublimated in academic research. "The social science literature contains only scattered evidence of what it means, feels, sounds, tastes, or looks like to commit a particular crime," Katz notes. "Readers of research on homicide and assault do not hear the slaps and curses, see the pushes and shoves, or feel the humiliation and rage that may build toward the attack, sometimes persisting after the victim's death" (1988, 3). But when we begin to experience crime from the criminal's perspective, we often see its rich and seductive dimensions. "Central to all these experiences in deviance is a member of the family of moral emotions: humiliation, righteousness, arrogance, ridicule, cynicism, defilement, and vengeance" (9). The crime most often does not emerge from a material gap. It is not motivated by the need to get a television set or some cash. It arises from the need to resolve moral tension.

> The closer one looks at crime, at least at the varieties examined here, the more vividly relevant become the moral emotions. Follow vandals and amateur shoplifters as they duck into alleys and dressing rooms and you will be moved by their delight in deviance; observe them under arrest and you may be stunned by their shame. Watch their strutting street display and you will be struck by the awesome fascination that symbols of evil hold for the young men who are linked in the groups we often call gangs. If we specify the opening moves in muggings and stickups, we describe an array of "games" or tricks that turn victims into fools before their pockets are turned out. The careers of persistent robbers show us, not the increasingly precise calculations and hedged risks of "professionals," but men for whom gambling and other vices are a way of life, who are "wise" in the cynical sense of the term, and take pride in a defiant reputation as "bad." And if we examine the lived sensuality behind events of cold-blooded "senseless" murder, we are compelled to acknowledge the power that may still be created in the modern world through the sensualities of defilement, spiritual chaos, and the apprehension of vengeance. (Katz 1988, 312)

The key to interpreting youths' gun carrying, then, may be precisely to explore, rather than ignore, what it feels like to carry a gun, what it means to pack heat, what gunpowder smells like, the kick of the gun, the appeal of those two baby nines. We may need to listen closely and carefully to the voices of the youths themselves.

THE POLITICAL DIMENSION

Guns also have a significant political-economic dimension. To many youths, handguns have important exchange value. They are a commodity to be sold for cash or traded for drugs. CMS-3, a sixteen-year-old Hispanic gang member, has a long record of selling drugs. He started selling them when he was in eighth grade, the year before he dropped out of school, and soon he was selling all kinds of stuff. "Whatever, whatever people needed," he says. "If people needed coke, I'd sell coke. If people needed pot, I'd sell pot. If they wanted some bud, I'd go serve them. I sold crack before, I sold rocks." When I asked whether this was gang related, he was adamant: "No, it was something I wanted to do on my own. Try to make money on my own" (CMS-3, 25). He insists that his dealing was not part of his gangbanging but his own enterprise. In the same sense, for him guns are "easy money" (CMS-3, 21)—a way to make money and participate in the market economy.

In this sense gun carrying may resemble other forms of criminality that have a political valence. Vandalism, for instance, is often a form of political expression, a mode of protest or resistance to a political-economic system that may appear to the vandal as foreign, alien, or oppressive. E. P. Thompson, in his wonderful essay "The Moral Economy of the English Crowd in the Eighteenth Century," describes how food riots in eighteenth-century England, rather than being merely spasmodic and occasional social disturbances brought about by a bad harvest, may actually have been politically engaged resistance to a relatively new laissez-faire political economy. These acts, Thompson argues, were "a highly complex form of direct popular action . . . operat[ing] within a popular consensus as to what were legitimate and what were illegitimate practices in marketing, milling, baking, etc." (1991, 188). The food riots were not about hunger but about the perceived violation of a moral economy. The rioting was aimed not at stealing food but at damaging the mills and machinery—acts that were counterproductive from the perspective of hunger. The riots were a response to the perceived violation of the legitimate beliefs and moral order of the economy. What really mattered was the affront to the *legitimate* moral order.

Drawing on Thompson's insight, there may be a parallel between the cultural outlook of some Catalina youths and late-modern entrepreneurial norms. Several of the boys perceive themselves as entrepreneurs—independent, self-motivated, market-driven, and street savvy. Like the start-up venture capitalist, these youths have a robust concept of individual responsibility and self-sufficiency. When asked if they have a role model, many respond that they are their *own* role models. "I am my own role model," one sixteen-year-old tells me. "I look up to my own self, my own accomplishments" (CMS-3, 12). "I look to myself," says another (CMS-17, 29). Or, as yet another claims, "[I'm] making my own way up" (CMS-54, 7). "I'm my own role model . . . I can't really be nobody's follower. I'm my own person, you know" (CMS-13, 9).

Some of these youths are and want to be fully responsible for themselves and their own success. They experience guns through a powerful desire for material wealth—for clothes, drugs, cars. They have a fine sense for making money, for bartering guns for drugs, cash, or other pleasures. They too want to make it on their own. They are entrepreneurs—in their own way. They resemble in many respects the informants in Philippe Bourgois's *In Search of Respect: Selling Crack in El Barrio* (1995), crack dealers who are emulating an entrepreneurial dream. As Bourgois contends, it is important "to place drug dealers and street-level criminals into their rightful position within the mainstream of U.S. society. They are not 'exotic others' operating in an irrational netherworld. On the contrary, they are 'made in America.' Highly motivated, ambitious inner-city youths have been attracted to the rapidly expanding, multibillion-dollar drug economy during the 1980s and 1990s precisely because they believe in Horatio Alger's version of the American Dream" (1995, 326).

CONFLICTS AND DESIRES

Throughout the interviews there are tensions and conflicts—ruptures between these different moral, sensual, and political dimensions. Most of the Catalina youths experience what seems to be genuine internal turmoil, existential angst between wanting to be "down" and wanting to straighten up. Many are negotiating a sharp conflict between wanting to burglarize homes, get rich quick, and party and use drugs and wanting to continue their education, go to college, and have a legitimate job.

Jesús is a good illustration—torn between gang life and getting straight. Recall that he wants to go to college and join the Marines. He realizes it may be difficult, that he has a long journey, and that he may in fact fail. He claims that he has, in effect, outgrown gang life. At the same time, though, when he gets back out on the street and returns to his neighborhood, his desires shift, he gets sucked back into delinquency. He explains how things changed for him after he came out of detention the last time, how he refused to make "beer runs" anymore.[9] But his homeys persisted:

"Remember back in the days when we used to do beer runs, like, every day? Remember? Remember? Remember right there at the Circle K, man? When we got caught that one time, they tried to catch us." And I was just thinking, "Damn, well, all right, well, I'll go do that." Cause I was thinking how fun it was. And I was like, "All right, I'll go do it." And I started doing it, like, every day. So some people, yeah, you could probably say, if different people look at it, they could probably say I was pressured into it, I guess.

But, to me, I knew I had my own choice. I could have still told them no. But I started thinking about how much fun it was. (CMS-16, 38)

Whether he was pressured or made his own choices, his preferences somehow shifted as he moved from one environment to another. And those different sets of preferences—going to college and joining the Marines or doing beer runs and burglarizing homes—are, in a sense, deeply incommensurable, sharply in conflict.

CMS-66, who opens this part of the book, is similarly torn between his dual lives—his friendship with drug dealers and his studies at the community college. Even though he has been incarcerated for the Glock .40 and is now incarcerated for the shotgun, he has a role model: Patch Adams. "You seen that movie, *Patch Adams*?" he asks me. "It's about the doctor who starts the Gesundheit Institute. He is, like—he's this doctor, he's talking about increasing the quality of life . . . He does all these things to help people. Doesn't just heal people. Medicine is about increasing the quality of life. He always inspired me. But I never felt I could make it through med school, so I'd try dental school. It's always, 'Mom, I'm gonna be a doctor no matter what. Either a doctor or a dentist. I'm gonna be one of those no matter what'" (CMS-66, 13).

Now, it may be that his desire to straighten up and go to college is pure rhetoric. Jesús may tell me, a straight-looking university professor conducting an interview in the administration building, that he would like to go to college when he is twenty-five, but maybe he is just trying to please me or merely repeating the Catalina Mountain School line. Maybe he is making it up. Perhaps he is playing a role. But this would not fully account for the depth of the tension between his sets of preferences.

The fact is, there are numerous examples of adjudicated youths—just like these Catalina boys—who have made it out of detention. Former senator Alan Simpson, now the director of the Institute of Politics at Harvard University, served two years on probation as a youth for destruction of federal property, shoplifting, and breach of the peace. District Attorney Terence Hallinan of San Francisco spent time in juvenile hall and the Marin County jail as a youth for fighting and assault. Ronald Laney, director of the Child Protection Division of the Office of Juvenile Justice and Delinquency Prevention of the U.S. Department of Justice, was adjudicated for larceny, fighting, and drinking as a minor, served a handful of sentences in juvenile detention, and spent almost a year at a state training school in Marianna, Florida. Luis Rodriguez, a poet, author, and journalist in Chicago, had a delinquency history including burglary, robbery, and attempted murder in connection with gang membership ("Second Chances" 2000).

All the youths I interviewed expect to be alive and well at age twenty-five, and the vast majority hope to be thriving. In response to the question what they would like to be doing in the next three to five years, twenty-one of the youths (70 percent) say they want to continue their education or go to college. Practically all of them have a good idea of what and where they want to be three years from the interview. Many can also distinguish what and where they want to be in three or five years versus when they will be twenty-five—suggesting that they are not "hyperbolic discounters." Seventeen of the youths specifically mention that they want to go to college, and another four say they want to continue their education. Ten of them want to join the military, either the Marines, the air force, or the MPs. Several want to start their own businesses. Others want to settle down and have a family—or, as one youth put it, "be a father to my kids" (CMS-10, 24). One wants to be a homicide detective, another a police officer, another a pilot, and yet another an architectural designer. Two of the youths want to pursue martial arts training. Two want to be rappers, and another wants to be a disc jockey. Others want to be a computer graphics specialist, an aviation mechanic, and a forest ranger. One of them wants to have a degree from Pima Community College and get a "damn good job" (CMS-2, 24). CMS-66, you will recall, wants to go to medical or dental school and be like Patch Adams (CMS-66, 28). And this is consistent with a lot of other research. In the RAND study, for instance, of the thirty-four youths interviewed in the Los Angeles Juvenile Hall in 1998, 75 percent had been in gangs and 52 percent claimed they planned to get out of their gangs (Goldberg and Schwabe 1999, 10). That study reflected very optimistic responses about positive future expectations (21).

The Catalina youths, for the most part, express a deep and sincere desire to straighten up and change the course of their lives. A seventeen-year-old Mexican American high school dropout, who had been using and selling a lot of hard drugs on the outside, explains:

> I got my GED in here. I have a baby on the outs[ide]. I want to get my shit together, I'm tired of that old lifestyle, you know. I just want to do something honest, make my mom proud, and I'm trying to get real involved in a lot of things. I'm not sure if I want to join the air force or what, but I am going to do something with my life, cause before I wanted to be the best at being the worst, you know, being crazy, going out beating people, drinking, stealing, making the most money selling drugs. This time I want to be the

best at doing good. I started off in here doing, you know, I got involved in anything possible in here, got my upper level on time, got my senior on time, and everything. Council, you know, I am pretty much way up there in the cottage, I'm never locked down. People, they got me to redirect, you know, trying to do something. Make the change, get involved and stay busy, so I can train myself in here for when I get out to not think about drugs, you know, maintain positive, you know. Get some self-restraint. I want to be something. (CMS-14, 5)

CMS-2 is another illustration. He is the sixteen-year-old European American youth living in the northwest suburbs of Tucson who dropped out of school and spent most of his time dealing drugs in his neighborhood. He had an extensive history of gun possession and gun carrying, his main source of guns being home burglaries. He describes how his preferences have changed:

When I was out, it was who could sell the most drugs. Who had the most money. Who had the nicest rims. Who had more straps. Who had more girls. That's what made them important. But now, what makes you important when I get out . . . is I'm going to look at the people more that don't do that stuff . . . The normal people. The normal kids because that is more normal than trying to be somebody that you're not . . . When I get out I'm not going to have shit to do with nothing. I'm not going to fall back into anything. I'm just going to keep my ass out of trouble. Stay clean. (CMS-2, 44, 45)

"I want to be something." "Stay clean." These desires are part of a whole set of preferences about family, learning, employment, and legitimacy. And they are deeply in conflict with another set of desires that lead to delinquency. In this sense, the youths experience dynamic, shifting, and conflicting desires—a constant, continuous flow of clashing preferences, changing from month to month, from one day to the next, from morning to night, from one conversation to the next. Their preferences are heavily sensitive to context. The context of being at the Catalina Mountain School itself strongly influences their choices and stated preferences. At Catalina the youths are, after all, in an institutional setting where they receive a lot of support, supervision, and counseling. They are daily encouraged and counseled to avoid negative thoughts. They are less exposed to drugs and alcohol. In contrast, on the street, in their neighborhoods, they experience a wholly different set of markers. There they experience the affirmative moral, political, and sensual dimensions of guns and gun carrying, the powerful forces that seduce them to embrace, in many cases willingly embrace, powerful handguns.

PART TWO
EXPLORING
METHODOLOGICAL
SENSIBILITIES

"It's too much time to fuck with guns." "If out there you don't have a strap, you're going to get killed." "I want to get my shit together." "I had me two baby nines. I fell in love with those. They look beautiful to me." "I never got into guns besides selling them." "I like to reload bullet shells." "You feel powerful when you have a gun. You get respect." "Anybody can fight with a gun." "I love guns. Hell, yeah, I love guns. I love everything about a gun." "Even myself, I'm still a child, I shouldn't be possessing guns."

The Catalina interviews are rich, and they provide stimulating material with which to explore the leading methodological approaches in the human sciences. Some passages corroborate instrumental theories of gun possession and deliberate decision making. Others suggest an impulsive attraction to guns—a sensual, almost sexual attraction far removed from deliberation. Still others point to scripts and recurring narratives—to what is taken for granted. Take the situation of CMS-66, for instance. Surely he felt a genuine need for protection when he was hanging out with his drug-dealing friends. But maybe he carried because that's what he saw around him. Maybe he was just imitating or absorbing the gestures of his friends. Yusuf wanted to make some pocket money, he says. But he would also carry a gun to parties. Maybe Yusuf wanted to impress his peers and wasn't making a deliberate choice. Or perhaps he was erotically attracted to guns. They are, after all, "pretty tight." Maybe he was suicidal. Perhaps he was just reckless, not really thinking about consequences. Or maybe, just maybe, he was *intentionally* repressing all rational thought. Jesús, for instance, tried to *avoid* thinking about the police when he was carrying a gun.

Embedded in any one of these interpretations, however, are assumptions about human behavior. As a result, the choice of methodological approach has significant implications for law and public policy. If gun carrying is about power and the search for respect—if gun carrying is instrumental to those ends—then perhaps it may make sense to use law or policy to try to change the symbolic meaning of guns. If gun carrying is related to the cost of apprehension, then it might make sense to increase the likelihood of detection or the amount of punishment. If gun carrying is all about social networks and making friends, then perhaps it might be better to offer these youths practice alternatives. The fact is, the various methodological traditions make distinct assumptions about human behavior that orient law and public policy in different directions.

Rather than proceeding blind to the tilt of behavioral assumptions, the chapters in part 2 turn the tradition on its head. Instead of drawing inferences from the Catalina interviews, these chapters use the interview material to explore the four major methodological traditions in the social sciences. The first is the phenomenological. It focuses minutely on individual decision making to determine exactly what the human subject is thinking, doing, deciding. From this perspective, the transcripts of the Catalina interviews offer clues about mental processes—about the way the Catalina youths actually think, deliberate, and consciously engage guns. By listening closely to their words, by watching their actions, by experiencing their histories, the phenomenological gaze seeks to detect the range of choices facing these youths: to discover how they are defining and giving meaning to their actions; to learn what they thought they were doing in carrying guns.

Take CMS-66 again. By possessing the shotgun, CMS-66 perhaps was choosing between his two lifestyles, abandoning his dream of becoming a doctor and opting instead for drug dealing. He knew, after all, the dangers of gun possession and the likelihood of being caught. He was aware that another gun offense would get him in serious trouble. He must have been making a conscious choice, weighing the risks and benefits. After all, he is smart; he's attending community college—against the odds. He must have been keenly aware of the risks of gun possession. Certainly he knew the danger of guns. He had been taught to respect firearms.

This interpretative approach is associated with a particular methodological perspective that focuses microscopically on subjective decision making, on the individual decision maker, on the subject. I call this approach phenomenological because it is so closely attuned to the subjective experience of decision making. From this phenomenological perspective, the focus is on the individual actor and the meanings he imposes on his surroundings. The perspective is methodologically individualist: trained on the actor alone, on his situation, on his life. The individual is the meaning giver, and it is *his* meanings that we seek to uncover—whether the rational pursuit of self-interest, a utopian idealist vision, or absurd, even meaningless desires. Numerous approaches fit under this phenomenological perspective, ranging from Sartrean existentialism to rational choice theory.

The phenomenological approach, though, raises a number of questions and some concerns. First, the method makes a set of assumptions about CMS-66's *ability* to choose his path and weigh the costs and benefits, about his *capability* to deliberate and privilege certain motives over others. These interpretations depend on his having control over his actions. Second, the method privileges *our* interpretation of *his* actions. Are we in fact uncovering the actor's meaning, or are we, in the very process of interpreting his meaning, imposing our own meanings, our own process of reasoning, our own desires and drives? Are we discovering the different reasons for action in the voices of the youths, or are we imposing our own ideas onto their responses? Once we assume that CMS-66 gives meaning to his actions, do we as researchers become the real source of meaning?

To avoid some of these problems, a second methodological perspective moves away from the individual actor and focuses instead on broader social meanings and societal structures. Rather than isolating the individual subject and the meaning he imposes on the gun or on gun carrying, this second perspective attempts to decipher the larger interpretive building blocks and social forces—whether linguistic, political-economic, institutional, or even biological—that may be operating *through* the individual. I call this second approach structuralist in order to capture a wide range of theoretic sensibilities, from social disorganization and moral poverty theory to Saussurean semiotics and even dialectical materialism.

The structuralist—here I have in mind the linguistic structuralist—may explore the language of guns or the common myths about gun carrying in order to detect the rules of the language, the common structures, the tools that the Catalina youths have at their disposal when they interact with guns. An individual youth may use the language of myth to justify gun carrying or alternatively to resist gun possession. By mapping out the basic building blocks, the structuralist can interpret particular expressions or make predictions about likely modes of expression, exchange, or action.

The trouble here is that linguistic structures impose some constraints on the way the youths talk, but not necessarily on what they say. They do not necessarily control behavior. The constraints of language coexist with freedom of individual expression, so the patterns that emerge are no more than that—patterns. They help make sense of individual expression but do not dictate how youths will deploy the language of guns. Unless the structures *influence* behavior. Unless the structures themselves are internalized by the individual actors, shape their consciousness in such as way that their thoughts, perceptions, reasoning, reactions, deliberations are molded by the structures. Unless the structures have ways of reproducing themselves.

This points to a third methodological sensibility—one that builds on the phenomenological *and* structuralist approaches to explore precisely how structures *influence* behavior. Here the researcher may treat structures, language, or myths as taken-for-granted scripts that condition future behavior. These narratives, tales, or codes become secondhand ways of doing things, cognitively inscribed in the mind, that shape the way the youths act, think, and perceive. Youths may see these scripts and begin to live them, to identify with them, to carry them out. This third approach I call practice oriented. It is reflected in a variety of methodological sensibilities ranging from practice theory, to "new institutional" approaches in sociology, to behavioral law and economics.

The hard question here, though, is whether the scripts contribute to gun carrying. Does CMS-66 *follow* a script—or is he instead making it up at every moment? Does this device help us understand what Yusuf or Jesús is doing with guns—or is it just the contrary, that what these youths do with guns *creates* the script and *shapes* the identity? Isn't the identity of the young, tough, gun-carrying youth—Jesús in the park or Marc on the lam—constantly being shaped, molded, formed *by* the gun carrying? Are gun identities not themselves being constituted in the very act of their own expression?

A fourth and final methodological sensibility raises precisely this last set of questions. From this perspective, the researcher explores scripts and identities not as causal antecedents of gun carrying but rather as themselves shaped by social and political forces. This approach dissolves the individual actor as a separate subject of study. From this vantage point—which I call performative—there is no individual actor behind the identity, choosing the script or negotiating another identity. There is only the identity, formed in part by the conduct of carrying a gun, by the institutions of juvenile correction, and by the practices of gang initiation. There is only the performance of identity—which changes through every action and interaction. Here action is modeled on the discursive—on how youths iterate and reiterate and, in the process of reiteration, slightly modify the meanings of what they are saying. From this perspective, youths have the ability to deliberately change the script by repeating lines differently, by subverting, exaggerating, mimicking. The discursive subject, plunged in discourse, is able to contest, resist, modify, or transform the constraints of discourse *through* discourse.

Each of these four methodological approaches brings with it a set of assumptions about human behavior that have significant implications for law and public policy. In this part, I investigate those assumptions in order to lay the groundwork for an examination, in part 3, of the law and public policy alternatives. I proceed by exploring a debate in late twentieth-century social thought surrounding structuralism on the Continent. During the second half of the twentieth century in Europe, there was a direct engagement between the phenomenological and the structural. It took the form of a sharp intellectual clash between two generations of intellectuals, the first represented by writers such as Jean-Paul Sartre, Albert Camus, and Maurice Merleau-Ponty, the second by authors such as Claude Lévi-Strauss and Roland Barthes. The intellectual clash ultimately produced another generation of thinkers who sought to overcome, in their own ways, the earlier debate—including writers such as Pierre Bourdieu and Michel Foucault on the Continent and Judith Butler in the United States.

In this part I focus attention specifically on the conflict between Sartre's existential phenomenology and Lévi-Strauss's linguistic structuralism, then follow the conversation through Pierre Bourdieu's writings of the 1970s and 1980s and subsequently to the performative turn generated by Judith Butler in the United States in the 1990s. I begin with the debates on the Continent because they are unique and unparalleled in the United States. Even though there were similar clashes between parallel perspectives—between, for instance, rational choice theory as an expression of a phenomenological approach and new institutionalism in sociology as an expression of practice theory—stronger disciplinary boundaries in the United States seem to have muted debate over the different methodological sensibilities.

Chapter 7 begins, then, with an analysis of the phenomenological approach embodied in the work of Jean-Paul Sartre. Sartre's play *Les mains sales* offers a brilliant illustration of this first approach. It represents one specific manifestation of the phenomenological that shares with other versions, such as rational action theory, game theory, or theories of emotions, an intense focus on individual decision making—on the deeply internal mental processes that dissect motivations, reasons, and desires and produce individual action. Chapter 8 turns to a structuralist response as expressed in the work of Claude Lévi-Strauss. Chapter 9 proceeds to practice theory and focuses on the writings of Pierre Bourdieu, who self-consciously intervened in an effort to overcome the debate between Sartre and Lévi-Strauss. Chapter 10 then explores the performative turn in the United States through a reading of Judith Butler. Finally, chapter 11 takes stock of the methodological controversies and offers a framework for examining laws and public policies in part 3. As an entry into the debate, then, let's turn the clock back to April 2, 1948, the opening night of *Les mains sales* at the Théâtre Antoine in Paris.

Les mains sales, act 6, scene 4. The German army has occupied the country and is engaged on the eastern front with the invading Soviet forces. The governing coalition consists of the regent, his conservative faction, and a liberal party headed by Karsky. The Communist Party is actively resisting the governing coalition—blowing up bridges, sabotaging factories, seizing munitions—but is internally fractured. Communications with the Soviet leadership have broken down. A hard-core faction within the Communist Party, led by Louis and Olga, wants to continue armed resistance in order to weaken the governing coalition and seize power when the Soviet forces invade. In contrast, the party secretary, Hoederer, is pursuing secret negotiations with the regent and Karsky to form a new coalition government that will surrender to the Soviet forces and rule together in a postwar regime.

Louis decides that Hoederer has to be assassinated to prevent further negotiations, and with some coaxing from Olga he assigns the task to Hugo. Young, intellectual, and anarchist, Hugo is desperate to prove himself. The son of a wealthy industrialist, Hugo runs the party newspaper, where he essentially transcribes the week-old radio broadcasts from the Soviet army. But this assignment will change everything. It will make him a true revolutionary. Hugo will pose as the new secretary to Hoederer, gain his confidence and trust, and then gun him down.

Hugo and his young wife, Jessica, move into Hoederer's walled complex. Hugo assumes his position as the new secretary. At great risk, he smuggles a revolver into the residence, but once inside, he can carry it at no risk. Every day, all day long, Hugo is with Hoederer. He takes dictation, writes correspondence, engages in conversation. At any moment he could freely shoot him. The bodyguards—Georges, Slick, and Léon—are stationed in the hallways outside the office. There is nothing stopping Hugo. Days go by. Yet Hugo still does not act.

Certainly it is not from lack of opportunity. Just moments earlier, Hoederer had turned his back on his young secretary and poured him a cup of coffee, giving him the chance to shoot him in the back without even having to look him in the eyes. The chance to overcome his own human frailty. But Hoederer had calculated right. Having learned of the plot, he had taken Hugo's measure perfectly. He had disarmed Hugo with words—offering him his confidence and trust, promising to be a father figure, a mentor, making him realize what it would really be like to pull a trigger.

Hugo leaves Hoederer's office but returns moments later, only to find his wife, Jessica, in his mentor's arms, her lipstick on his chin. Hugo grabs his revolver, levels it at the Communist leader, looks him unflinchingly in the eyes, and fires three shots. Hoederer falls to the ground and dies.

Two years later, on his early release from prison, Hugo remains disoriented, bewildered, and perplexed as to why he murdered Hoederer, a man whom he had come to care for, respect, even love. "I loved him more than I have loved anyone else in this world," Hugo would later admit. "I liked to see him, to listen to him; I loved his hands and his face, and when I was with him, all my inner storms were calm" (Sartre 1948, 238). For two long years, Hugo has obsessed about his act, replaying it over and over, trying hard to understand why he shot Hoederer.

Was it out of jealousy, on the mistaken belief that Hoederer was sleeping with Jessica? Surely, finding them in each other's arms had somehow triggered the act. "Jealous? Perhaps. But not of Jessica," Hugo mumbles (235). Was it out of anger or a feeling of betrayal? Did Hugo believe at that moment that he had been duped by Hoederer—that Hoederer wanted him to stay on as his secretary only because of his wife? Or was it out of love for Olga, the charismatic leader of his revolutionary cell—a woman of principle, someone who would never lie to her comrades? In part, perhaps. But she had betrayed him. She herself had tried to kill Hoederer with a bomb while Hugo was in his office. She had given up on Hugo. She might even have killed him.

Was it out of hatred for his father, who mocked his political idealism? "Me too, in my time," his father had told him; "I was part of a revolutionary group. I wrote in their journal. You'll get over it just as I did" (44). Was it to prove himself as a true revolutionary? Or was it to commit suicide? "Olga," Hugo confessed, "I do not want to live" (46). Was it for the principle—for the idea of never compromising, of never collaborating with fascists and the bourgeois? "I left my family and my class the day I understood what oppression really is. Under no circumstances will I accept to compromise with it," Hugo exclaimed (51). But that was well before he met Hoederer. Or was it because he was under orders from the party? Not entirely, Hugo explained. "Even with the greatest intentions in the world, what you do is never what the party orders you to do . . . The order? There was no order any more. Orders, they leave you all alone after a while. The order stayed behind and I went forward alone, and I killed all alone and . . . I do not even know why" (21).

These questions frame *Les mains sales*. They frame the plot of Sartre's work, but they also provide the theoretical framework: the answers to these questions, it turns out, determine whether Hugo shall live or die—whether Hugo can be brought back into the fold or must be gunned down by his Communist comrades. While Hugo was in prison, Olga and the radical faction of the Communist Party entered into the exact arrangement with the fascist government and the liberal opposition that Hoederer had been pursuing. If Hugo killed Hoederer because of his politics, then he too must now be eliminated. But if he killed out of jealousy, then he still may be useful to the party.

Two years have passed, and Hugo is still unable to give a motive, to explain the act, to find the cause. "It's an idiotic story, like all stories," Hugo says. "If you look at it from afar, it hangs together, more or less. But if you get close, it makes no sense. An act goes too fast. It comes out of you brusquely, and you don't know if it's because you wanted it or because you could not restrain it" (33). When pushed by Olga, Hugo is not even sure he committed the act. He feels no responsibility for the murder. He bears no weight. "Did I even do it? It was not me who killed, it was chance. If I had opened the door two minutes earlier or two minutes later, I would not have surprised them in each other's arms, I would not have shot. I was coming to tell him that I would accept his guidance . . . Chance fired three gunshots . . . But me. *Me*, in all this, what have I become? It's an assassination without an assassin" (235–36).

All that changes in the final moments of the play, when Olga explains that she too has changed politics and that her comrades are on their way to gun Hugo down. Olga asks Hugo to renounce his act, and it is only then, in a flash, that he is able to see the possible meaning of his act. At that moment Hugo sees what his act *might* mean: if he renounces the murder and returns to the party, then Hoederer will have died by chance. He will have been shot out of jealousy. He will have been murdered for a lover. But if Hugo claims his act as a political act, then Hoederer will not have died by accident. Hoederer will have died because of what he believed in.

At that moment, Hugo sees the light. A door is opened through which he can see what his action might mean. And at that moment Hugo finally invents himself. He explains to Olga:

Listen: I don't know why I killed Hoederer, but I know why I should have killed him: because he was engaging in bad politics, because he was lying to his comrades, and because he risked corrupting the party. If I had the courage to fire when I was alone with him in his office, he would be dead because of that and I could look at myself in the mirror. I am ashamed of myself because I killed him . . . later. And you, you are asking me to carry even more shame and say that I killed him for nothing. Olga, what I thought about Hoederer's politics, I continue to believe. When I was in prison, I believed that you agreed with me and that kept me going. I realize now that I am alone on this, but I will not change my opinion. (247–48)

In the dramatic conclusion to *Les mains sales*, Hugo finally gives meaning to his act. He intentionally claims the murder. He no longer lets chance hold sway. He assumes responsibility. In the very final exchange, Hugo declares: "I have not yet killed Hoederer, Olga. Not yet. It is now that I will kill him, and myself with him" (248). And as the armed comrades come to the door, over Olga's cries telling them to go away, Hugo screams, "Not salvageable" (249).

THE SUBJECT AS SIGNIFIER

Sartre's play is a brilliant illustration of the first methodological sensibility. Hugo's final words are the quintessential free act that propels him out of his bad faith and gives meaning to his earlier act. Before that moment, he had not assumed responsibility. He attributed his choice to chance, to the haphazard, to myriad influences and external forces. He allowed himself to be controlled by his situation. He did not know why he had acted; in fact, he was not even sure he had acted at all. It is only when he fully realizes his situation—when he learns from Olga what the party has done during his time in prison—that he recognizes the possible meaning of his act and sees the chance to vindicate his politics and to rehabilitate Hoederer. It is at that turning point—when he understands *what it would mean* to be gunned down by his comrades—that he exercises his full subjectivity with eyes wide open: that he creates himself. It is then that Hugo finally liberates himself from his handlers and from bad faith. It is at that point that he *invents* himself.

The idea of giving meaning to an act—so central to Sartre's work—is distinctively captured in a little-known interview with Pierre Verstraeten in the *Revue d'Esthétique* in 1965. In the interview, Sartre is asked whether he draws a distinction between signification and the signified—central terms of art in Saussurean structural linguistics that are intended to capture the distinction between word and object. More specifically, Sartre is asked: "Do you draw a distinction between signification and the signified?"[10] Sartre responds:

> Yes, for me the signified is the object. I define my own language, which may not necessarily be the same as linguists': this *"chair,"* it is the object, thus it is the signified; then, there is signification, it is the logical set that will be constituted by words, the signification of a phrase. If I say, "This table is in front of the window," I am aiming at a signified that is the table by signifi-cations that are the set of phrases that are constituted, and *I consider me, myself, as the signifier*. The signification, that is, the *noema*, the correlate of the set of vocal elements proffered. (Sartre 1965, 311; emphasis added)[11]

Sartre's response is stunning. By interjecting "the signifier" and identifying with it, Sartre boldly turns the focus back on the individual subject as the one *who gives meaning*. There is no mediation through what structural linguists would traditionally call the signifier—the socially constructed relations of concepts. For Sartre, the *actor* imposes meaning by himself. The individual actor is the agent who gives meaning—who decides, who deliberates, who chooses, who acts. It is in this way that Hugo gave meaning to his homicide by committing suicide. And to foreshadow later discussion, it is in this way that CMS-66 may have given meaning to his prior acts by deciding to possess a shotgun.

This is the point of departure for existential phenomenology. What defines our being, as humans, is precisely our ability to negate our situation—to create nothingness in the heart of our being—through our own acts and interpreta-tions. In contrast to inanimate objects, human subjects have the ability to negate, to reject, to repel, to alter, to change their own condition by imposing meaning on the world (Sartre 1943, 56). It is in this sense, Sartre declares in *L'être et le néant*, that "man is the being through which nothingness comes to the world" (1943, 59). It is in the act of negation that possibilities present them-selves. It is through the process of negation that the subject can seek alterna-tives to his present condition.[12] As Sartre writes:

> It is important to invert general opinion and recognize that it is not the dif-ficulty of a situation or the suffering that it imposes that are the reasons we conceive of another state of being where everyone would be better off; on the contrary, it is on the day when we can conceive of that other state of being that a new light falls on our troubles and on our suffering and that we *decide* they are insufferable. (Sartre 1943, 489)

This focus on subjectivity and intentionality characterizes Sartre's phenomenological gaze. "One has to start from subjectivity," Sartre emphasizes in his lecture of 1945, *L'existentialisme est un humanisme* (1958, 17). As Sartre explains:

> Our point of departure is in effect the subjectivity of the individual, and this for strictly philosophical reasons. Not because we are bourgeois, but because we want a doctrine based on truth, and not on a set of pretty theories full of hope but without real foundation. There can be no other truth, to start with, than this: *I think, therefore I am*. It is here that we find the absolute truth of conscience finding itself . . . In other words, for there to be any truth, there has to be absolute truth; and this one is simple, easy to attain, accessible to all. It consists in seizing oneself without intermediary. (1958, 64–65)

From this subjective perspective, the individual invents himself through his actions. Simply put, he is nothing more than the actions he takes. "Man is nothing else than what he makes himself" (1958, 21–22). And his actions become his project. "Man is nothing else than his project. He exists only insofar as he realizes himself. He is nothing else than the set of his actions, nothing else than his life" (1958, 55).[13] As a result—and somewhat paradoxically—voluntary deliberation for Sartre is often already loaded. The life project already shapes the likely outcome of deliberation. "When I deliberate, the chips have already been played" (1943, 506–7).

Sartre is here negotiating the space between freedom and constraint. First, freedom. The fact that subjects shape the world through acts of negation produces a radical sense of freedom. Here there are no external factors or forces that *make* an individual do anything. "If, in effect, existence precedes essence," Sartre argues, "then we can never explain actions by reference to a given and fixed human nature. In other words, there is no determinism, man is free, man is freedom" (1958, 36–37).[14] But second, there is constraint, which is captured in the concept of the situation. The situation, or facticity, is precisely the other side of freedom—or, as Sartre wrote, "l'autre aspect de la liberté, son 'revers'" (1943, 538). The individual is *en situation*—in a complex web of influences that pull and tug him in different directions. Each of us has a family history, a place, relations with others, memories, and habits. Sartre acknowledges that these ties are influential, sometimes limiting: the freedom of the other, for instance, can limit my freedom in ways that I can have no control over. Even though I must submit freely, my submission is decisive. I cannot avoid it. In this case there is a limit to my freedom: "I exist in a situation that has *an outside* and that has, by this very fact, a dimension of alienation that I cannot escape" (1943, 582).

But the *situation* is not, for Sartre, proof of the absence of freedom. It is, rather, proof of its existence. Adverse circumstances do not establish that there is no freedom, because it is precisely our free choice that creates the situation *as adverse to us*. We experience our situation as oppressive or liberating only because of the project we have chosen. The situation itself is created by our goals: "This rock, which is profoundly resistant if I want to move it, will be, in contrast, a precious aid if I want to climb it to view the landscape. In itself, the rock is neutral; in other words, it has to wait to be enlightened by a project to manifest itself as adversary or auxiliary" (1943, 538–39).

This raises the paradox of freedom—the fact that "there is freedom only *in situation* and there are situations only by reason of freedom" (1943, 546). It is our free project that creates and defines our situation, and at the same time, our freedom is always located within a situation. Sartre's point is that ultimately there is always the decision whether to let oneself be pulled and tugged by the situation—whether to reject, to negate, or to change that situation. There is always room for choice, for taking responsibility. Denying this possibility, believing in determinism, Sartre contended, is acting in bad faith (1943, 80). "Any man who seeks refuge behind the excuse of his passions, any man who invents a determinism, is a man of bad faith" (1958, 80–81). He denies that he gives meaning. He ignores the fact that he is *the signifier*.

HUGO BARINE AS SIGNIFIER

"If it is true that man is free in a given situation and that he chooses himself *in* and *by* that situation," Sartre said, "then the theater must show simple and human situations, and liberties that are chosen in those situations" (Jeanson 1955, 7–8). *Les mains sales* did just that. It is precisely a play about being *en situation*. When Hugo, for example, attributes the death of Hoederer to chance, he is deceiving himself. He is making excuses for himself. He is allowing himself to be buffeted by his situation rather than assuming responsibility for his action. He is, in effect, acting in bad faith. In contrast, when he asserts himself in the final exchange of the play, Hugo begins to act fully human; he begins to make himself, to invent himself intentionally. And in the process Hugo is not only inventing himself but reinventing his past. As one commentator explains, there is only one means by which the characters can "really" decide who they are, what they did, and why they did it: they must go on acting in such a way that their future acts confirm or refute the "past" they have chosen as the "real" one. It is not the mere hypothesis of the action, or of the sociologist or historian, that fixes the what and why of the act. It is future acts and events that determine our view of the facticity and meaning of the past. The behaviorist concept of motivation is thus turned on its head. It is not the stimulus that caused the response; it is through man's choice of action in the present that he knows what were its causes in the past. The historical process, as well as the daily praxis of human existence, is thus an ongoing dialectical struggle of individuals and groups for their liberty and authenticity (Brown 1978, 169).

When Hugo finally takes control of his life in the last exchange of the play, he is *defining* his past, *creating* himself.[15] This is the pivotal moment in the play. It is the moment that allows him to negate his condition and see the possibility of another project. When Olga confesses to Hugo, everything falls into place. Hugo sees a new possibility, a new project—and he makes up his mind. He tells Olga, "Hoederer, Louis, you, you are all of the same kind. Of the *good* kind. Of the tough, the conquerors, the leaders. I'm the only one who took the wrong door" (1948, 246).

"The wrong door": this brings to mind a passage in *L'être et le néant* where Sartre discusses a story by Kafka: A merchant goes to plead his case at the castle. A terrible guard blocks his entry. The merchant does not dare go past him; he waits, and he dies waiting. At the hour of his death, he asks the guard: "How come I was the only one waiting?" And the guard responds, "This door was made for only you" (Sartre 1943, 609). The guard was an obstacle to the merchant because he kept *wanting* to plead his case. The point is that we each make our own door.

Les mains sales. Final stage directions: "Hugo kicks the door open and screams: '*Non récupérable.*'"

THE CATALINA YOUTHS

Jesús, Yusuf, Marc, CMS-66: Are they making their own door? Are they creating their own obstacles? How do guns and gun carrying figure in their projects? And how do they relate to their situations?

CMS-66 gives new meaning to his earlier act of gun carrying—his earlier possession of the Glock .40—when he later decides to possess a shotgun. The decision to take home a shotgun seems to represent a deliberate choice between his two lives—between his academic pursuits at the community college and his allegiance to his drug-dealing friends. The shotgun gives meaning to the Glock .40: no longer a youthful mistake, it is now a true indicator. Was there a moment when CMS-66 made that choice? Was there a conversation, an exchange, a look? How did he get the shotgun, and what was he thinking when he took it home?

There is also a sense in which CMS-66 is giving a different meaning to his earlier acts of gun carrying when he says, "Even myself, I'm still a child, I shouldn't be possessing guns." Those words seem intended to resignify his earlier actions as childhood mistakes. He is disowning his past, choosing instead a path of maturity. He is redefining his life project—opting for Patch Adams over drugs and vice. Are there any actions that go with these words? Has CMS-66 done anything at the Catalina school that would lend credence to this reinvention?

When Jesús resumes doing "beer runs," he too is redefining himself, choosing between his gang life and going straight. He slips back into gang habits slowly, reluctantly, romantically. "I was thinking how fun it was." He knew he could make his own choice—he resists the idea of peer pressure. Nevertheless, he seems to be treating the delinquent acts differently than before. Back then, there were guns and drugs—violence and crime. Now there are beer runs. Acts that seem more childish, more fun, more innocent. neither serious nor harmful. Is Jesús trying to give new meaning to his prior delinquency? Does it reflect an element of maturity, or at least a desire for maturity?

When Marc was on the lam, he carried a .38. He carried it on his ankle and never took it off except to take a shower. He didn't play with it. He cleaned it. He test fired it. He kept it in a holster. The fact that he was carrying a gun, it seems, emphasized the seriousness of his running away from home. The .38 added a layer of reality and danger to his experience. Marc knew he should take guns seriously. He had been trained in their use and safety. He considered the gun a tool—here, a tool for protection. Carrying the gun gave meaning to how serious his situation really was. Marc was only thirteen years old, but in running away *with a gun*, he was an adult. The gun gave him self-sufficiency. It helped create a situation for Marc. It opened a door to an intense experience.

That Yusuf admits he carried his "Russian nine" a few times "just to try to be cool" may give a slightly different meaning to his act of selling guns. Dealing the Glock .45, it seems, is not just about money. It's not just about $200. The commodification of guns also gives status. It may offer respect. It may ingratiate. Recall that Yusuf sold a 9-mm to the mother of a girlfriend. Did he feel like the protector of the family? Was he assuming the role of the father, while being in an intimate relationship with the daughter? Had he become the man of the house? Clearly there was more to that situation than a purely commercial exchange. Was Yusuf trying to open a door to adulthood?

The phenomenological approach tries to read subjects' meanings and intentions from their deliberate actions and expressions. Because they are so dangerous and freighted with meaning, guns are a central and important mechanism for youths to give meaning to their actions. At times gun possession seems to represent an obstacle for these Catalina youths—a hurdle they have set for themselves. Certainly this seems true of CMS-66 and his shotgun. At other times gun possession seems to present a way to open a door—to create a new role, to assume, for instance, the responsibilities of an adult.

It is important, from this perspective, to analyze the gun carrying not in isolation but as part of a larger life project—to try to read how the Catalina youths are giving meaning to their past selves within the complex situation they find themselves in. This involves the difficult task of distinguishing between acting in bad faith and acting freely—between letting the situation control and controlling the situation. Recall that much of the gun possession described in the Catalina interviews began passively. The gun *was given* to the youth for protection. But the fact is, the youth *took* the gun. He did not refuse it. The existential phenomenological task is to determine whether this was a free act or an action in bad faith—whether it was a conscious decision or whether it was made with conscious avoidance.

Sartre's approach focuses on how the Catalina youths, as signifiers, give meaning to their situation and projects *by means of* guns and gun possession, and how they give meaning to gun carrying *by means of* subsequent acts and expressions. Other phenomenological approaches focus elsewhere. Rational action theory, for instance, focuses on the individual's reasoning and rational decision making. It might take the act of gun possession as signifying delinquency or deviance and then compare different cost regimes to determine whether the youths are internalizing the price of carrying a gun and changing their behaviors accordingly. What these different approaches share, though, is the intense focus on the individual decision making and on the subject's mental processes.

GIVING MEANING TO ACTS

The phenomenological method, however, introduces some troubling concerns. First, how do we know that the subject has the ability to act freely? What are we assuming about CMS-66's *capability* to give meaning to his actions, to weigh the significance of an act, to evaluate costs and benefits? Is it realistic to assume that any of these Catalina youths, when they are in situation—on the street, among their peers, dealing drugs—have the ability to deliberate and the freedom to choose a path? Does the approach depend too much on their exerting—or being able to exert—autonomous control over their conduct?

In part the answer depends on how thick a notion of intention, autonomy, deliberation, or rationality we assume. Within rational action theory, for example, there is a wide range. Some commentators adopt an extremely thin conception of rationality. Richard Posner, for instance, defines it simply as "choosing the best means to the chooser's end" (Posner 1998a, 1551). From this perspective, "Rats are at least as rational as human beings when rationality is defined as achieving one's ends (survival and reproduction, in the case of rats) at least cost" (1551). John Elster gives the following illustration of a "thin" theory of rationality: "If an agent has a compulsive desire to kill another person, and believes that the best way (or a way) of killing that person is to stick a pin through a doll representing him, then he acts rationally if he sticks a pin through the doll" (Elster 1983, 3). This thin conception of rationality rests only on an assumption of consistency of desires and beliefs—minimally, on the criterion of transitivity: "If I prefer *a* to *b* and *b* to *c*, I should prefer *a* to *c*" (6).

In contrast, a thicker or broader conception of rationality goes beyond the formal criteria of transitivity and "allows scrutiny of the substantive nature of the desires and beliefs involved in action" (Elster 1983, 15). Under a thicker conception of rationality, we might ask not only whether preferences and desires are consistent but whether they are themselves reasonable. From this perspective, not only is the voodoo doll irrational, but the very desire to kill may be entirely irrational as well.

The trouble is, the moment we move away from a minimalist notion of rationality or intentionality—the moment we stop equating action with rationality or intent, as do the thinner conceptions—the phenomenological approach runs up against the issue of capabilities: Are the Catalina youths themselves able to impose meaning? Are they able to rationally weigh costs and benefits—or are they moved to act because of other forces, such as the sensual attraction to guns, moral righteousness and indignity, or the political economy of the border?

Second, and equally important: Who is it, really, that is imposing meaning on their actions? Is it the youths themselves? Or is it us when we read meaning into their words? These youths, after all, say a lot of things. They often say contradictory things. How do we faithfully interpret their words? How do we give meaning to their gestures? More precisely, are we giving expression to their meanings or simply imposing our own interpretations and theoretical framework on their actions? How do we interpret CMS-66's enrolling in community college *and* carrying a Glock .40? How do we interpret Marc's respect for gun safety *and* the ankle holster? Are we not, in fact, the ones privileging one set of actions over the other and imposing meaning?

Further, when we give meaning, are we not using the intermediary of the larger symbolic realm in which the Catalina youths operate? CMS-66, Jesús, Yusuf, Marc—they alone cannot impose meaning on their acts. *And neither can we.* The claim "I am the signifier" goes only so far. Every one of these youths is stuck in a rich symbolic world that confers already established meanings and ways of interpreting their actions. CMS-66 alone does not control the meaning of his action. He does not control how others in his social environment will interpret his acts. The local prosecutor, a judge, a probation officer, a college counselor, his peers—all these people participate in giving CMS-66's act its meaning. They locate the act within rich social, political, cultural, and historical contexts and help give it meaning by their own interpretations.

Third, the giving of meaning never really ends. There is no "final" act in life—there are no final stage directions. Time does not stop. It does not stop for CMS-66. He will have another chance to redefine himself, and with it an opportunity to make good—to transform the shotgun possession into an aberration. Yusuf may have the chance to redeem himself and prove his mother right—"My momma always said that guns, they bring trouble automatically" (CMS-13, 26). Marc may have the opportunity to become the skilled marksman he idolizes rather than a stowaway youth. Meanings will continue to change.

The same is true for Hugo in *Les mains sales*: time does not stop even though Hugo has just committed suicide. As the curtain goes down and the audience applauds, shocked and riveted by Hugo's last words, Hugo—one can only assume—is gunned down like a dog by his Communist comrades. And by that very act, he loses control over his actions. As he drops to the floor, bleeding, gasping, the comrades get to write the next act—or at least get to *try* to write the next act. Perhaps they mutilate his body, and he is never identified as Hoederer's assassin. Retrieved in a gutter somewhere, his remains are placed in an unmarked grave. Or he is left in circumstances suggesting suicide or a foiled armed robbery: a recidivist, just released from prison, shot dead in the act. Perhaps he is a victim of the invading Soviet forces. Perhaps a john killed by a pimp on his first night out of prison. As for Hoederer, he still goes down in history as having been shot for having an affair with his secretary's wife. A typical politician. A victim of his lust. As one commentator suggests, "Hugo's suicide changes nothing. What he has done remains irrevocable; Hoederer is dead, and the Party will continue to use its own version of his murder" (McCall 1969, 77). Hugo no longer has any control over that.

READING *LES MAINS SALES*

It turns out, somewhat ironically, that Jean-Paul Sartre himself struggled unsuccessfully to give Hugo's final act the meaning that *he* had intended—he, Sartre, as *signifier*. Much to his chagrin, *Les mains sales* was roundly attacked by Communists and praised by conservatives. The liberal press, as well as the Communist press, interpreted the play as *anti*-Communist. It was often referred to in newspapers as "Sartre's anti-Communist play" (McCall 1969, 54; see generally Beauvoir 1963, 166–69). "For thirty cents and a plate of American lentils, Jean-Paul Sartre sold whatever was left of his honor and integrity," wrote a Soviet critic (Beauvoir 1963, 168).

Sartre vehemently rejected this characterization. "I still think, subjectively, that is to say as far as what I wrote is concerned," Sartre emphasized, "that it is not an anticommunist work but just the opposite, a work of a fellow-traveler" (Sartre 1976, 213). Yet Sartre had a hard time convincing even sympathetic readers of his intended meaning. "The play's meaning," Sartre emphasized, "does not coincide with Hugo's fate" (Sartre 1976, 219). Sartre did not himself identify with Hugo, he repeatedly maintained. "I can entirely appreciate Hugo's attitude, but you are wrong in thinking that he is an embodiment of myself," Sartre told a friend and critic. "Hoederer's role is myself. Hoederer is the person I should like to be if I were a revolutionary, so I am Hoederer, if only on a symbolic level" (Sartre 1976, 219–20).

The objective of the play, Sartre insisted, was not to valorize Hugo's final act but to explore "the dialectic necessity within a praxis" (Sartre 1976, 217). Sartre explained in an interview:

I have never found Hugo a sympathetic character, and I have never thought he was in the right as against Hoederer. But I was trying to present in him the torments of a certain type of youth which, though it is emotionally inclined to a protest of a kind which is very specifically communist, does not go as far as joining the party because of its humanist educational background. I did not want to say whether they were right or wrong; if I had, my play would have been propagandist. I simply tried to describe them. But Hoederer's is the only attitude I think sound. (Sartre 1976, 210)

Sartre tried to give this *malentendu* a positive spin. It reflected the dogmatism of Stalinism—"that is to say," in his words, "the fact that a *critical* 'fellow-traveler' was not tolerated at that time" (Sartre 1976, 215). Olga and Louis represented this Stalinist tendency, one that required all things to be black or white and that did not allow for the nuance of Hoederer's politics. For Olga and Louis, any criticism, any opposition whatever, meant betrayal and had to be met with a rewriting of history. Hoederer opposed their views, and thus he was a social traitor (McCall 1969, 55). "Falsification of the past was a systematic practice of Stalinism," Sartre emphasized (Sartre 1976, 217).

According to Sartre, the attacks on his play reflected a similar dogmatism— and were entirely misguided. The assassination of Hoederer and the death of Hugo were not intended to impugn the socialist project or the Communist Party, he protested. They were meant, instead, to "examine dialectically the problems of the imperatives of praxis at the time"—here, the fact that Olga could not repudiate Hoederer anymore (Sartre 1976, 219). Sartre nevertheless had great difficulty convincing others of the meaning he wanted to project onto Hugo's final act.

In 1952 Sartre prohibited further productions of the play in any country in which the local Communist Party would not agree to the performance (Sartre 1976, 210).

8

LÉVI-STRAUSS AND
THE STRUCTURAL MAP
PARIS, THE TROPICS,
AND THE UNTAMED
MIND

Jean-Paul Sartre alone could not impose meaning on his play, and neither can CMS-66 alone impose meaning on his possession of the Glock .40. CMS-66 is embedded in a rich symbolic realm that already has structure, patterns, and associations. He alone does not control the meaning of his action. He does not control how others in his social environment will hear and interpret his acts. His college peers, his mother, his drug-dealing friends all participate in giving meaning to his actions, through the intermediary of a shared symbolic realm.

Like language, there is already an existing range of possible symbolic meanings that may be attributed to CMS-66's act of gun carrying: he could be trying to fit in, or protect himself, or feel powerful. The act itself, it turns out, functions as a symbol that can have a number of meanings. These meanings make up a symbolic language shared and contested among the Catalina youths. In other words, CMS-66's act functions within a system of signs: the act relates to other acts very much as a word or utterance might relate to other words or language as a whole. Claude Lévi-Strauss's work represents a classic expression of this insight and a particularly appropriate historical contrast to existentialism, given the clash in the 1960s between existential phenomenology and the writings that became known as "structuralist."

THE SCIENCE OF MYTHOLOGY

There are several points of contact between Lévi-Strauss and Sartre. The most direct confrontation occurred in the mid-1960s after Sartre published his second major philosophical work, *Critique de la raison dialectique* (1960), a work intended to harmonize his earlier existentialist thought with Marxism. Lévi-Strauss devoted the concluding chapter of his book *La pensée sauvage* (1962) to a criticism of Sartre's *Critique*, focusing on the tension between the historical nature of Marxist thought and the static nature of the structuralist method. Sartre responded in interviews (Sartre, *Arc*, 1966; Sartre, *Revue d'Esthétique*, 1965), and most of the secondary literature discusses this episode (see, e.g., Delacampagne and Traimond 1997; Caws 1992;

Brown 1978; Silverman 1978; Rosen 1971; Hartmann 1971; Abel 1970; Pouillon 1965). But given our focus on Sartre's earlier existentialist writings, a more appropriate place to start is Lévi-Strauss's study of mythology.[16]

From this angle, the structuralist would view the Catalina interviews as presenting variations on a "passage to adulthood" myth. The Catalina transcripts represent different versions of the larger constellation of myths about how young men enter manhood. The structuralist task would be to decipher clusters of common relations between elements of the interviews in order to better understand the individual versions and the myth collectively. Lévi-Strauss dedicated a series of books to this enterprise, beginning with *La pensée sauvage* but then writing four volumes specifically on the "science of mythology" (Lévi-Strauss [1964] 1969).

According to Lévi-Strauss, there are patterns of similarity and difference within certain genres of myths—for instance, within the Oedipus myth—despite the apparent arbitrariness and contingency of any one specific rendition of the myth. Lévi-Strauss's work attempts to resolve this apparent tension by drawing on structural linguistic writings and mapping the relations between the basic elements of the myth (Lévi-Strauss 1967d, 206–7). For illustration, it may be useful here to first map the structure of Sartre's play *Les mains sales*, using Lévi-Strauss's method. Hypothetically, the structure of the play could be represented as shown in table 8.1.

On this reading, the first column has as its common feature *betrayal by a loved one*. It assembles, first, the original betrayal by Hugo's father, who viciously mocked Hugo's political commitment by telling him that he—now one of the wealthiest industrialists—had also been a member of a revolutionary group in his youth and had also been assigned to write their newspaper. "You'll get over it just like I did" (Sartre 1948, 44). It contains the moment when Hugo's wife Jessica mocks him and tells him, "You could never be an assassin, my poor little honeybee" (73). It also collects the ultimate moments of betrayal when Hugo discovers Hoederer embracing his wife and when Olga, the only person left in Hugo's life after prison, informs him that she has adopted the very strategy for which Hugo was to assassinate Hoederer.

The second column is related to the first but represents its inverse: *fidelity*. This column captures moments in the play where Hugo recognizes acts of faithfulness. It collects, for instance, the moment when Olga persuades Louis to assign Hugo the task of assassinating Hoederer—a moment of fidelity that transforms Hugo's life. "Before the end of the week," Hugo dreams aloud to Olga and Louis, "You'll be here, both of you, and you'll be waiting for news; and you'll

TABLE 8.1. *Mythological structure of* Les mains sales

BETRAYAL	FIDELITY	BAD FAITH	GOOD FAITH
		Hugo consents to be the news reporter for the Communist Party	
Hugo's father mocks Hugo's membership in the Communist Party		Hugo tells Olga he wants to commit suicide	
	Olga and Louis assign Hugo to kill Hoederer		
Jessica mocks Hugo's ability to kill Hoederer	Hoederer offers to guide Hugo in life and politics		Hugo argues with Hoederer's body-guards about his privilege
Hoederer lets himself be seduced by Jessica		Hugo shoots Hoederer without thinking	
		Hugo is released from prison and still does not understand why he killed Hoederer	
Olga tells Hugo that the Party has changed course and will enter into a coalition government		Hugo claims he did not kill Hoederer, that the gun killed him	
	Olga tries to save Hugo		Hugo screams out *"non récupérable"*

be worried and you'll talk about me and I will matter to you. And you'll ask your-selves, What is he doing? And then, there will be a telephone call, or someone will knock on the door, and you will smile at each other and say to each other, 'He did it'" (Sartre 1948, 56). It also contains the pivotal moment when Hoederer manages to gain Hugo's confidence and helps him negotiate his failure to accomplish his mission. "I have confidence in you," Hoederer exclaims. "You're a kid having a hard time becoming a man, but you'll make a very good man if someone facilitates the passage. If I can escape their guns and their bombs, I'll keep you close to me and will help you" (1948, 220).

The third column represents acts done in bad faith. This column assembles the multiple moments when Hugo denies his agency and his freedom. These are the times, for instance, when Hugo denies that he even shot Hoederer: "It's an assassination without an assassin" (Sartre 1948, 236). Or when Hugo actually shoots Hoederer in a reflex, without thinking through his action, without taking responsibility for his act. Or when he tells Olga unthinkingly that he wants to commit suicide. Finally, the fourth column represents the inverse of the third: actions done in good faith. The pivotal moment here is the very last exchange of the play, when Hugo decides to commit suicide in order to redeem the assassination of Hoederer.

The structure of the play, then, can be represented in a simple schema, and we might translate it in Lévi-Strauss's shorthand into the chart in figure 8.1.

This schema gives the meaning of the play. As Lévi-Strauss explained, "Were we to *tell* the myth, we would disregard the columns and read the rows from left to right and from top to bottom. But if we want to *understand* the myth, then we will have to disregard one half of the diachronic dimension (top to bottom) and read from left to right, column after column, each one being considered as a unit" (Lévi-Strauss 1967d, 211).

On this reading, *Les mains sales* represents one version of the myth about the passage to manhood. In this variation—one exemplar set in war-torn Europe in the mid-twentieth century—we observe the central role of betrayal and faithful-

		3	
1		3	
	2		
1	2		4
1		3	
		3	
1		3	
	2		4

FIGURE 8.1. *Schema of the mythological structure of* Les mains sales

ness and how these relate to the human subject acting in bad faith or good faith. Multiple acts of betrayal trigger a loss of bad faith, as if the human subject is shaken out of his slumber by the pain of betrayal. There is also a cyclical motion between the first and second columns, and between the third and fourth, like a pendulum swinging from betrayal to fidelity and from bad faith to good faith. We can also identify three major tropes that represent vital moments in any coming-of-age myth: political commitment, murder, and suicide. These elements can be deployed in many ways depending on the myth but are often central to the narrative. The structural reading discerns, then, the central building blocks of the myth (murder/suicide), the pivotal relations in the plot structure (betrayal/fidelity), and the possible impact of these relations (betrayal/good faith).

REREADING THE CATALINA INTERVIEWS

A structural analysis might approach the Catalina interviews in much the same way. The transcripts reveal important experiences of betrayal and fidelity. Recall CMS-66, for instance. Surely he experienced the death of his father when he was only thirteen as an act of betrayal. Conversely, his relationship with his older friend in the drug business—someone who paid for extra math classes and gave financial support to his mother—represents a bond of fidelity. That strong allegiance may have led CMS-66 to passively accept the Glock .40—unthinkingly, in bad faith. He may originally have experienced his first incarceration for possession of the handgun as betrayal by his older friend—who placed him in a position where he could be arrested and imprisoned. But later he may have reinterpreted that experience as betrayal by society at large, leading him to act consciously and deliberately in acquiring the shotgun. Taking the shotgun home may have represented, then, a free act, an act in good faith. (Acts in good faith are not necessarily wise.)

Let's take the cases of other Catalina youths. Let me first tell their stories, ignoring the columns and, as Lévi-Strauss suggests, "reading the rows from left to right and from top to bottom." CMS-40—I'll call him Paul—identifies himself as, in his own words, "excuse my language, a bastard" (CMS-40, 7). Paul has a hard time describing his family background. His mother was from Montana and is now somewhere in Texas. He never knew his father. Paul lived off and on with his mother. She first gave him up to her mother, who raised him for a while. Then when he was seven years old she gave him up to foster care. He has been in and out of foster homes and juvenile detention since then. Paul is a ward of the state.

Paul first got in trouble with the law for shoplifting when he was about eight years old. By the time he was twelve, he had run away from his foster placement and was caught trying to hot-wire a car. He was placed on probation. When he was fifteen, Paul got into more serious trouble—this time it involved a gun.

Paul had few experiences with guns growing up. He went hunting a few times with an uncle in Montana, and when he was about five years old his mother had a 9-mm handgun. He remembers because his older brother got in trouble for taking the gun without permission and shooting into the air. But overall he was not—and is not today—overly attracted to guns. "Truthfully, I never owned a gun. I've owned a BB gun, but that's it. I remember shooting at targets, that's it . . . I really don't think guns are so fascinating that I really sit and talk and talk about them. I know that they're nice to have around for protection or even to look at, or sometimes, clean, or even use once in a while. But for hunting, or protection, that's it" (CMS-40, 11).

When Paul was fifteen, he was living with a foster family that owned a car lot. Paul is fascinated by cars, he confesses, and one day he took a truck on the lot that belonged to a friend for a ride—without permission. Paul found a 9-mm in the glove compartment. He returned the truck but kept the gun overnight. It was a long night, a night during which Paul seriously contemplated committing suicide. He didn't shoot himself, ultimately, but he also didn't return the gun on his own. He didn't want to tell his friend he had taken it because he didn't want his friend to lose trust in him (CMS-40, 15). But that made matters worse—and the next day his friend came with the police to retrieve the gun.

This is his second time at Catalina. Paul has been here for eight months on charges of absconding from placement and grand theft auto. He is now seventeen and is a senior upper-level student. That's an accomplishment. He has behaved well at Catalina this time around and has earned the highest privileges accorded an upper-level student. He can walk around the campus freely. He has more free time. He can buy food and other items at the canteen. He has worked hard for his privileges. He is trying hard to redeem himself.

Another youth, CMS-8—I'll call him John—is an old hand at the Catalina school, here for the third time. He too has spent a long time in institutional settings. His father disappeared when he was four years old, and he was raised for a while by his mother and her boyfriend. This is the boyfriend, you may recall, who had a lot of guns: "20-gauges, 12-gauges, 14-gauges, 16-gauges, elephant gun, 9-mms, .45s, .44 Desert Eagles, Berettas, SKSs, Tech-9s, Tech-11s, .22s, .22 full auto, total .25s" (CMS-8, 7). He would take John shooting when he was nine years old.

John had an early history of delinquency with guns. When he was eleven, he got in trouble for threatening to shoot someone with a BB gun. When he was thirteen, he bought a 9-mm from an older friend for about $65. He usually kept it in a locked box in his closet, but now and then he would carry it in a shoulder holster: "Sometimes, when they said there was going to be something stupid happening on my street or something. Cause it's your neighborhood, you try to keep your neighborhood protected" (CMS-8, 14).

He and his friends were arrested while riding around in a car and charged with possession of the 9-mm, but the charges were ultimately dropped because the police could not pin the weapon on any one of the youths. The next gun he got, about a month later, was a .44 Desert Eagle. He got it from the same friend, this one for about $150. "That one stayed in my house all the time," John says. "It was too big" (CMS-8, 16–17). "When I fired it, it knocked me on my butt . . . They're hard to control. I didn't like it very much. It's too big. They're heavy" (CMS-8, 17).

That was the last gun John played around with. Since that time, he has moved away from guns—not entirely on his own. At fourteen, John was sent to the Catalina school for an aggravated assault involving substantial disfigurement. He served two years. When he was released, he was taken away from his mother and sent to a group home in Phoenix. He doesn't know what happened to his mother or where she is now. "When I was in here my mom just kind of faded away" (CMS-8, 6). The group home in Phoenix housed seven or eight kids and usually had one or two adults on a shift. He didn't have guns there because there was too much supervision. "It wasn't safe to have one" (CMS-8, 19).

John was sent back to Catalina for a second time from the group home for simple assault and disruption of an educational institution. He originally was sentenced to a three-month term, but he assaulted a staff member and got six extra months. After his release, John was charged with grand theft auto and sent back to Catalina for a third time. He has been at Catalina for a month now. He recently got his GED and is now taking the equivalent of college courses.

John claims he is not into guns anymore. And he has not been charged with a gun offense since he was thirteen. To be sure, he has a record of delinquency—aggravated assault and disfigurement, simple assault, staff assault, and grand theft auto—but no recent gun violations. Over the past few years, he has begun to see himself in the role of protector—his new self-described identity. He protects his neighborhood. He protects his friends. He feels that he earns respect by "being a protector": "That's how I earn my respect. I mean, people don't come in my neighborhood and disrespect me for no reason. I protect people. 'Yeah, he's cool. He's just protect[ing] people. He don't go starting trouble for no reason,'" John claims (CMS-8, 44). According to him, you *can't* earn that kind of respect with guns. Guns get you "the wrong kind of respect . . . Scared respect. That's not the respect you want. People respect you cause they're scared of you, and that's not the kind of respect that people want" (CMS-8, 44).

These two accounts reflect important moments of betrayal, especially by parents. The death or disappearance of a father. Early abandonment by a mother—at age seven for Paul. *Seven.* How unimaginable. Fourteen for John. Also, in Paul's case, the betrayal by his friend who comes for the gun with the police. These two accounts also reveal instances of fidelity. John, for instance, views himself as a protector of his friends and of his neighborhood. This is in large part his new identity. Paul has been working hard at Catalina and is being treated fairly by the administration. He is reaping the benefit of his efforts. At the same time, the swing between betrayal and fidelity triggers important moments of action. For Paul, it triggers a suicidal night. Was he acting in bad faith—or good? Could that night have been a turning point for Paul? Could it be that the subsequent betrayal by his friend led him, ultimately, to turn a page and become a senior upper-level student? What about John? Has he appropriated the role of protector as a reaction against his mother's betrayal and abandonment?

In order to *"understand* the myth," as Lévi-Strauss explains, we may need to read only the columns. A structural analysis of the Catalina interviews may suggest, then, a complex relation between betrayal and fidelity that triggers another intricate relation between acts in good faith and in bad faith. To be sure, this structural account does not help us *predict* how the Catalina youths might act. It does not help us predict whether any one of them will carry a gun. But it might offer a better understanding of the interviews as the instantiation of one particular coming-of-age narrative in relation to others: to see the building blocks (commitment, betrayal, possession, carrying, and suicide, among others), to appreciate the bundles of relation in any one particular life story, and to see how the elements of the structure relate to each other. This could help us predict the elements and relations that would form the narratives in these youths' lives. In this way, we could draw on Lévi-Strauss's science of mythology to interpret the Catalina interviews.[17]

A STRUCTURALIST MODEL OF ACTION

It may be useful to back up slightly and get a more systematic view of the structuralist method. Lévi-Strauss set out the basic tenets of his structuralist approach most succinctly in his essay "Structural Analysis," where, following the phonologist Nikolai Troubetzkoy, he reduced the structuralist model to four tenets:

> First, structural linguistics shifts from the study of *conscious* linguistic phenomena to study of their *unconscious* infrastructure; second, it does not treat *terms* as independent entities, taking instead as its basis of analysis the *relations* between terms; third, it introduces the concept of *system* . . . ; finally, structural linguistics aims at discovering *general laws*, either by induction "or . . . by logical deduction, which would give them an absolute character." (1967a, 31; see also Lévi-Strauss and Éribon 1988, 158)

The second tenet is perhaps the most familiar today, and it represents the idea that meaning in language derives from the relations of difference and similarity between terms, and not from the terms themselves. As Ferdinand de Saussure contended, language is a system of differences, without positive terms; it is a set of relations of difference and similarity rather than a set of terms that are differentiated. *"In the language itself, there are only differences,"* Saussure emphasized. "Even more important than that is the fact that, although in general a difference presupposes positive terms between which the difference holds, in a language there are only differences, *and no positive terms*" (Saussure 1989, 118 [166]; see also Pettit 1975, 8; Caws 1988, 72–73). This fundamental insight of structural linguistics has had important implications for the social sciences. As applied to symbolic action, it suggests that the meaning of behaviors cannot be deciphered in isolation and that acts derive their meaning not from themselves alone but rather from the distinctions and similarities between different meanings. As Lévi-Strauss writes, "The error of traditional anthropology, like that of traditional linguistics, was to consider the terms, and not the relations between the terms" (1967a, 45).

The third tenet is the idea that the relations of difference and similarity form a structure or system. To Saussure, "A language is a system in which all the elements fit together, and in which the value of any one element depends on the simultaneous coexistence of all the others" (1989, 113 [159]; see also Caws 1988, 72). One consequence is that as the structure becomes more apparent, patterns become evident. As Duncan Kennedy suggests, "The power of structuralist methodology is that it shows that what at first appears to be an infinitely various, essentially contextual mass of utterances (parole) is in fact less internally various and less contextual than that appearance" (Kennedy 1994, 343).

The first tenet is that these relations of difference and the overall structure of relations are second nature. They operate at the level of the unconscious. They are taken for granted. This too has its source in Saussure, who suggested that language is not produced intentionally and consciously but is the work of unconscious mechanisms. "People use their language without conscious reflexion, being largely unaware of the laws which govern it" (Saussure 1989, 72–73 [106]; see generally Pettit 1975, 10). Lévi-Strauss endorsed this notion of the unconscious, referring to the collective nature of culture as being "no more than the expression, on the level of individual thought and behavior, of certain time and space modalities of the universal laws which make up the unconscious activity of the mind" (1967b, 64). An essential fact in the social sciences, according to Lévi-Strauss, is precisely this idea that "the laws of language function at the unconscious level, beyond the control of the speaking subjects, and we can therefore study them as objective phenomena, representative in this sense of other social facts" (Lévi-Strauss and Éribon 1988, 59).

The fourth basic tenet of structuralism is that structural analysis can help discover general laws with universal character. In Lévi-Strauss's structuralism especially, there is a strong tendency toward both binarism and universalism.[18] Lévi-Strauss attempted to derive generally applicable laws not only in the area of kinship relations, but relating as well to all other social phenomena— including legal systems. He wanted to relate the structures of kinship to structures of linguistics, and from there to a wide range of social phenomena. The goal was to find patterns, a structure that helps understand behavior. "Ethnographic analysis tries to arrive at invariants beyond the empirical diversity of human societies" (Lévi-Strauss 1966, 247 [1962, 326]).

These invariants represent fundamental characteristics of mental processes— of the way we think, the way we analyze, the way we categorize and relate concepts. Lévi-Strauss's project was, in this sense, very ambitious. His ultimate goal was to appropriate structural linguistics to understand human thought and action. As he explains in "Language and the Analysis of Social Laws,"

> The road will then be open for a comparative structural analysis of customs, institutions and accepted patterns of behavior. We shall be in a position to understand basic similarities between forms of social life, such as language, art, law, and religion, that on the surface seem to differ greatly. At the same time, we shall have the hope of overcoming the opposition between the collective nature of culture and its manifestations in the individual, since the so-called "collective consciousness" would, in the final analysis, be no more

than the expression, on the level of individual thought and behavior, of certain time and space modalities of the universal laws which make up the unconscious activity of the mind. (Lévi-Strauss 1967b, 64)

In *The Savage Mind*, Lévi-Strauss sets out precisely to uncover these "universal laws which make up the unconscious activity of the mind." He explores there how North American and South American native peoples classify plants and animals and relate concepts to each other. He attempts to decipher the "untamed" mind—the *ways of thinking* of non-Western indigenous peoples. In his analysis, Lévi-Strauss compares their mode of thinking, as reflected in their legends and myths, with European scientific modes of thought during the eighteenth through the twentieth centuries.[19]

In his discussion, Lévi-Strauss offers a fascinating illustration of different modes of thought. It is in the context of a contemporary—at least, at the time—political debate, and it offers a perfect window to visualize the implications of his theory for the Catalina interviews. Lévi-Strauss recounts the following exchange at the conclusion of an academic conference:

M. Bertrand de Jouvenel: M. Priouret, would you like to say a few words in conclusion?

M. Roger Priouret: It seems to me that we are faced with two diametrically opposed theories. Raymond Aron follows the views of André Siegfried, according to which there are two basic political attitudes in France. This country is sometimes Bonapartist and sometimes Orleanist. Bonapartism consists in the acceptance and even desire for personal power, Orleanism in leaving the administration of public affairs to representatives. In the face of crises like the defeat of 1871 or a protracted war like the one in Algiers, France changes in attitude, that is, turns from Bonapartism to Orleanism as in 1871 or from Orleanism to Bonapartism, as on 13 May 1958.

In my own view, on the other hand, the actual change, although not entirely independent of these constants in French political temperament, is connected with the upheavals which industrialization brings into society. A different political analogy occurs to me. The *coup d'état* of 2 December 1851 corresponds to the first industrial revolution and the *coup d'état* of 13 May 1958 to the second. In other words, history shows that upheaval in the conditions of production and consumption seems incompatible with parliamentary government and leads this country to the form of authoritarian power which suits its temperament, namely, personal power. (Lévi-Strauss 1966, 70 [1962, 94])

These two positions represent, according to Lévi-Strauss, the two dominant theoretical positions vying for the public's imagination in France at the time. The first—which I shall refer to as the "cultural account"—privileges structure over the event. The cultural account suggests that there is a binary structural opposition between two forms of political engagement and that this structural opposition is the most important or foundational element in understanding French politics. The binary opposition constructs the field of politics and influences actual political opinion. Important historical events, such as the defeat in the Franco-Prussian War or in the Algerian War, act as a catalyst that moves French political institutions from one side of the binary structure to the other. The historical events, though, are essentially fungible. They have no substantive importance in themselves. They are consequential only insofar as they trigger a movement in the binary structure, which, in contrast, is what explains the political shift.

The second theoretical position—which I shall refer to as the "material account"—privileges certain events over the structure. The material account suggests that there are certain events, specifically those related to industrialization and upheavals in the conditions of production and consumption, that are most fundamental to understanding French politics. These material events are what bring about changes in political institutions. The primary forces are the material events, which then have a secondary effect on the structure of political opinions. The material account does not entirely dismiss the structure of French politics. There remains the opposition between authoritarian power, which M. Priouret claims suits the temperament of the French, and parliamentary government. But the structure is, in an important sense, superstructural. It is not what drives or explains the political change. What does is, instead, the evolution in modes of production and consumption.

These two accounts offer competing explanations regarding the shift to more authoritarian political institutions in France in 1851 (with the rise to power of Napoleon III) and 1958 (with the rise of Charles de Gaulle first as premier, with the power to rule by decree for six months, and then as first president of the Fifth Republic) and the shift to parliamentary institutions in 1871 after the French defeat in the Franco-Prussian War. The cultural account suggests a recurring binary opposition, the materialist account evolving modes of production. And these different explanations bear differently on future predictions. The Middle Eastern conflict may, for instance, amount to a significant enough political event to trigger a movement in the cultural account. Whether it is a significant enough material event under the material account depends on whether it reflects anything about upheavals in the conditions of production and consumption. It may, in the sense that it may reflect globalization and some form of an industrial reorganization. But the question turns on the relation of that event to economic change, and not simply to the abstract historical importance.

In terms of the dominant theoretical positions vying for the public's acceptance at the time, the cultural account represents what could be considered a more "structuralist" account. It focuses on the structural relation between the two political attitudes and on the symbolic realm insofar as these attitudes reflect aggregated political opinions or social norms. It is, in this sense, the more "synchronic" of the two—an account that focuses on the present *statis*, the current structure of the present state of affairs. The material account, in contrast, focuses on the historical event and at the time would have been considered the more Marxist account. The causal explanation here is more materialist, concrete, down-to-earth. What drives political change is not the structural relation between Bonapartism and Orleanism but rather the infrastructural conflict in modes of production. In this sense, the material account is the more "diachronic" of the two. It is an account that focuses on the historical evolution and changes of social conditions, in this case economic.

Lévi-Strauss suggests that, among his contemporaries, a choice between these two alternatives—between the cultural and the material account— would have to have been made. He indicates that his contemporaries would expect to be able to, and would in fact "pretend" to, choose between them (Lévi-Strauss 1962, 95 [1966, 70]). In contrast, Lévi-Strauss argues, the study of the legends and myths of the Osage—an Indian tribe—suggests that they would approach these competing accounts differently. The Osage, Lévi-Strauss suggests, would seek to harmonize the two in their mythical accounts. "The Osage would probably have used these two types of opposition, one synchronic and the other diachronic, as a point of departure. Instead of expecting to be able to choose between them they would have accepted both on the same footing and would have tried to work out a single scheme which allowed them to combine the standpoint of structure with that of event" (Lévi-Strauss 1966, 70 [1962, 95]).

Insofar as Lévi-Strauss identifies the intellectual move that the Osage would perform in the debate between cultural and material accounts of political change, it is probably fair to conclude that he considers himself sophisticated enough not to be purely "structuralist" according to the cultural account. Lévi-Strauss, it seems, negotiates the cultural and material accounts.

MAPPING THE CATALINA INTERVIEWS

How exactly does this relate to the choices the Catalina youths make? Can we decipher the way CMS-66, Jesús, Yusuf, Marc, Paul, or John *thinks*? Are there binary cultural accounts reflected in the Catalina interviews?

Perhaps. Drawing on the work of Elijah Anderson, we might discover in the interviews different ways of negotiating urban conditions in late-modern postindustrialized cities. In *Code of the Street* (1999), Anderson identifies a tension between "street codes" and "decent family codes" in certain neighborhoods in Philadelphia. Street codes represent tougher, meaner, more survivalist and individualist ways of negotiating the urban space. Decent family codes reflect more family-oriented, moralistic, possibly religious ways of dealing with the same urban space. Using these categories, we could explore whether the Catalina youths draw on these competing cultural models, whether they move fluidly between them, or whether the pendulum swings from one category to the other. Are there any material events—economic recession, an epidemic of gun violence, a spike in the supply of guns—that trigger movement from one code to the other? Does the temptation to adopt a particular code increase gun carrying? Do these codes ebb and flow?

Alternatively, we could explore youths' gun carrying from a more materialist perspective. Perhaps guns reflect something about the economic condition of inner-city youths. Is there a connection between the experience of economic change and the sale of guns? Have the fluctuations in the number of postindustrial, minimum-wage service jobs in the inner city affected gang membership and gun carrying? This second perspective could still leave room for the cultural account, as in Lévi-Strauss. It could still recognize an opposition between street codes and decent codes. But it would privilege the material account. It would privilege the narrative of economic transition. A third approach—associated with the Osage—would seek to blend the two previous stories, interweaving competing codes with material accounts.

What would these different accounts actually sound like in the situation of the Catalina youths? Do the youths have to be fully aware of the binary opposition between street codes and decent codes, or of the economic forces pushing them toward or away from gun carrying? Would we hear them talking about these forces in their interviews?

Yusuf views guns as a commodity. Might that be connected in some way to a materialist interpretation? Surely the economic value of handguns in the Southwest is directly related to the drug trade and the war on drugs, which is also connected, along materialist lines, with our postindustrial economic condition—and the dependence in many less developed countries on international drug revenues. Yusuf's gun trafficking may also be related to his lack of opportunity in the service-oriented economy of the Southwest. Jesús turns to gun carrying as a direct result of his drug trafficking. For Jesús, there is a direct link to the drug economy and its material role in the construction of the Southwest. CMS-66, on the other hand, is fully conscious of his "dual life"—of the "decent" life he lived with his mother, attending community college, aspiring to be a dentist, and the "street" life he led with his drug-dealing friends. He is aware of the dueling codes and seems to navigate between the two. Are there particular material events that push him from one to the other?

THE REGISTERS OF GUN TALK

Rather than focus on the relation between betrayal and fidelity, or on the duality of street codes and decent family codes, it may be more promising from a structuralist perspective to return instead to the three registers of gun talk that I identified in the interviews. Perhaps the Catalina youths deploy the different registers—commodity, recreation, self-protection—as ways of justifying or resisting gun possession. A youth, for instance, might use the fact that he hunts a lot with guns and his feeling that "guns have to be respected" to help him resist when his friends hand him a gun. Or a youth may say that he needs a gun "because it's my life or his" as a way to promote his own gun carrying. The categories or codes are precisely the registers of gun talk.

The structuralist insight, then, is that there are identifiable patterns of meaning associated with gun carrying, and that the Catalina youths may be bound by those registers. An individual youth can assign a purely subjective meaning to his act of gun possession—for example, guns are a "tool"—but this subjective meaning will have little effect if it is out of line with the dominant codes. In fact, if it is too far off it may be treated as delusional or insane. Individuals have freedom to act and give meaning, but their freedom is constrained by the community's rules of construction—rules that are themselves imposed on the individual, not freely chosen. Writing about the invariability of the signifier, Ferdinand de Saussure noted that "the signal, in relation to the idea it represents, may seem to be freely chosen. However, from the point of view of the linguistic community, the signal is imposed rather than freely chosen . . . No individual is able, even if he wished, to modify in any way a choice already established in the language. Nor can the linguistic community exercise its authority to change even a single word. The community, as much as the individual, is bound to its language" (1989, 71 [104]).

The Catalina youths are not free to express themselves in any manner they desire—as long as they want to be understood by their peers. The language of guns is inherited and, for the most part, employed without choice. This is not to suggest, of course, that language never changes. The point, rather, is that for the most part we take our language for granted. We place ourselves within a structure rather than creating it ourselves. "No society," Saussure emphasized, "has ever known its language to be anything other than something inherited from previous generations, which it has no choice but to accept" (Saussure 1989, 72 [105]).

The structuralist account, then, would sound like this: There are three clusters of ways of thinking about guns among the Catalina youths—the "action/protection" cluster, the "recreation/respect" cluster, and the "commodity/dislike" cluster. The first cluster is associated with heavy gun carrying, the other two with, respectively, less and less carrying. What makes youths gravitate toward the first cluster and actually carry guns, perhaps, is low economic opportunity and lack of parental supervision, which promote drug use and gang affiliation. What encourages youths to gravitate toward the second cluster is parental intervention—a strong emphasis on safety and precaution. Mixed parental messages and supervision tend to promote the third "commodity/dislike" cluster. On this interpretation, the cultural account plays an important role but is pushed along by material events.

In relation to the phenomenological reading, this structuralist account would contest the centrality of the individual life project: it is not the case that youths have a fundamental project that shapes how they deliberate and decide whether to carry guns. Nor are they free to impose whatever meaning they want on guns. On the contrary, there is a set of meanings that is already established—a language of guns. And the youths are influenced by certain events, such as parental intervention or economic conditions, to gravitate toward one or another cultural meaning. The Catalina youths can give meaning to the guns only by negotiating the codes they inherit.

There is, as a result, a wide methodological gap between the two approaches. Instead of focusing on CMS-66 and his individual decision making, the structuralist is interested in analyzing the patterns and relations formed when the Catalina youths think about, discuss, and make decisions about guns. To the structuralist, the phenomenological focus on the individual is incapable of generating useful findings. Lévi-Strauss emphasized these strong methodological reservations in *The Savage Mind*, where he wrote:

He who begins by steeping himself in the allegedly self-evident truths of introspection never emerges from them. Knowledge of men sometimes seems easier to those who allow themselves to be caught up in the snare of personal identity. But they thus shut the door on knowledge of man . . . Sartre in fact becomes the prisoner of his Cogito: Descartes made it possible to attain universality, but conditionally on remaining psychological and individual; by sociologizing the Cogito, Sartre merely exchanges one prison for another. Each subject's group and period now take the place of timeless consciousness. (Lévi-Strauss 1966, 249 [1962, 329–30])

Focusing narrowly on the individual's decision making says little, if anything, about men more generally—about patterns of behavior, about cultural opposition, about material events.[20]

THE PROBLEMS OF STRUCTURAL CHANGE AND INFLUENCE

The trouble is, the structuralist account does not readily answer the question of structural change. If we focus on the structures themselves, then how do we explain structural metamorphosis? If the analysis is static, how are we to understand the dynamism of structures? How is it, exactly, that the language of guns among the Catalina youths changes over time? Moreover, the structuralist account also does not offer a ready answer to the question of structural influence. Do the structures shape individual behavior, and if so, how? Do structures influence practice in a way that would allow us to predict future behavior? Do they affect human action in a way that perpetuates the structures themselves—or undermines them? How do structures *interrelate* with practice?

The turn to structuralism, after all, is intended to give us a better purchase—a more scientific perspective—on human behavior. The goal is to improve our ability to understand action and predict behavior. The purpose is to decipher *necessary* patterns. "Throughout, my intention remains unchanged," Lévi-Strauss emphasized in *The Raw and the Cooked*. "Starting from ethnographic experience, I have always aimed at drawing up an inventory of mental patterns, to reduce apparently arbitrary data to some kind of order, and to attain a level at which a kind of necessity becomes apparent, underlying the illusions of liberty" (Lévi-Strauss [1964] 1969, 10).

But once we have identified the necessary patterns, how do we connect them back to individual practice? The registers of gun talk may well constrain how the Catalina youths express themselves, but how do we know whether they influence what the youths actually do? Do the registers constrain their individual actions?

A HISTORICAL ASIDE: SARTRE VERSUS LÉVI-STRAUSS

It is here that the debate between Sartre and Lévi-Strauss ultimately foundered—on the question of history, on the interaction between structure and individual behavior. As I noted earlier, Sartre attempted a reconciliation of existentialism and dialectical materialism in his book *Critique de la raison dialectique*—an ambitious feat given the tension between the freedom of good faith and the determinism of dialectical materialism.[21] Lévi-Strauss dedicated the final chapter of *The Savage Mind*, titled "History and Dialectic," to a critique of Sartre and attacked Sartre's reliance on history. Lévi-Strauss argued that historical interpretations are for the most part misleading reflections of our own ideologies—in essence, that they are a social artifact. They are more often than not the victor's history, what Lévi-Strauss refers to as "*faulty acts* which have 'made it' socially" (1966, 254 [1962, 336]).

"In Sartre's system," Lévi-Strauss writes, "history plays exactly the part of a myth" (1966, 254 [1962, 336]). He continues:

> Sartre is certainly not the only contemporary philosopher to have valued history above the other human sciences and formed an almost mystical conception of it. The anthropologist respects history, but he does not accord it a special value. He conceives it as a study complementary to his own: one of them unfurls the range of human societies in time, the other in space. (Lévi-Strauss 1966, 256 [1962, 338–39])

In a set of interviews, Sartre responded to Lévi-Strauss by criticizing structuralist methods for evincing, in turn, a "rejection of history" (Sartre 1966, 87). According to Sartre, the structuralist enterprise misses the most interesting question: it fails to address how men pass from one pattern of thinking to another (Sartre 1966, 87). Structuralist analysis misleadingly focuses on the synchronic, on the static condition of patterns, at the expense of the historic or diachronic. According to Sartre, the structuralist tendency of the 1960s represented nothing more than a veiled attack on Marxism. Referring specifically to Michel Foucault, but intending structuralism more generally, Sartre wrote: "The real target is not history, but Marxism. The project is to develop a new ideology . . . Unable to 'overcome' Marxism, we will just suppress it. We'll say that history cannot be known as such . . . [and] we will oppose to history, domain of the unknown, the analysis of *structures* that, alone, permit true scientific investigation" (Sartre 1966, 88).

Though Sartre acknowledged the existence of structures, he was simply not prepared to recognize their importance as a topic of study. The focus, for him, had to be on how subjects *overcome* structures, *surpass* them, and make room for *new* structures: "Man is, for me, the product of a structure, but only insofar as he surpasses it. If you like, there are 'stases' of history that are structures. Man received these structures—and in this sense, we can say that they make him. But he receives them only insofar as he is engaged himself in history, and engaged in such a way that he cannot not destroy them, to constitute new ones which, in turn, will condition him" (Sartre 1966, 90–91).

As these exchanges reveal, the clash between existentialism and structuralism was not only conceptual but also—perhaps even primarily—political. The structuralist movement flourished in France in the 1960s in a climate critical of dogmatic Marxism and, in particular, Stalinism. Jean-Paul Sartre was at his apogee, but to many he had failed to offer a convincing account of Stalinism. Structuralism offered such an account. Politically, it suggested that the larger structure of institutions and discourses forms the functional equivalent of a language that sustains certain practices within a political community, that acts as a mythical narrative, and that has symbolic efficacy. This provided a way of understanding how institutions that seemed appalling could nevertheless gain legitimacy.

Structuralism offered a critique both of dogmatic Marxism and of liberal institutions in the period leading up to the student protests of May 1968. As Vincent Descombes explains,

> The semiological theorem of the exteriority of the signifier has thus a political corollary. The self-styled "political ideologies" of our societies are, very precisely, myths, and their symbolic efficacy (the trust of the faithful, the adherence of the masses) is no guarantee of their correspondence with the reality which they claim to describe. Lévi-Strauss is explicit on this point. "Nothing resembles mythological thought more than political ideology." A myth is the account of a founding event, of a privileged episode belonging at once to a certain time (its origin) and to all time (since festivals are given over to repeating it). (Descombes 1980, 107)

Structuralism, in this sense, offered a legitimation story that functioned much like critical theory—like the writings of Lukács, Gramsci, and the early Frankfurt school. For Lévi-Strauss, Sartre's philosophy was precisely a specimen of contemporary political ideology. Lévi-Strauss wrote in *The Savage Mind* that "[Sartre's] philosophy (like all the others) affords a first-class ethnographic document, the study of which is essential to an understanding of the mythology of our own time" (Lévi-Strauss 1966, 249n* [1962, 330n*]; see also Lévi-Strauss and Éribon 1988, 165). Whereas critical theory had been deployed principally to expose the false consciousness of the proletariat, though, structuralist theory was used primarily against Stalinism and dogmatic Marxism—and also against Sartrean existentialism. The result, as Mark Lilla suggests, is that "in the Paris of the late Fifties, the cool structuralism of Lévi-Strauss seemed at once more radically democratic and less naive than the engaged humanism of Sartre" (Lilla 2001, 167).[22]

The ensuing dialogue between Sartre and Lévi-Strauss, though, was short-lived. Sartre did not respond in writing to Lévi-Strauss's criticisms, and Lévi-Strauss did not earnestly respond to Sartre's comments (Lévi-Strauss and Éribon 1988, 164). Though much has been written about the dispute (see Delacampagne and Traimond 1997; Caws 1992; Brown 1978; Silverman 1978; Rosen 1971; Hartmann 1971; Abel 1970; Pouillon 1965), it did not lead to further productive exchanges between Sartre and Lévi-Strauss.

9

BOURDIEU AND PRACTICE THEORY
FROM THE KABYLE HOUSE TO THE STREET CORNER

It fell on the next generation to negotiate the space left open by Sartre and Lévi-Strauss and to resolve the question left hanging: How does structure relate to individual decision making? In the case of the Catalina interviews, how are the registers of gun talk connected to the practice of carrying guns? Do they help us understand why the Catalina youths possess guns, and can they help us predict which youths carry? Do the registers influence practice so as to perpetuate or undermine the language itself? Do the structures change over time? And what would account for the change? In sum, how do the registers of gun talk relate to the individual decisions to carry guns?

Pierre Bourdieu specifically addressed these questions, and the approach he helped develop—known as "practice theory"—represents the perfect illustration of a third methodological approach to social science. "The social world," Bourdieu writes in *Outline of a Theory of Practice* (originally published in 1972), "may be the object of three modes of theoretical knowledge, each of which implies a set of (usually tacit) anthropological theses" (Bourdieu 1977, 3). The first mode of theoretical knowledge is what I have called the phenomenological. Bourdieu associates it with Jean-Paul Sartre. This mode of knowledge "sets out to make explicit the truth of primary experience of the social world" (3). The second mode of theoretical knowledge is what I have called structuralism. Bourdieu calls it an "objectivist" approach and associates it with Claude Lévi-Strauss. This mode focuses on the linguistic relations that structure primary knowledge of the social world. The third mode of knowledge Bourdieu attributes to himself: it is a theory of practice, and it represents a break from both the phenomenological and structuralist modes of knowledge.

This third mode begins with an inquiry into the limits of the objective and the objectifying standpoint "which grasps practices from outside, as a *fait accompli*, instead of constructing their generative principle by situating itself within the very movement of their accomplishment" (Bourdieu 1977, 3). This mode aims "to make possible a science of the *dialectical* relations between the objective structures to which the objectivist mode of knowledge gives us access and the structured dispositions within which those structures are actualized and which tend to reproduce them" (3). It is a mode of knowledge that treats actors as ensconced within structures—semiotic and material—that are internalized and taken for granted, and who navigate these structures strategically. Actors understand the rules of the game and play by, manipulate, and strategize the rules, often in a secondhand way. It incorporates both the Lévi-Straussian moment of unconscious structures and the Sartrean moment of subjectivity in a theory of practice that is intended to let us better understand and predict actions. In this sense, Pierre Bourdieu's work addresses precisely the questions left open by the Sartre–Lévi-Strauss debate.

For Bourdieu, that dispute crystallized the central problem in contemporary thought and social science—the lack of a theory of human agency. The thrust of Bourdieu's intervention was to emphasize how Sartre, but also or especially Lévi-Strauss, circumvented the main problem—the problem of human action, the question of how practice relates to the explanatory structures that we are able to discern in our scientific inquiry.

BOURDIEU'S CRITIQUE OF PHENOMENOLOGY
AND STRUCTURALISM

Bourdieu's critique of the phenomenological approach is that it places too much confidence in the generative powers of the self and of the imagination. For instance, Sartre's idea that the individual subject has the power to give meaning to his situation by the mere act of imagining a different state of being does not have any power to explain history or social formation. It represents a fanciful flight toward an idealized notion of subjectivity that is far detached from reality (Bourdieu 1977, 74).

At the methodological level as well, Bourdieu finds fault with Sartre's approach. Bourdieu homes in on the passage in *L'être et le néant* where Sartre describes the condition of the *garçon de café*—the café waiter. In that passage, Sartre describes the excessive mannerisms of the typical Parisian *garçon de café*: his quick step, his extreme solicitude (or haughtiness, perhaps, to Americans), the way he carries his *plateau*. Sartre asks himself why the *garçon* appears to be acting or playing the role of the *garçon*, and he comes to the conclusion that the man is, in fact, playing at being the *garçon*: "Il joue *à être* garçon de café" (Sartre 1943, 95). In other words, he is playing the role in order to realize his condition. Sartre explores these issues by placing himself directly in the waiter's shoes, by inquiring how he himself would be a waiter, would attempt to realize the in-itselfness of being a waiter, of being what he is not.

Bourdieu trenchantly criticizes Sartre's phenomenological method. Taking a page from Lévi-Strauss, Bourdieu treats Sartre's passage *"as an anthropological document"*—a document that reflects, more than anything, the naïveté of the removed intellectual. Bourdieu writes:

> One could dwell on every word of this almost miraculous product of the social unconscious which . . . projects an intellectual's consciousness into a café waiter's practice . . . No doubt one needs to have the freedom to stay in bed without being fired to be able to see the person who gets up at five to sweep the floors and start up the coffee pot before the customers arrive as freeing himself (freely?) from the freedom to stay in bed, at the cost of being fired. The logic seen here, that of identification with a phantasm, is the one which has enabled others, presenting the "intellectual" relation to the working-class condition as the working-class relation to that condition, to produce a worker entirely engaged in "struggles" or, alternately, by simple inversion, as in myths, a worker desperately resigned to being only what he is, his "being-in-itself" as a worker, lacking the freedom that comes from being able to count among one's possibles positions like those of diplomat or journalist. (Bourdieu 2000, 155)

How could Sartre simply place himself in the waiter's shoes? Bourdieu asks. How is it possible to make any inferences about how the waiter experiences his being from introspection into how the bourgeois customer feels or thinks? It is impossible to draw any conclusions from such a fanciful approach. It would be necessary, at the very least, to begin by mapping out patterns of thought and behavior and then investigating how individuals who are waiters negotiate those patterns. In this sense, the break with primary experience—the move from the phenomenological to the structural—is necessary for Bourdieu. Methodological objectivism is, according to him, "a necessary moment in all research" (1977, 72).

Bourdieu's critique of Saussurean structuralism, on the other hand, is that it relies on a mode of knowledge of "applying rules"—of speech acts' being viewed as applying rules of language. So he writes, "The limits of Saussurian objectivism are never more clearly visible than in its inability to conceive of speech and more generally of practice other than as *execution*, within a logic which, though it does not use the word, is that of the rule to be applied" (1977, 24). Bourdieu argues that the underlying logic of the relation between language and expression—or between culture and practice in the system of structural anthropologists—is a logic of execution: the speech acts are understood only by deciphering the rules that are being applied. This approach, Bourdieu argues, is fatally flawed because it does not incorporate a theory of practice, a theory of how people act. It relies on a legalist formalist perspective that does not properly distinguish between the outsider's understanding of how natives follow rules and the native's or insider's view of how to act and how action requires a subtle appreciation of all the intricate nuances of those rules.

Bourdieu illustrates this by critiquing Lévi-Strauss's discussion of gift exchange. The successful exchange of gifts, Bourdieu argues, requires a certain form of strategizing that is not captured entirely by Lévi-Strauss's analysis of the cycle of reciprocity—"the unconscious principle of the obligation to give, the obligation to give in return, and the obligation to receive" (Bourdieu 1977, 5). In contrast to Marcel Mauss's phenomenological approach to gift exchange and Lévi-Strauss's structural perspective, Bourdieu offers a theory of practice that focuses on the subtle time differentials (the "interval") between receiving and giving and on the actor's strategic use of that period. "To abolish the interval is also to abolish strategy," Bourdieu complains. "The period interposed, which must be neither too short (as is clearly seen in gift exchange) nor too long (especially in the exchange of revenge murders), is quite the opposite of the inert gap of time, the time-lag which the objectivist model makes of it" (6). Actors in the structure understand all the meanings associated with a short delay, a long delay, or too rapid an exchange. One's reputation can be damaged, one's social capital can increase or decrease by playing on the interval. "When the unfolding of the action is heavily ritualized," Bourdieu explains, "there is still room for strategies which consist of playing on the time" (7).

A "FEEL FOR THE GAME"

We experience this playing on time every day—for example, when we delay an hour, a day, or more in responding to an e-mail, in returning a call, in exchanging an invitation. We know what all the rules are, we know the structure well, we have internalized it, and as a result, in our practice we do not play by the rules, we play the rules. Bourdieu often plays on this notion of gaming the rules. As players in a complex game, actors start to know the rules of the game at second hand. They follow certain scripts in different contexts, knowing what others will do. Even though they may be acting strategically, and in this sense instrumentally, they are not calculating based on preferences and options. They know what to do because they know the rules and outcomes and have developed a "feel for the game." In many situations they will be doing their strategizing without even consciously focusing, in a taken-for-granted way. In this way, Bourdieu hopes to take account of "the real principle behind strategies, namely the practical sense, or, if you prefer . . . the practical mastery of the logic or of the immanent necessity of a game—a mastery acquired by experience of the game, and one which works outside conscious control and discourse" (Bourdieu 1990, 61).

Bent Flyvbjerg, in *Making Social Science Matter* (2001), writes in the tradition of Bourdieu and illustrates well this notion of "feel for the game." He too draws heavily on the metaphor of sports. He discusses at length the virtuoso expertise on the field of the soccer player—or "soccer angel." Drawing on the writings of the Danish novelist Hans-Jørgen Nielsen, he describes the intuitive, unpracticed, nonchalant, but perfect free-kick pass that results in a goal. There is no plan or communication between the two players before the goal. "We don't exchange a word before I take the free kick, not even a telling glance, everything happens during the run-up, completely natural . . . It is a shared knowledge, from the perspective of the bodies and the eyes, ready to become reality, and it is prior to our being able to speak about it as a language and an ego" (Flyvbjerg 2001, 18, quoting Nielsen). He describes this to make the point that "experts operate from a mature, holistic well-tried understanding, intuitively and without conscious deliberation. Intuitive understanding comes primarily from experiences on one's own body and is in this way at one with the performer . . . Their skills have become so much a part of themselves that they are no more aware of them than they are of their own bodies" (Flyvbjerg 2001, 18–19).

Flyvbjerg's writings are helpful in conceptualizing notions of practice in Bourdeiu's work. In *Making Social Science Matter*, Flyvbjerg discusses the Dreyfus model of human learning—a model developed by Hubert and Stuart Dreyfus—which bears resemblance to ideas of practice theory. The Dreyfus model is a model of the phases or levels that people pass through as they learn skills. Although there are five levels—novice, advanced beginner, competent performer, proficient performer, and expert—the most important distinction is between the first three and the last two, between the realm of rule-based thinking and its replacement by context and intuition. Or as Flyvbjerg writes, "from rule-based, context-independent to experience-based, situational behavior" (2001, 22).

From the novice to the competent performer, the Dreyfus model shows, our actions are predominantly based on following context-independent rules we have been taught. The driver of a stick-shift car is told to change gears when the car makes a certain noise or when the engine revolutions reach a certain level. He or she may do so at first, following the rules, looking at the tachometer or listening for the right noise. This is rule-following, rational and technical.

It differs significantly from the experienced or expert driver, who changes gears unconsciously. In the later stages of proficiency and expertise, our actions are no longer guided by rules. Expert performances—by doctors, commodity traders, or athletes—rest on more than the application of preset rules. "The best performances within a given area require a qualitatively different expertise based on intuition, experience, and judgment" (Flyvbjerg 2001, 21). Flyvbjerg explains "intuition" as follows:

> Intuition is the ability to draw directly on one's own experience—bodily, emotional, intellectual—and to recognize similarities between these experiences and new situations. Intuition is internalized; it is part of the individual. Existing research provides no evidence that intuition and judgment can be externalized into rules and explanations, which, if followed, lead to the same result as intuitive behavior. Such externalization is possible only for analytical rationality, that is, for those skills which characterize the lower levels in the learning process. (Flyvbjerg 2001, 21)

The Dreyfus model does not suggest that there is an exclusive choice between rationality and intuition, but rather proposes that the two are complementary and, with experts, hierarchically related. "The Dreyfus model does not present a situation of 'either rationality or intuition' but of both of them in their proper context: the position of intuition is not beyond rationality but alongside it, complementary to it, and insofar as we speak of experts, above rationality" (Flyvbjerg 2001, 23).

This illustrates well how actors, as I suggested earlier, do not simply play *by* the rules, but *play* the rules. There is here an important notion of "second nature"—of the significant assumptions that underlie our ability to engage in practice. "I am talking about dispositions *acquired through experience* . . . This 'feel for the game,' as we call it, is what enables an infinite number of 'moves' to be made, adapted to the infinite number of possible situations which no rule, however complex, can foresee" (Bourdieu 1990, 9).

In this sense, Bourdieu is especially critical of Lévi-Strauss, who, he argues, deploys a number of obfuscating concepts to skirt the central issue of agency. Lévi-Strauss deploys concepts like the "unconscious," "models," or "structures" to describe ways of understanding the social world, and he goes back and forth between notions of knowing or being aware of these rules to notions of them as unconscious. Bourdieu writes, "Lévi-Strauss' use of the notion of the unconscious masks the contradictions generated by the implicit theory of practice which 'structural anthropology' accepts at least by default, restoring the old entelechies of the metaphysics of nature in the apparently secularized form of a structure structured in the absence of any structuring principle" (Bourdieu 1977, 27). The result is an undertheorized—or untheorized—conception of human agency and actual human practices. By failing to think properly about practices, Bourdieu argues, structuralist approaches are

> condemned either to ignore the whole question of the principle underlying the production of the regularities which it then contents itself with recording; or to reify abstractions, by the fallacy of treating the objects constructed by science, whether "culture," "structures," or "modes of production," as realities endowed with a social efficacy, capable of acting as agents responsible for historical actions or as a power capable of constraining practices; or to save appearances by means of concepts as ambiguous as the notions of the rule or the unconscious, which make it possible to avoid choosing between incompatible theories of practice. (Bourdieu 1977, 26–27)

THE CONCEPT OF HABITUS

At the heart of Bourdieu's affirmative theory of practice is the concept of *habitus*. Habitus represents Bourdieu's conceptualization of how objective structures influence individual action. It is the notion he uses to negotiate the space between the individual subjectivity of the phenomenologists and the objective structures of the structuralist. His intention in using the concept of habitus is to "escape from under the philosophy of the subject without doing away with the agent, as well as from under the philosophy of the structure but without forgetting to take into account the effects it wields upon and through the agent" (Bourdieu and Wacquant 1992, 121–22).

Habitus is the system of categories, of ways of thinking, perceiving, and acting, that the individual internalizes by growing up in a certain milieu, time, and place. It reflects the way our minds are socially structured. Bourdieu offers several definitions of habitus in order to communicate the various dimensions of this structured subjectivity, or what he calls "socialized subjectivity" (Bourdieu and Wacquant 1992, 126). He defines habitus as "the durably installed generative principle of regulated improvisations" (Bourdieu 1977, 78) or "the strategy-generating principle enabling agents to cope with unforeseen and ever-changing situations" (72). He also describes it as

> systems of durable, transposable *dispositions*, structured structures predisposed to function as structuring structures, that is, as principles of the generation and structuring of practices and representations which can be

objectively "regulated" and "regular" without in any way being the product of obedience to rules, objectively adapted to their goals without presupposing a conscious aiming at ends or an express mastery of the operations necessary to attain them and, being all this, collectively orchestrated without being the product of the orchestrating action of a conductor. (Bourdieu 1977, 72)

Notice the emphasis on coordinated activity in the absence of one central-ized coordinator—in the absence of imposed obedience to rules of coordina-tion. The concept of habitus contains both the moment of coordination (of rules, of shared understandings) and the moment of individual action (of strategies). Bourdieu is negotiating here the space of practice, where practice in effect reproduces the very principles that render intelligible the practices themselves: the practices at the same time "tend to reproduce the objective structures of which they are the product" and "are determined by the past con-ditions which have produced the principle of their production" (Bourdieu 1977, 72). Habitus depends on shared, though contested, understandings of how things operate, in such a way that there need not be explicit reference to intentions. Things are understood, they are known at second hand. They are taken for granted. Here is how Bourdieu describes it:

One of the fundamental effects of the orchestration of habitus is the pro-duction of a commonsense world endowed with the *objectivity* secured by consensus on the meaning (*sens*) of practices and the world, in other words the harmonization of agents' experiences and the continuous reinforce-ment that each of them receives from the expression, individual or collec-tive (in festivals, for example), improvised or programmed (commonplaces, sayings), of similar or identical experiences. The homogeneity of habitus is what . . . causes practices and works to be immediately intelligible and foreseeable, and hence taken for granted. This practical comprehension obviates the "intention" and "intentional transfer into the Other" dear to phenomenologists, by dispensing, for the ordinary occasions of life, with close analysis of the nuances of another's practice and tacit or explicit inquiry ("What do you *mean*?") into his intentions. (Bourdieu 1977, 80)

PRACTICE THEORY

It is here that Bourdieu answers the central question that plagued the Sartre–Lévi-Strauss debate: Do structures *influence* practice? His answer: Yes. The structures, as part of the environmental physiognomy, are absorbed by subjects and thus transmitted (and transformed) from generation to generation. The transmission occurs in practice. It need not, according to Bourdieu, attain the level of discourse. "The child imitates not 'models' but other people's actions" (1977, 87). In this sense, "schemes are able to pass from practice to practice without going through discourse or consciousness" (1977, 87).

Bourdieu illustrates this process of transmission in his noted study of the Kabyle house, the traditional home of members of the Berber tribes in Algeria. Transmission occurs through "the dialectical relationship between the body and a space structured according to the mythico-ritual oppositions" (1977, 89). The interior of the Kabyle house is organized along structural lines that the young internalize in their earliest learning. The division between male and female space, between the public and the private, structures the world in a way that is easily internalized. Here the structural relations of the Kabyle study serve as a segue to Bourdieu's notion of habitus: the structures are internalized and become part of practice from early childhood:

> This analysis of the relationship between the objectified schemes and the schemes incorporated or being incorporated presupposes a structural analysis of the social organization of the internal space of the house and the relation of this internal space to external space, an analysis which is not an end in itself but which, precisely on account of the (dangerous) affinity between objectivism and all that is already objectified, is the only means of fully grasping the structuring structures which, remaining obscure to themselves, are revealed only in the objects they structure. The house, an *opus operatum*, lends itself as such to a deciphering, but only to a deciphering which does not forget that the "book" from which the children learn their vision of the world is read with the body, in and through the movements and displacements which make the space within which they are enacted as much as they are made by it. (Bourdieu 1977, 90)

Children absorb the structural relations of the house in their everyday practice. They learn the fundamental oppositions that structure their lives: male/female, day/night, cooked/raw, fertilizing/able to be fertilized, high/low (Bourdieu 1977, 90). As the youths master these structures, they become second nature. And as they act, they then instantiate these structures, strategize through them, reinstating but also playing off the different relations. They use the oppositions to define their identity, to understand their psyches, to organize their relations with others, to relate to their own bodies, to represent their sexuality.

THE CATALINA SCRIPTS

The implications for interpretation and prediction are significant. In the context of the Catalina interviews, the registers of gun talk represent cognitive scripts shared by the youths. They embody taken-for-granted, second-hand ways of talking about guns, of reacting to guns in a social setting, of engaging with guns in social interaction. The primary meanings are, in a sense, well-trodden paths: comfortable, cozy, familiar. They are paths of least resistance. So, for instance, the youth who wants to resist gun carrying may feel comfortable telling a peer that guns are to be "respected"; that guns are for hunting or target practice; that he is a sharpshooter and does not need to act macho; that he is familiar with guns and does not play with them; or that it is more fun to scrap the old-fashioned way, to fight with your hands. These are familiar, comfortable ways for the youths to communicate with peers and resist gun carrying. At the other extreme, dogging others and talking shit are convenient, conventional ways to get some action going, to draw some heat, to play around.

Bourdieu's work might suggest, then, that youths growing up in proximity to these registers of gun talk in Tucson absorb these ways of thinking about, talking about, and interacting with guns. These relations between structured meanings and practices reflect known scripts. We saw, for instance, that there are contexts in which guns seem to be carried more—gangs, drug dealing, parties. And we heard recurring scripts of how youths interact with guns. Based on these types of scripts, we can predict how youths are going to react in certain circumstances, whether they are going to carry guns or not, whether they are going to use guns or not. We can see how youths might deploy one register against the other to avoid gun carrying. How a youth, for instance, might deploy the fact that he hunts a lot or is a sharpshooter as a way to *resist* taking the gun that is being handed to him by a friend in the middle of an attempted burglary. Or the opposite. How a youth might talk about the power of guns to encourage himself to carry.

Recall John, who is at the Catalina school for the third time. John recounts an incident that occurred while he was hanging out with some friends at the Rillito River. At the time, he was still carrying his 9-mm:

> We were by the Tohono Center down in the wash. And we were just sitting there . . . They were walking by . . . They kept on dogging me . . . Staring down. Like not saying anything. Just staring . . . hard . . . [And they] started talking crap. Like, you know, your instinct is to talk crap back . . . Like,

"You're a pussy." "No, you're a bitch." "I'm gonna kick your ass." Just talking. "Fuck your mother." They get mad. "Yeah, whatever." "Fuck you." "You ain't down." . . . So we were talking crap and then like, "Yeah, whatever . . . ," he was all, "I'll shoot you." I said, "Do it then." So he pulled out a gun. And I pulled out mine really quick. And then we just stood there and I said, right at the end, I was all like, "You know both you and me aren't gonna pull the trigger, so why don't you shut up and leave?" (CMS-8, 29)

Notice how perfectly scripted this sounds. The "dogging" and "talking shit": these Catalina youths know what to do and what to say. There is a cadence to talking shit, and you learn how to do it by listening to others. You practice. You hear it. You play it. Over time, it becomes second nature. "What, bitch?" "I ain't no bitch." "I got your bitch." It's like a good volley. It has a sweet rhythm. Others watch and listen. They see how things are done. Likely they will relive an episode just like it. It seems pretty cool. It's a lot of fun. "I think shit talking is the funnest thing in the world," John says (CMS-8, 30). It reflects a real feel for the game.

These youths know how their interactions are played out. They are *playing* the rules, strategizing, pushing the limits, and at the same time protecting themselves. One of the most remarkable facts about John's script is how it is deployed to *avoid* using the guns. It leads to a climax and a standoff—and no one is hurt. These Catalina youths have a real appreciation for the rules of the game. Theirs is a rapid game, almost second nature.

Jeffrey Fagan and Deanna Wilkinson, in their research on the processual dynamics of youths' aggression and violence, rely in part on a resonant notion of "violence scripts," by which they mean a preset cognitive framework within which youths act. Scripts are the "cognitive structure or framework that organizes a person's understanding of typical situations, allowing the person to have expectations and to make conclusions about the potential result of a set of events" (Fagan 1999a, 535–36). Different contextual junctures trigger different scripts, automatic behaviors by youths that are scripted in previous and repetitive encounters. Fagan locates the notion of "violence scripts" in Derek Cornish's use of "procedural scripts" to explain the decision-making processes of violent offenders (Fagan 1999a, 536). In this sense, Fagan uses "violence scripts" as a way to enrich rational choice perspectives on offending. "The script framework," Fagan suggests, "provides a useful way of understanding the decision-making process, including the calculation of risks, strategic decisions, and the assessments of available choices" (1999a, 536). Fagan and Wilkinson's work on violence scripts also ties in to conceptions of identity.

The scripts relate importantly—reinforcing at times, undermining at others—central identities tied to gun carrying, such as the identity of the "herb" who is punked all the time, of the "hold your own" type of carrier who gets respect, or the "wild" or "crazy" guys who are trigger-happy and to be avoided. These identities are themselves scripted.

In this way, practice-oriented theory brings together the symbolic realm (the gun registers) and the practical realm (gun carrying). It is a model of action in which conduct is often second nature, taken for granted, and scripted along contextual lines. A number of contemporary approaches fit in this third perspective, including not only Pierre Bourdieu's practice theory but also the fascinating work of Ronald Breiger and John Mohr,[23] Calvin Morrill's notion of action tales,[24] and the idea of violence scripts (Fagan 1999a), as well as new institutionalism and other strands in sociology and anthropology that focus on scripts and identities. These approaches all negotiate the space of intentional action within internalized cognitive structures.

10

BUTLER AND THE PERFORMATIVE
FROM IDENTITY AND SCRIPTS TO THE DISCURSIVE

What progress have we made with the Catalina interviews? Are we in a better position to interpret them? To understand the Catalina youths? To predict their behavior? Practice theory has taken us from the realm of the deeply subjective, phenomenological approach that focuses on the mental processes of the individual youths, through the realm of recurring patterns of thought and action that reflect a structure to their language of guns, and finally to a realm of practical action where the youths negotiate the registers of gun talk in a secondhand way, with a special feel for the game.

Practice theory is a realm that brings together decision making and symbolism in a dynamic relationship—a relationship that produces a more fluid conception of structures and a more structured notion of decision making. But it raises its own set of difficult questions. Do these scripts, identities, or habitus really shape conduct in a predictable way? Or are the scripted actions of the Catalina youths merely performances that *create* the scripts and *form* the identities? Are the youths merely enacting in their performances the stereotypes that we attribute to them ex post? Is it an illusion to believe that youths act *in accordance with* scripts, that they *pursue* identifiable identities, or that they *internalize* their surrounding structures in a way that would give the researcher power to predict their behavior? Could it be that these identities, scripts, and habitus, rather than shaping their interactions with guns, are simply the *product* of these interactions?

A FOURTH METHODOLOGICAL SENSIBILITY

Judith Butler raises precisely these kinds of questions in the context of gender identities in *Gender Trouble: Feminism and the Subversion of Identity* (1990), offering yet another approach to interpreting the Catalina interviews. Butler presents a critique of the role that gender identities—in particular the feminine—play in and through identity politics. She argues that the very conception of the identity "woman" is deeply problematic: instead of providing a way of uniting women in a struggle against patriarchal social structures, the identity has the effect of marginalizing many women because the category itself is laced with heterosexual and male hierarchical preferences. The category is constructed through a discourse permeated with compulsory heterosexuality. As a result, it produces resistance among many women who are supposed to be its beneficiaries, even though, Butler emphasizes, the category is being deployed for emancipatory purposes.

Butler's critique challenges the notion that gender identities are in any way fixed or natural. It undermines the idea that gender identities could *make* subjects do things—that the feminine identity, for instance, would cause women to act in certain ways. Butler contests the notion that there are genuine or authentic identities. On the contrary, she argues, our identities are the product of institutions, practices, and discourses. Moreover, identities are created in the very performance of imagined identities. Gender identities are, in this sense, performative: not the source of our conduct, but the product of our practices and of institutional forces. What Butler offers, in effect, is a "critique of the categories of identity that contemporary juridical structures engender, naturalize, and immobilize" (Butler 1990, 5).

Gender is performative in the sense that it is "constituting the identity it is purported to be" (Butler 1990, 25). In other words, it is constantly being produced as a category. As Butler explains,

> Gender is always a doing, though not a doing by a subject who might be said to preexist the deed. The challenge for rethinking gender categories outside of the metaphysics of substance will have to consider the relevance of Nietzsche's claim in *On the Genealogy of Morals* that "there is no 'being' behind the doing, effecting, becoming; 'the doer' is merely a fiction added to the deed—the deed is everything." In an application that Nietzsche himself would not have anticipated or condoned, we might state as a corollary: There is no gender identity behind the expressions of gender; that identity is performatively constituted by the very "expressions" that are said to be its results. (Butler 1990, 24–25)

It may be worth adding that the "doer"—who does not exist behind the deed—is not alone. The performance of gender is inextricably interpersonal or intersubjective. Others are also performing identity in their very interactions with the missing "doer." They too are doing, without being "doers." Butler's point is that the resulting identity is not what *makes* any of them act, it is rather *produced* itself by them *through* their actions.

Richard Ford gives a powerful illustration of this in "Beyond 'Difference': A Reluctant Critique of Legal Identity Politics":

When a well meaning but misguided white liberal shakes the hand of my white friend the same way he would shake the hand of [a] Fortune 500 CEO but holds out an open palm to me to "give me five" or awkwardly tries to give me the "soul" handshake, he is performing my identity. By the same token, if another black man gives me the "soul" handshake, he is performing my identity. This is true even if giving the soul handshake strikes me as the most natural thing in the world—in fact that is perhaps when it is most true. (Ford 2002, 19)

By means of a performative conception of identity, Butler pushes critical theory one step further into and against the realm of identity politics. Social reformers perform a critique—like the critique of the social construction of sex—but then allow gender itself to become a fixed category. Repeatedly we destabilize, but we restabilize along new axes. This is the sense in which, Butler suggests, "[a] great deal of feminist theory and literature has nevertheless assumed that there is a 'doer' behind the deed" (Butler 1990, 25). It assumes that there is a gender identity behind the expressions of gender: that there are gender identities, rather than just performances of them. "For the most part," Butler writes, "feminist theory has assumed that there is some existing identity, understood through the category of women, who not only initiates feminist interests and goals within discourse, but constitutes the subject for whom political representation is pursued" (1).

Butler's project is to destabilize the notion of gender by means of a genealogical critique, in order to decenter the institutions that benefit from these constructed identities. The terms "feminine" and "masculine," taken as universals, are coercive to women even though they are elaborated for the purpose of liberation. "These domains of exclusion reveal the coercive and regulatory consequences of that construction, even when the construction has been elaborated for emancipatory purposes" (Butler 1990, 4). Rather than searching for true underlying identities or genuine identities, Butler's project is to focus on how those identities are constructed, what power and knowledge purposes are served:

A genealogical critique refuses to search for the origins of gender, the inner truth of female desire, a genuine or authentic sexual identity that repression has kept from view; rather, a genealogy investigates the political stakes in designating as an *origin* and *cause* those identity categories that are in fact the *effects* of institutions, practices, discourses with multiple and diffuse points of origin. The task of this inquiry is to center on—and decenter—such defining institutions: phallogocentrism and compulsory heterosexuality. (Butler 1990, viii–ix)

CRITIQUING THE ALTERNATIVE METHODOLOGICAL APPROACHES

Gender Trouble performs just this kind of genealogical critique. In the process, it critiques and highlights the assumptions underlying the three other methodological sensibilities.

First, structuralism. This approach, Butler argues, focuses myopically on *binary* structures—the self and the other, freedom and constraint—as a way to better understand practices. But these binary structures do not simply shed light on social phenomena; they constrain how we think about them. They constrain our imagination. The question to ask, then, is not whether the structures are correct, but how it has come about that they have been accepted as universal and dominant.

Butler discusses this point in relation to the category of the feminine. She questions the very questions we have chosen to ask about the construction of the category itself. She explores whether the questions allow for choice on the part of the subject: "Is gender as variable and volitional as Beauvoir's account seems to suggest? Can 'construction' in such case be reduced to a form of choice?" These questions themselves, she argues, are misguided. They "founder on the conventional philosophical polarity between free will and determinism" (Butler 1990, 8). The debate between free will and determinism is itself caught in the structuralist trap of binarity: the very way the questions are posed reflects the constraints *of structuralism*. It is only because we assume the either/or that we struggle with these issues. It is modern consciousness— here the "binary structures" in language that appear as "universal rationality"—that accounts for the limits on free expression of identities (9):

> Whether gender or sex is fixed or free is a function of a discourse which, it will be suggested, seeks to set certain limits to analysis or to safeguard certain tenets of humanism as presuppositional to any analysis of gender. The locus of intractability, whether in "sex" or "gender" or in the very meaning of "construction," provides a clue to what cultural possibilities can and cannot become mobilized through any further analysis. The limits of the discursive analysis of gender presuppose and preempt the possibilities of imaginable and realizable gender configurations within culture. This is not to say that any and all gendered possibilities are open, but that the boundaries of analysis suggest the limits of a discursively conditioned experience.

These limits are always set within the terms of a hegemonic cultural discourse predicated on binary structures that appear as the language of universal rationality. Constraint is thus built into what that language constitutes as the imaginable domain of gender. (Butler 1990, 9)

This is a critique of the *discourse* of structuralism: a critique of the way conceptions of structuralism are already themselves always mediated through discourse, and in the process, loaded with assumptions. One such assumption in the case of Lévi-Strauss, Butler suggests, is the heterosexual male prerogative. In the context of his discussion of gift exchange, she argues, the structural binarisms of male/female, active/passive, giver/gift, and nature/culture presume both heterosexuality and the masculine viewpoint. "The naturalization of both heterosexuality and masculine sexual agency are discursive constructions nowhere accounted for but everywhere assumed within this founding structuralist frame" (Butler 1990, 42–43). In this sense, the binary structures limit our sight or vision. They constrain the realm of our imagination. They naturalize the heterosexual male viewpoint.

Second, existentialism. This approach also fails to recognize the important role of discourse. Butler's writings do, at times, have a strikingly existentialist flavor, especially when she refers back to the Nietzschean aphorism that there is "no doer behind the deed"—an idea that bears much resemblance to Jean-Paul Sartre's claim that existence precedes essence, or his contention that man is his project. Butler in fact recognizes and acknowledges the resemblance. But in the concluding chapter of *Gender Trouble*, she distinguishes her theory of the performative from Sartre's writings by focusing precisely on the notion of discourse:

The foundationalist reasoning of identity politics tends to assume that an identity must first be in place in order for political interests to be elaborated and, subsequently, political action to be taken. My argument is that there need not be a "doer behind the deed," but that the "doer" is variably constructed in and through the deed. *This is not a return to an existential theory of the self as constituted through its acts, for the existential theory maintains a prediscursive structure for both the self and its acts.* It is precisely the discursively variable construction of each in and through the other that has interested me here. (Butler 1990, 142; emphasis added)

The thrust of Butler's critique, then, is that the existentialist approach does not take proper account of the role of language in the construction of categories and in the giving of meaning. In contrast to Sartre, who viewed *himself* as giving meaning, Butler focuses on discourse and how *the discursive* distributes meaning.

To this specific charge, existentialism—at least Sartrean existentialism— must plead guilty. Sartre's approach is prediscursive in precisely the meaning that Butler suggests. For Sartre, as we saw earlier, the subject gives meaning. The individual subject is the signifier: "I consider me, myself, as the signifier" (Sartre 1965, 311).

The charge of "prediscursive" picks up on the structuralist critique of existentialism but goes further in one important respect. For Butler, discursivity not only constitutes the categories through which we relate to others, such as gender, but also functions as a model for action. Butler in a sense displaces existential action with a model of action in a discursive key.

Third and finally, practice theory. This approach, as I noted earlier, assumes a subject behind the performance. It improperly assumes an intentional agent performing a known script or pursuing a known identity. But here too Butler's critique goes further. Practice theory also fails to recognize the centrality of the discursive as a model for action. Practice is not a mere vague or nebulous playing out of a script. It is not simply a mystery that produces coordinated activity. Practice is far more familiar to us. It is something we do day in and day out. It is, very precisely, discourse, language—the discursive.

A DISCURSIVE MODEL OF ACTION

In her work, Butler develops a theory of action modeled on the discursive, a theory based on the idea of speech, repetition, and linguistic transformation. The central idea is that although we are inevitably discursively situated—located in language and discourse, constructed by these—we are nevertheless not determined by discourse. We are socially and culturally constructed, but not completely constrained by culture. There is room, flexibility, and it is reflected in the notions of iteration and reiteration.

The model for this fluidity is the linguistic. Signification—the giving of meaning—involves a repetitive task of speech, description, identification. This repetitiveness opens us to the possibility of slight changes, of gradual transformations, of tweaking the repetition. Butler writes, "All signification takes place within the orbit of the compulsion to repeat; 'agency,' then, is to be located within the possibility of a variation on that repetition" (1990, 145).

Butler's point is that we have no choice but to perform our identities. There is no place beyond discourse. "The task in not whether to repeat, but how to repeat or, indeed, to repeat and, through a radical proliferation of gender, *to displace* the very gender norms that enable the repetition itself" (1990, 148). The illustration Butler uses in *Gender Trouble* is of gender-bending performances—drag shows, cross-dressing, and butch/femme identities. These performances challenge the coherence of the sex/gender relationship and create a space within which we can imagine different alignments of sex and gender and gender performance. At the same time, these acts reveal the element of performance embedded in all gender identities and destabilize the naturalness of so many gender performances. "*In imitating gender,*" Butler emphasizes, "*drag implicitly reveals the imitative structure of gender itself—as well as its contingency*" (137; emphasis in original). In disclosing its contingency, these performances challenge the very claim to natural gender identities. Another illustration of this is how the derogatory term "queer" was appropriated by gay men and lesbians and given new meaning through a process of resignification. In *Excitable Speech: A Politics of the Performative* Butler writes, "The revaluation of terms such as 'queer' suggest that speech can be 'returned' to its speaker in a different form, that it can be cited against its originary purposes, and perform a reversal of effects. More generally, then, this suggests that the changeable power of such terms marks a kind of discursive performativity that is not a discrete series of speech acts, but a ritual chain of resignifications whose origin and end remain unfixed and unfixable" (1997, 14).

In *Excitable Speech*, Butler advocates these kinds of nonjuridical, nonregulatory forms of resistance, everyday forms of opposition and organized group resistance, instead of state regulation (1997, 23). So, for instance, she argues against Catharine MacKinnon's proposal to regulate pornography because of her concern that regulation may give too much power to the state. The risk, according to Butler, is that the state will then deploy its regulatory power against the interests of minority groups. Butler warns that "such strategies tend to enhance state regulation over the issues in question, potentially empowering the state to invoke such precedents against the very social movements that pushed for their acceptance as legal doctrine" (24). She suggests that "this very extension of state power . . . comes to represent one of the greatest threats to the discursive operation of lesbian and gay politics" (22).

In this sense, Butler wants to emphasize that there is room for change, room for agency, room for transformation *through* a performative conception of action. "Construction is not opposed to agency," Butler emphasizes; "it is the necessary scene of agency, the very terms in which agency is articulated and becomes culturally intelligible" (1990, 147). Butler's political program seizes on this notion of discursivity: "The critical task for feminism is not to establish a point of view outside of constructed identities . . . The critical task is, rather, to locate strategies of subversive repetition enabled by those constructions, to affirm the local possibilities of intervention through participating in precisely those practices of repetition that constitute identity and, therefore, present the immanent possibility of contesting them" (147).

The difference between Butler's approach and the three other methodological sensibilities, then, is more than simply a discursive critique of the other methods. More important, it is Butler's use of discourse *as a model of action.*

Butler's work does not end in genealogy. It subscribes, instead, to a model of how we act: a model that asserts resistance, choice, and free will by means of repetition and reiteration along a discursive paradigm. We are inextricably in discourse, yet not bound by it, not fully determined by it. This represents an affirmative conception of action, a substantive commitment to the idea that subjects perform shifting identities by means of recurrence. Subjects have the ability to change the script, in a deliberate way, by repeating lines differently, by subverting, exaggerating, mimicking what is expected. The discursive subject, who is totally plunged in discourse, constructed by intersubjectivity, shaped by relations to others, is nevertheless able to contest, resist, modify, transform these constraints.

PERFORMANCE AND THE CATALINA INTERVIEWS

In relation to the Catalina interviews, the performative approach might focus our attention on the moments of resistance to the dominant discourses of gun carrying, as a way to explore how the registers of gun talk change. Rather than focusing exclusively on the registers of gun talk—the action/protection, commodity/dislike, and recreation/respect clusters—we could explore how youths rhetorically mimic those ways of speaking, how they deploy the registers in ways that effectively modify them.

Many of the Catalina youths, for instance, recounted narratives involving gunfights. In relatively few cases, though—thank goodness—are any of the youths actually shot. Hearing these stories, one can only wonder whether these youths are shooting with an intent to hit one another or shooting out of range simply to unload some shots and scare their rivals.

Here is a good illustration. CMS-2 is a sixteen-year-old Anglo youth from the suburbs of Tucson. He is not himself a gang member. He had dropped out of school and was dealing drugs—and had a long history of gun possession and carrying. CMS-2 tells this story:

Jack-in-the-Box on the corner of Twenty-second and Craycroft. We were eating normal. We were just eating normal. It was a Sunday night. We were listening to slow jams, Sunday night slow jams. We were just sitting there at Jack-in-the-Box . . . parked in the parking lot . . . eating in the car . . . [My friend was] from Sur Trece, the gang . . . [These other guys] came into the parking lot, and they parked next to us and we didn't know. And they got out and they were all dressed in red . . . [My friend] went and parked in another parking spot on the other side of the parking lot. Right there are Twenty-second and Craycroft. He got out, and went over there and [was] standing there waiting for them to come out. And they came out and he's like said, "Wuz up? This is Sur Trece." You know, started his gang and shit. And I was sitting in the car and he started yelling at them. Then they got around their car, and he was talking shit like, "What's up, fool? You want to get it or something?" You know, he was talking shit. And that fool was just, "Nah, fool. Chill up and kick back. Fool, get out of here." And [my friend] had [his gun] in his hand and I know they could see it. And they went to get into their car, and that fool came out with a strap. And [the other guy] got up on the car and was all, "Boom." . . . And he shot like two or three times. And then my homey jumped behind them, right there was a little garbage can, next to the bus stop, and he went to the little bus stop thing. And he shot like twice and I guess he hit his car because he got pissed. And started shooting. He shot like four times . . . They took off. (CMS-2, 18–20)

Is it possible that these youths are imitating a TV or Hollywood gang script but intentionally changing the script to avoid getting in deep trouble? To avoid hitting another youth and exposing themselves to serious criminal liability? I'm not sure. But there were enough narratives like this one—where one would have expected someone to get shot, dead, and yet no one is harmed—to make me begin wondering whether the made-for-TV gang script is actually being modified as it is played out, as it is reiterated. Could it be that they are playing with the script, following along, going through the motions, but actually subverting it intentionally so as not to hurt one another?

Listen closely to this other narrative. You may recall CMS-10, a seventeen-year-old gang member—the youth who identifies as "pure Mexican. I'm straight Mexican, that's all I am" (CMS-10, 32). Here is what he says:

Walking on the street to the liquor store, me and my friend, a van pulls up from a neighborhood I didn't even know, ain't my rivals, I never even heard of them . . . We're walking right here and they pass us a few feet in front of us. They stop. The van door opens and some guy gets out with a 12-gauge and another one with a big-ass .357, and they go, "Where are you fools from?" I tell them my neighborhood, my friend tells them the neighborhood, and they be like, "You guys ain't from 213?" That's another neighborhood. We said no. They said, "You better not be from 213." "Like, I told you where I'm from." Then he kept pointing the gun to my face, had it in front of me, and I moved it. He said, "What the fuck you doing?" I said, "Don't put that in my face." And they did that thing to my boy, my boy just stood there. They take it from his face again, he said, "Don't be pointing that to my face." They said, "You lucky you ain't from that neighborhood." I said, "I told you where I'm from." My boy says, "If you're gonna shoot us, shoot us." Then one of the guys from inside the van says, "Let's go, let's go," and as they pulled away they started shooting, but not at us, they just shot. If I had a gun, I would have shot them. (CMS-10, 24–25)

Could it be that these rivals tweak the script to keep things safe? Recall John in the Rillito River wash. They both pulled out guns. But that kept them safe. They drew but did not fire. Were they playing out a script according to practice theory, or reiterating it in a manner that subverts the western, to keep things safe?

The performative approach might also focus our attention on the way *others* perform our identity. The Catalina youths are not the only ones performing. People around them are also performing *their* identity as dangerous youths. So, for instance, the police officer who is following the Catalina youths down Sixth Avenue while they cruise the boulevard on a Saturday night is performing *their* identity as troublemakers. The police officer is participating as an equal in the identity of these youths as at-risk, troubled, suspicious, dangerous, about-to-get-in-trouble juveniles. The police officer is helping to create a certain identity that the youths are performing.

Alternatively, though, the performative might go further and contest the very idea that the registers of gun talk hold any sway over the youths: there are no scripts, there are only performances. There is no such thing as an identity of "the punk" or "the wild one" that has any purchase on future action, that can help us predict how youths will act. There is no doer behind the deed. There are just performances that result in these identities. At the extreme, the performative stops predicting and only interprets. It is a methodological sensibility that ultimately defies the social science project.

But if this is true, then how do we, as researchers, get any leverage on these performances? How do we begin to interpret youths' speech, and how can we make any predictions about where youths are going? How do we even get our hands around their performances? How can we predict youths' behavior?

11 EMBRACING THE PARADIGM OF DIRTY HANDS

The Catalina interviews lend support to each of the four methodological approaches. But at the same time, they expose the assumptions about human behavior embedded in each. The interviews reveal moments of individual decision making, of instrumental reasoning and deliberate choice. "I didn't want my mom to know that I had a gun in the house, cause she would probably call the police on me." CMS-6 here is weighing the costs, addressing the risks, taking some responsibility. But recall Jesús as well, who avoided thinking about the police when he carried. "Because I just think that's kind of like jinxing myself." This links back to Jon Elster's example of the voodoo doll: only on a very thin conception of rationality is Jesús engaged in rational action. The Catalina interviews also reveal recurring registers of gun talk. "I just have guns to sell them. Make some money off them. That's actually what they're for." Commodities, protection, suicide—there are patterns in the way the Catalina youths talk about guns. But how do those patterns become necessary, and why should we assume that they influence behavior? The youths recount recurring scripts about gun carrying—"dogging" and "talking shit." They seem to know well how to play these encounters. At the same time, the reiteration seems to modify the performance. Sometimes it leads to gunfire, at other times to a standoff.

The empirical data from the Catalina school raise more questions than they answer. Gun carrying is heavily associated with a felt need for self-protection, but does that mean that the Catalina youths are carrying because they feel a need to protect themselves? How do we know when these associations become motives? Is it true that youths "follow" scripts they have seen? How, then, do they change the scripts and modify the symbols? Where does this agency come from? What does it represent? Does it reflect an existing identity, or does it define that very identity? In the end, which of these four sensibilities helps us better understand and predict gun carrying among the Catalina youths?

This central question does not have a scientific answer. The four approaches all rest on different assumptions about human agency and, as a result, are nonfalsifiable. They each have some evidence to support them. They each have some compelling features. They each make sense and contribute to our understanding of youths' gun carrying. But not one of them can be proved wrong.

It is impossible to disprove, for instance, the existential insight: situations *are* of our own making, and we have the ability to imagine a different project and, in that very process, to act in good faith with deliberate choice. It is also impossible to falsify the structuralist perspective. The Catalina interviews reveal recurring patterns in the way the youths think, categorize, and relate ideas. We experience this in everyday life: recurring dichotomies between the self and the other; between altruism and egoism; between freedom and constraint. It is equally impossible to disprove the model of practice theory. The concept of having a "feel for the game" is so familiar and correct. How many times can we choreograph the next stage of a script? By the same token, it is impossible to falsify the performative conception of identity. Without a doubt, the actor constructs identity in the very performance of the script. The slight resistance, the modification, the exaggeration—these undoubtedly transform and simultaneously reconstitute the script.

There is evidence—anecdotal, statistical, and commonsense—for each one of these competing theories of action. Yet there is no way to rule out any one of them. As a result, to adopt any one methodological perspective requires a leap of faith. It requires making assumptions. Whether it is about the ability of a Catalina youths to make a free choice, about the influence that structures exert on the youths, about the constraint of scripts, or the absence of a doer behind the doing—each one of these methodological approaches makes a significant assumption about human behavior.

In the human sciences, the realm of consciousness interrupts every methodological approach and, as a result, radically undermines the scientific project. Mediating all human action is consciousness—a black box we have not yet penetrated. The different methodological approaches represent competing ways of modeling that black box. They offer different ways of thinking about motivation, self-interest, attraction, desire, and repulsion. But in the end they remain unproved, ambiguous, uncertain. We deal with this uncertainty by projecting our theories onto our data in order to make sense of our findings and to draw inferences. We deploy our theories—rational choice, practice theory, psychoanalysis, behavioral law and economics—to better understand human agency, to discover causes, to make predictions. Most of the time we look inward and extrapolate from subjective experience. We observe our own deterrence, script following, or subconscious motivations. And when a theory works, when the data conform, when a prediction comes true, we celebrate that moment of knowledge. We revel in it. We cling to it. We bask in having satisfied our deep desire to know. But, truth be told, we are merely taking a leap of faith—a positivist leap of faith, to be sure. It is data driven and empirical, which of course is far better than superstition, religious faith, or logic alone. But we are no closer to knowing human action than we were before. We are no closer to knowing the source of motivation.

Here is another way to say this. Even if we assume, for instance, that gun carrying among male youths is heavily associated with the felt need to protect yourself from being punked or disrespected in everyday encounters, is it right to say that the need for self-protection causes gun carrying? Might it not be the reverse? That carrying a gun makes you feel you need protection? Or might it be a justification for carrying—something that legitimizes your gun carrying in the eyes of our wider society? Or might the youths themselves be aggressive, and the talk of self-protection be merely a subliminal proxy for their own aggression? How do we unravel these possibilities and get a handle on human action?

The answer is, not very scientifically—if by science we have in mind empirical falsification. Instead, we take that leap of faith. We have a certain sensibility. We are trained in a certain discipline. We are comfortable with certain assumptions. We are raised with certain beliefs. We follow—and in rare moments, create—certain trends. Often a fashion develops and becomes a useful tool for social or professional advancement. Vogues change and bring in their wake a body of research. A good example, in the criminal justice field, is the monumental shift we have witnessed from a generalized acceptance of the rehabilitative model in the 1960s or 1970s to prevailing faith in incapacitation in the 1980s and 1990s. These represent, after all, huge swings in assumptions about human action—from a belief in people's ability to change, to improve, to rehabilitate to a conviction that many people are just plain evil and must be incarcerated for a long time. Different assumptions about human agency. Different leaps of faith.

A DIFFERENT SET OF QUESTIONS

The question to ask, then, when presented with a predictive hypothesis involving human action, is not whether the approach has been verified or falsified but rather how it is that the approach has come to be accepted. We need to pose a different set of questions. How is it that we come to believe that a theory about youths' gun carrying is right? What are the stakes and interests that are promoted by endorsing one theory over another? Who benefits when we adopt one particular theory of action, and how? As social scientists and policy makers, we need to stop guessing—to stop assuming that individuals are pursuing self-interest, to stop pretending that there are scripts, to stop imposing meaning on actions retroactively—and instead begin examining the theories of human action and the policy responses in light of our best appreciation of how those theories operate: what assumptions they make about human action, how they construct youths politically, socially, and economically, how they distribute power and respect.

The central question is, How does a theoretical approach become believable at any particular time under specific historical conditions, and at what price? This asks a different set of questions than does existentialism, structuralism, or practice theory. Rather than evaluating substantively those accounts of action, it probes the history of that knowledge and rationality. How is it possible that any of these discourses about youths' gun carrying could be received as correct, useful, intelligible? How does the process of making a discourse "true" shape the way we, as subjects, judge, think, categorize, desire the other? How is it that we turn ourselves into objects of study? This is not to suggest, of course, that discourses do not become "true." They certainly have done so. But that is not the issue. The real question is, How is it that they have come to be seen as true at this particular time?

This different set of questions is not paralyzing from a policy perspective. On the contrary, it overcomes the worn debates between free will and determinism and offers a clear path for research: critically explore what it takes to believe any one of these discourses of youths' gun possession, how they construct the human subject and social relations, what makes them convincing, how they become true, what toll they take on youths, what we have to do to ourselves and to others in order to believe these theories.

We need to embrace the idea of dirty hands in the field of law and social science. The fact is, the social science methods and models of action—rational choice, structuralism, or practice theory—are not determinate. They are not falsifiable. Accordingly, we need to evaluate theories of action in light of their ramifications for the individual and for society and then choose between them based on stated values. We need, in other words, to get our hands dirty. The decision is an ethical one. That, ultimately, is how we must decide between social science approaches.

DIRTY HANDS

Let's turn the clock back again to 1943. Act 5, scene 3. Hugo has been secretary to Hoederer for ten days. Olga has given up on him and throws a bomb into Hoederer's complex. The attempt coincides with a secret meeting between Hoederer, the regent, and Karsky. The bomb explodes outside. No one is seriously hurt. That night, Hugo confronts Hoederer. He tries to persuade him not to deal with the opposition. Collaborating with the regent and Karsky, Hugo argues, would mean years of deception before gaining power. It would mean compromising with the enemy and defending reactionary policies. It would weaken the party.

Hoederer responds with brute realism. Whichever government comes to power after the war will have to implement unpopular austerity measures. The economy will be a shambles. If the Communists are part of the coalition and a minority in the cabinet, they can resist the austerity measures and gradually gain popularity. They would become far more popular than if they were put in power by the Soviet army and perceived as a foreign-imposed government. Gradually they would gain the confidence of the people and seize power legitimately.

But it would mean lying to the comrades and compromising their ideals, Hugo protests. It would mean deceiving them. Gradually, over time, one compromise would lead to another, and soon enough there would be nothing left of the party to save. "Not all means are acceptable," Hugo pleads. "Any means are good if they are effective," Hoederer exclaims. "How you cling to your purity, my friend! How scared you are of dirtying your hands!" (Sartre 1948, 199–200).

Hoederer is the leader with dirty hands. He is prepared to use all effective means to achieve his goal—a goal, he believes, that will save lives. Hoederer sincerely believes that his strategy will save the lives of many compatriots. If the Communists do not collaborate with the regent, Karsky's army will fight fiercely against the invading Soviet army, and there will be hundreds of thousands of casualties on both sides. If they deal with the regent, the army will disarm voluntarily and allow the Soviets in. Hugo responds: "You don't make a revolution with flowers." "You see," Hoederer replies. "You see well. You don't like men, Hugo. You only like principles" (201).

This is the moral dilemma—the problem of "dirty hands"—and, as Michael Walzer rightly points out, "It is typically stated by the Communist leader Hoederer in Sartre's play of that name: 'I have dirty hands right up to the elbows. I've plunged them in filth and blood. Do you think you can govern innocently?'" Walzer's answer is no. "I don't think I could govern innocently" (Walzer 1973, 161).

In "Political Action: The Problem of Dirty Hands," Walzer offers several ways of thinking about the moral dilemma of dirty hands and ultimately endorses an approach that draws on an Albert Camus play, *The Just Assassins*. It is an approach that requires the person with dirty hands to acknowledge responsibility and accept punishment. It is an approach that "requires us at least to imagine a punishment or a penance that fits the crime and so to examine closely the nature of the crime" (1973, 179). With regard to Hoederer, Walzer writes:

> "We shall not abolish lying by refusing to tell lies," says Hoederer, "but by using every means at hand to abolish social classes." I suspect we shall not abolish lying at all, but we might see to it that fewer lies were told if we contrived to deny power and glory to the greatest liars—except, of course, in the case of those lucky few whose extraordinary achievements make us forget the lies they told. If Hoederer succeeds in abolishing social classes, perhaps he will join the lucky few. Meanwhile he lies, manipulates, and kills, and we must make sure he pays the price. We won't be able to do that, however, without getting our own hands dirty, and then we must find some way of paying the price ourselves. (1973, 180)

This is an attractive reading of the problem of dirty hands: it requires us to acknowledge the moral dilemma, to price it, and to be willing to pay for it. And it resonates well in the field of law and social science. Every model of social science comes at a price. It is our job to figure out what that price is and be sure we are willing to pay it. There is no scientific purity. There are no clean hands in the relationship between law and social sciences. We cannot proceed deductively from social science models. Instead, we need to explore options and evaluate how they are going to affect us as contemporary subjects.

The decision to adopt a particular social science method, to draw the policy implications, and to choose a policy outcome necessarily involves significant ethical choices, choices that will shape the way we conceive of men and women, the way we develop as human subjects, and the shape and kind of society we create. At its most abstract level, the decision whether to adopt, say, a rational action model or a new institutionalist framework will have long-term and large-scale implications for the way we conceptualize human subjects—whether we come to believe they are calculating, utility-maximizing, rational actors or people who are shaped by the scripts that surround them and by their social environment. The two models will have different long-range implications for individuals and for society. The choice is not dictated by science. We must choose—and in so doing, we make an ethical decision about who we will become. This decision has a price. We need to know what that price is and whether we are willing to pay it.

How exactly does the dirty hands analogy work? It turns on treating social science models as we would moral principles. The scholar with dirty hands starts from the position that there is no right methodological approach in social science. Every method, she contends, makes untestable assumptions about human agency. Each model traverses, at some point, the black hole of consciousness. Choosing a methodological approach, however, has significant implications for law and public policy. So the scholar tries to tease them out. Then she rolls up her sleeves to figure out which method, laws, and policies to choose in order to achieve what she considers best for the human subject and for society. She engages in an ethical choice.

The problem with embracing the dirty hands rubric is that it is generally understood to mean that *any* means are justified by the end. I am not suggesting that we can adopt *any* social science method. I am not that cynical, or that skeptical of social science. Nor do I suggest that we lie, deceive, or compromise for the purpose of convincing others. Instead, I suggest that we acknowledge that no choice is morally costless and recognize that we are dirtying our hands when we make these ethical choices. I suggest that we evaluate valid models of social science—models that have evidentiary support—in order to compare them and determine which will best promote our vision of an ethical life. Looking to acceptable methods—to those approaches that pass an empirical test—we then need to choose between them. And each one requires a leap of faith.

So let me be careful to recapitulate what I am *not* saying. First, I am not arguing that we should lie or deceive. Second, I am not suggesting that we can never know anything social scientifically. We do at times run across natural experiments from which we can draw tentative conclusions about whether policies do or do not seem to have their intended consequences. I am not taking the extreme position that *nothing* can be known in human science. We may have some evidence for deterrence, other evidence for scripts. And we could well adopt a smorgasbord approach and implement a number of different policies, hoping to achieve a combined or cumulative effect. But there is more indeterminacy than determinacy in the policy area; and given that indeterminacy, we should be thinking more critically about the social science models we use when we do intervene.

In the field of youth gun studies, then, the critical task is to trace the structures of belief that produce law and public policy frameworks. To explore what it takes to make a methodological approach convincing, how it becomes accepted, what toll it takes on the human subject. To investigate what we have to do to ourselves and to others in order to make a policy orientation acceptable and persuasive. To figure out the moral and ethical costs to the human subject, and then to dirty our hands. We have to choose between interpretive frameworks based on an ethical evaluation, recognizing and acknowledging the significant implications for society and the contemporary subject.

PART THREE

MAPPING LAW AND PUBLIC POLICY

The task in this final part is to map the law and public policy alternatives in the youth gun field onto the four methodological approaches, in order first to unveil the hidden assumptions about human behavior that are embedded in the various law and policy orientations and then to open a door for ethical choice. Not surprisingly, a significant number of laws and policies have been proposed and implemented in the context of youths' gun carrying at the turn of the twenty-first century. In response to a perceived epidemic of youth gun violence at the close of the 1980s and in the early 1990s, politicians, policy makers, and law enforcement administrators made monumental changes to the juvenile justice system in the United States. Across the country, in jurisdiction after jurisdiction, federal, state, and municipal authorities fundamentally altered the laws and policies regarding juvenile gun delinquency.

Many states enacted laws requiring the automatic transfer of juveniles to adult court for serious gun offenses. Other states lowered the age for discretionary judicial transfer, and still others increased the prosecutor's power and discretion about filing juvenile gun cases directly in the adult system. Some states created blended juvenile and adult sentences for youthful gun offenders, and others increased the penalties for youthful offenses committed with a firearm. Some counties and cities created juvenile gun courts—courts specializing in first-time gun offenders—to punish gun possession and violence more severely.

Other jurisdictions turned to federal prosecution of young gun offenders, on the model of Project Exile in Richmond, Virginia, in order to take advantage of stiffer federal sentencing schemes, pretrial detention, and exile to distant federal penitentiaries. Major metropolitan police departments, like the one in New York City, began implementing gun-oriented policing strategies that targeted youths for aggressive "stop and frisks." Other cities adopted strategies, such as Operation Ceasefire in Boston, that communicated directly with youth gang members and increased supervision of youths on probation. The federal Bureau of Alcohol, Tobacco, and Firearms (ATF) started a Youth Crime Gun Interdiction Initiative to trace the chain of ownership of guns confiscated from youths. A number of jurisdictions passed safe storage laws, and others enacted negligent storage laws, firearm safety training, boot camps, educational programs, and mentor programs for at-risk youths.

Overall, the United States witnessed a fundamental transformation of its juvenile justice system. As Jeffrey Fagan and Franklin Zimring observe, "Between 1990 and 1996, no fewer than forty of the fifty states passed legislation creating new standards for transfer decisions. Without exception, these new laws were designed to expand the number and kind of cases where transfer occurs" (Fagan and Zimring 2000a, 2). These measures have had wide repercussions, resulting in the virtual dismantling of juvenile courts in many jurisdictions and a general reconceptualization of how to treat young offenders.

Part 3 addresses these laws and public policies. Consistent with the framework of this book, though, it turns the analysis on its head: rather than asking what law and policy conclusions we should draw from the Catalina interviews, it explores how these particular laws and public policies have come to be proposed and implemented. It maps the terrain of law and policy onto the discussion of methodological approaches in order to highlight the assumptions about human agency.

An analysis along these lines begins with a genealogical inquiry: How did these law and policy alternatives emerge, develop, fragment, and reproduce over time? What are the disciplines, institutions, and practices that engendered these policies—or alternatively, that were themselves born of these projects? Such an inquiry involves two tasks. First, we need to trace the intellectual history of the field of youth gun studies. For obvious historical and technological reasons, the study of youths and guns blossomed in the last third of the twentieth century. But it grew out of a rich tradition of biological, sociological, and economic analyses of deviance and juvenile delinquency. The first task, then, is to trace the genealogy of the larger research field in order to locate the birth of youth gun studies. The second task is to explore the micropolitics of the laws and policies surrounding youth gun possession at the turn of the twenty-first century. How is it that youth gun possession became such a hot political issue in the mid- to late-1990s? Chapter 12 addresses these two lines of inquiry.

Chapter 13 then maps the leading law and policy positions in the youth gun field. These include moral poverty theory, the economic model of crime, new progressive approaches, institutional legitimacy, and self-control theories as well as critical cultural approaches. The chapter explores these various positions and maps them onto the discussion of methodological approaches in order to expose the assumptions about human behavior embedded in each. Chapter 14 then puts the central thesis of this book to a test. It explores in greater detail two of the leading works in the field—one from the economics camp, Steven Levitt's rigorous "Juvenile Crime and Punishment" (1998), and one from the critical cultural camp, Philippe Bourgois's remarkable ethnography, *In Search of Respect: Selling Crack in El Barrio* (1995)—and demonstrates that neither of these works avoids taking a leap of faith. This opens the door, in a concluding chapter, for ethical choice. It is, to be sure, the door I have made for myself. But in chapter 15 I invite you to walk through it with me.

12

A GENEALOGY OF THE YOUTH GUN FIELD

In the second half of the twentieth century, the study of youths and guns emerged almost full grown from the larger field of research on deviance and youth delinquency. By that time the larger field was well formed, shaped by decades of disciplinary battles between biology, sociology, and economics—internecine struggles that had punctuated the first century of criminology. The battles generated three major traditions of empirical research and ultimately left scars that would help define and demarcate the youth gun field.

A first tradition focused on individual-level predictors of criminality. Following in the footsteps of the early positive criminologists—pioneers like Cesare Lombroso, Enrico Ferri, and Charles Goring, who had focused on the individual physical, anatomical, and mental traits of delinquents—positive research in deviance and youth delinquency continued to expand the number and range of individual traits studied during the early twentieth century. Ernest Burgess, a noted sociologist at the University of Chicago, conducted an empirical study in 1927 of three thousand paroled inmates to determine what accounted for their success or failure on parole. Burgess identified twenty-two predictive factors, including the race or nationality of inmates' fathers, their marital status and that of their parents, and their personality type, mental age, and psychiatric prognosis (see generally Harcourt 2006). By the mid-twentieth century, the positive tradition registered a long catalog of individual-level explanations for crime that included not only genetic makeup but also education, employment history, prior delinquency, and family status, among other traits.

A second tradition focused on particular features of social life. Inspired by the early pioneers of sociology, Émile Durkheim and Auguste Comte on the Continent and Robert Park and Burgess in this country, and growing out of the positive tradition—in some cases, developing explicitly *against* biological determinism—social-level theories emerged in the 1920s and 1930s. These theories traced youth deviance back to social disorganization in the case of Clifford Shaw and Henry McKay (1942), to social strain and class conflict in the work of Robert Merton (1938), or to subcultural groups and social relations in the case of Albert Cohen (1955). These sociological models of delinquency emphasized social structure—such as community ties, economic conditions, and peer groups. The tradition entered the public imagination later, through more popular writings such as Oscar Lewis's *La Vida: A Puerto Rican Family in the Culture of Poverty—San Juan and New York* (1966). *La Vida* offered a structural theory about how the culture of poverty, passing from generation to generation, could generate criminality and deviance.

A third tradition, this one tracing back even further to the classical school of criminology founded by Cesare Beccaria and Jeremy Bentham, was revived in the mid-twentieth century by scholars such as Gary Becker in economics and Richard Posner in law. The classical model was premised on the idea that individuals pursue self-interest by trying to avoid pain and seek pleasure: they maximize their overall satisfaction or utility by choosing those opportunities that optimize their preferences. Gary Becker reinvigorated this tradition with his seminal paper "Crime and Punishment: An Economic Approach," published in 1968. Becker's economic model of crime suggested that criminal behavior was influenced by calculation of the costs and benefits of committing crime. In this sense the model did away with many of the other explanations offered by psychologists and sociologists—whether individual-level or social-level. Becker's model generated a swell of research and attracted a coterie of young economists and Ph.D. students to the field of crime and punishment.

FRAGMENTATION: 1960S AND 1970S

The field would undergo significant change in the 1960s and 1970s. First, radical theorists in sociology attacked the more conventional sociological approaches and, in the process, politicized and polarized the academic debates. Alvin Gouldner played an important role here, especially in his challenge to Howard Becker, who had founded labeling theory in the early 1960s (see Becker 1963). Becker had positioned himself on the left of the political spectrum, but Gouldner and others nevertheless attacked him for not being politically engaged enough (see Gouldner 1968, 1970), thus carving out a radical position to the left of the liberal sociological mainstream. The student movement of the 1960s also contributed in this respect. The New Left positioned itself in a peculiar relationship to older Marxist approaches. Though strongly influenced by the Frankfurt school and structural linguistics, the student movement nevertheless tried to forge a path beyond these structuralist approaches and further to the left—a new space to replace the old rhetoric of cultures of poverty and "root cause" liberalism.

The publication in 1965 of Patrick Moynihan's report *The Negro Family* further fractured the liberal sociological tradition. The book was savaged by the liberal establishment, which perceived the report as a threat to its political prominence, and at the same time fueled a newly emerging conservative trend in juvenile justice. In alienating whole segments of the left intelligentsia, Moynihan's report pushed many former liberals toward new progressive positions that rejected both the older liberal and new conservative shibboleths.

At the same time, the civil rights movement fomented and solidified a centrist, rule-of-law position that took control of many of the institutions and practices of juvenile justice. Through impact litigation and advocacy, civil rights organizations such as the American Civil Liberties Union extended the procedural due process revolution of the Warren Court to the juvenile context, displacing the discretion that had previously guided the exercise of authority. In cases such as *In re Gault*, 387 U.S. 1 (1967)—where the court extended the due process requirements of notice, counsel, confrontation, and cross-examination to the juvenile delinquency hearing—the Warren Court significantly transformed the juvenile court from a system modeled on parental and discretionary supervision to one modeled on the adult, adversarial process.

On the right, more conservative social thinkers such as Edward C. Banfield in *The Moral Basis of a Backward Society* (1958) and *The Unheavenly City* (1970) and James Q. Wilson in *Thinking about Crime* (1975) began blending individual-level approaches—the biological and the economic models—with elements of the culture-of-poverty thesis in an effort to dismantle the reigning rehabilitative model. Banfield developed a theory about lower-class individuals and present-orientedness. In a series of writings addressing the urban crises of the 1960s and 1970s, he argued that the norm of present-orientedness was precisely what gave rise to crime and delinquency, poverty and squalor, broken families and illegitimacy (Banfield 1974, 240; 1991, 320–21). Other conservative theorists, influenced by Banfield, also began borrowing from multiple traditions—including the classical model of criminology, biological determinism, and sociological conditioning—to develop theories that associated crime with moral poverty and human nature.

FURTHER SPLINTERING: 1980S AND 1990S

The field was further disrupted in the 1980s and 1990s with the collapse of Marxism and the emergence of poststructuralist thought in the West. First free market ideology, and with it the discipline of economics, took off. Rational choice, decision, and game theories flourished in this climate. The increasingly technical nature of economics resulted in refinements in rational action theory that then colonized the other social science disciplines. The field of political science, for instance, became dominated by rational action theory. In criminology, the economic model of crime, originally associated with Gary Becker, continued to be refined and developed and was extended to the field of juvenile crime by, among others, Steven Levitt, in "Juvenile Crime and Punishment" (1998), John Donohue, and John Lott. In his controversial book *More Guns, Less Crime* (1998) Lott argued, using the tools of econometrics, that the private carrying of concealed weapons reduces crime. Using similar econometric methods, John Donohue and Steven Levitt argued in "The Impact of Legalized Abortion on Crime" (2001) that the increased incidence of abortions following the Supreme Court's decision in *Roe v. Wade*, 410 U.S. 113 (1973), accounted for the decline in crime during the 1990s.

On the left, the emergence of poststructuralist thought further fractured left liberal criminology.[25] A wave of writings influenced by Continental social theory—especially Michel Foucault's critique of the rehabilitative model in *Surveiller et punir* (1975)—stepped into the space that had been carved out earlier by radical criminology. These writings denounced the politically conservative results of liberal criminology. In the process they further eroded the structural accounts of crime and pointed to the social construction of crime problems. Katherine Beckett's *Making Crime Pay* (1997) documented how public concern with crime was the product not of crime waves but of media attention and political initiatives in the crime area. Beckett argued that the focus on "the undeserving poor" and their criminal inclinations was the outgrowth of a long-term conservative political strategy to tarnish the less well-off and dismantle the social welfare state.

There also emerged, on the far left, a set of critical ethnographic writings on youth culture, informed by poststructuralism, cultural studies, and practice theory. Scholars in this tradition engaged in thick descriptions of youth culture and criminal subcultures and tended to be explicitly radical in their policy orientation. Representative works here include Philippe Bourgois's ethnography *In Search of Respect: Selling Crack in El Barrio* (1995) as well as Ralph Cintron's *Angels' Town*: Chero *Ways, Gang Life, and Rhetorics of the Everyday* (1997). Through ethnographic research and narrative descriptions, these works depicted the lives of youths in their full context. Though situated in a tense relationship with public policy debates, many of these authors addressed the policy questions and generally advocated deep, structural reform of society.

On the far right, the campaign against "root cause" criminology produced even more radical theories of moral poverty and helped create the threatening specter of the young "superpredator." In *Body Count: Moral Poverty—and How to Win America's War against Crime and Drugs* (1996), William Bennett, John DiIulio, and John Walters traced crime back to inadequate moral education— ineffective parenting and socialization, lack of moral and religious education, child abuse, drug use, and lax criminal law enforcement. The most dangerous offenders are youngsters whose family and society have neglected them or, worse, abused them. These Bennett, DiIulio, and Walters refer to as "super-predators": "the youngest, biggest, and baddest generation any society has ever known" (1996, 26). They represent "a new young breed of super-predators who have been raised in practically perfect criminogenic environ-ments, who are already destroying lives and, as their ranks thicken and unless radical changes are made, may soon terrorize our nation" (194). Also on the far right, the positivist tradition continued to produce biological determinist theories that offer a pure individual-level biological explanation for crime (see, e.g., Mednick, Moffitt, and Stack 1987; see generally Wilson and Herrnstein 1985, 90–102).

The double assault from the far left and the far right severely weakened the liberal sociological mainstream but nevertheless produced several reconstruc-tion projects. In *A General Theory of Crime* (1990), Travis Hirschi and Michael Gottfredson tried to pick up some of the pieces by integrating elements of the sociological tradition with both the positivist and classical model of criminol-ogy. Hirschi and Gottfredson developed a theory of self-control that ultimately attributes criminality to child-rearing practices in the first six to eight years of childhood (1990, 272). As a result, they endorse efforts primarily aimed at encouraging parental supervision.

Another reconstruction project focused on institutional legitimacy and pro-cedural justice. Tom Tyler, in *Why People Obey the Law* (1990) and in essays including "Trust and Democratic Governance" (1998), argued that institutions that respect youths and treat them fairly are likely to shape them into more law-abiding adults. The central idea here is that procedural due process and fair treatment in criminal justice institutions such as the juvenile court, cor-rectional facilities, and treatment programs have an influence on individual youths. Specific proposals that emanate from this approach include teen courts, community conferencing, and other youth-oriented procedural inno-vations. The policy prescriptions focus on maintaining the due process requirements and substantive practices of the juvenile court system, especially in the face of efforts to dismantle the courts, and ensuring constitutional criminal procedure guarantees in police encounters with youths.

Disillusioned with conservative culture-of-poverty explanations on the one hand and traditional liberal solutions on the other, "new progressive" scholars began focusing on other criminogenic factors such as joblessness in the inner city or lack of trust and social capital in crime-ridden neighborhoods. The writings of William Julius Wilson, especially *The Truly Disadvantaged* (1987), as well as the research of Robert J. Sampson, helped launch this new approach that drew attention to the problem of lack of investment in the inner city. In the legal and public policy arena, Dan Kahan and Tracey Meares built on this work, offering a set of policies including order-maintenance crackdowns, reverse sting operations, antigang loitering ordinances, and youth curfews that were intended to bolster neighborhood social capital.

THE FOCUS ON YOUTHS AND GUNS

Against this backdrop, the turn of the twenty-first century witnessed an intense focus on *youths and guns*. This produced a new, more focused research field within the larger field of deviance and youth delinquency and an astounding number of public policies addressing youth gun possession, carrying, and violence. The new focus on youths and guns was born of complex micropolitical forces resulting from the combination of several factors: first, a sharp increase in youth gun violence that fueled a crime wave during the late 1980s and early 1990s; second, Democratic control of the White House from 1992 to 2000, resulting in a pro–gun control administration looking for politically palatable crime control initiatives; third, a liberal political tendency to focus on children as innocent victims when faced with a difficult policy area; and fourth, a Republican crime strategy of cracking down on young "super-predators" and gun offenders in order to satisfy pro-gun and tough-on-crime constituencies.

The United States experienced a crime wave in the early 1990s that was fueled in large part by a significant increase in youth gun homicides. This crime wave marked the third and final peak of the high-crime period that extended from the late 1960s to the early 1990s. The first peak was in 1974, when the national homicide rate hit 9.8 per 100,000, up from 5.1 in 1960; the second was in 1982, with a record high of 10.2 homicides per 100,000; and the third was in 1991, with a rate of 9.8 per 100,000.

During 1985 to 1991, the percentage of total homicides represented by youth firearm events increased consistently, and at the same time homicides involving weapons other than firearms declined steadily though slowly (U.S. Department of Justice 2004). As Alfred Blumstein reports, "The growth [in national homicides during the period 1985 to 1991] was attributed to more than a *doubling of homicide by young people during that period* . . . The growth among the younger offenders was associated predominantly with *an increased use of handguns,* and with no increase in the use of non-handgun weapons" (Blumstein 1998, 965). The national trend was also reflected at the regional, state, and local level, though at times with a slight delay (see generally Harcourt 2001, 234–37). The national trend is vividly illustrated in figure 12.1, compiled by the U.S. Bureau of Justice Statistics.

As Franklin Zimring demonstrates in his 1996 essay "Kids, Guns, and Homicide," trends in youth gun homicide explain most of the variance in national

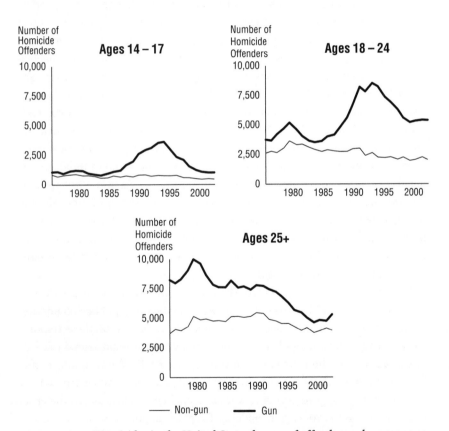

FIGURE 12.1. *Homicides in the United States by age of offender and weapon use, 1976–2002 (from http://www.ojp.usdoj.gov/bjs/homicide/weapons.htm)*

homicide rates during 1984 to 1992. During that period, the "total homicide volume attributable to the age group ten to seventeen doubles in less than a decade and gun use is the only visible cause . . . [F]luctuations in the proportion of youth homicide committed with guns might explain eighty percent of the variation in total homicide rates" (Zimring 1996, 29). Zimring ties the increase in youth gun homicides to increased availability of guns among youths and increased willingness to use them. "What we know," Zimring writes, "is that a larger number of guns than earlier are under the control of kids by the early 1990s" (1996, 31).

A leading explanation for the trend in youth gun violence was increased gun availability among youths associated with the epidemic of crack cocaine—what is referred to as the drug market–firearm diffusion hypothesis (Blumstein and Rosenfeld 1998, 1209; Blumstein 1995; Blumstein and Cork 1996; Blumstein 1998). In "Linking Gun Availability to Youth Gun Violence" (1996), Alfred Blumstein and Daniel Cork find that "the diffusion of guns played an important part in the growth of youth homicide rates" (1996, 12). They trace the diffusion of guns to the recruitment of youths into illicit drug markets, especially the crack cocaine market (Blumstein 1995, 30; see also Cork 1999; Grogger and Willis 2000). On this view, the diffusion fueled increased homicides because ordinary youth disputes escalated into gunfights. "In view of both the recklessness and bravado that is often characteristic of teenagers, and their low level of skill in settling disputes other than through the use of physical force, many of the fights that would otherwise have taken place and resulted in nothing more serious than a bloody nose can now turn into shootings as a result of the presence of guns" (Blumstein 1995, 30–31). According to Blumstein, this held true even in Tucson, Arizona. "The market recruits kids to sell drugs and provides the guns for protection," Blumstein explains. "This makes for a cycle that has turned fistfights into fatalities among youths, even in smaller cities such as Tucson" (Haussler 1995).

Although these trends in youth gun violence later would ebb (see fig. 12.2),[26] by the mid-1990s they had deeply marked the public imagination. Or more precisely, the media and political initiatives seized on these trends—on what they called an epidemic of youth gun violence—and seared the public's imagination. The facts alone, of course, never tell us how to interpret or how to respond. What happened, in effect, is that a Democratic Party in favor of gun control, eager to outmaneuver its Republican opposition on the crime issue, seized on the youth gun epidemic for political purposes.

President Bill Clinton, a southern Democrat who favored gun control but at the same time was cautious about the National Rifle Association and

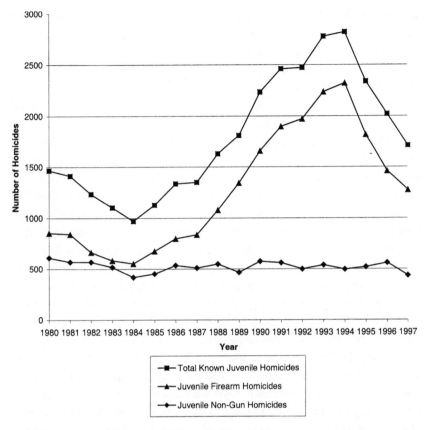

FIGURE 12.2. *Juvenile homicide trends, 1980–97*

aggressive on crime issues, took office in 1992. He and his advisers felt a strong need to offer concrete crime control policies as an alternative to tough-on-crime Republican proposals such as "three strikes and you're out" laws, habitual offender enhancements, and mandatory minimum sentences. The youth gun epidemic—identified by liberal academics such as Alfred Blumstein, Philip Cook, and Franklin Zimring—offered a perfect vehicle to advance gun control measures under the guise of crime control. For the Democrats, it was a way to kill two birds with one stone: it offered an avenue for concrete, tangible crime policies *and* it favored gun control.

It also offered a strong rhetorical advantage in the gun debates. Advocating gun control measures in the United States has always been difficult but is generally far less difficult if the measures concern children. Here, in the context of innocent third-party harm, the liberal harm argument is at its strongest. For this reason, children have always served as a policy gateway. The focus on youthful innocence is a well-worn strategy—one that has been used successfully in a number of contexts, including welfare programs, homelessness advocacy, health care, and the death penalty, to name a few. As a strategic matter, it has always been important to lead with the most attractive victim—a good plaintiff—and innocent children tend to satisfy that criterion.

In this case the focus on youth offered a way for Democrats to get their foot in the door of gun control. The mere use of the word "youth" was a useful device. A good illustration of this was the ATF's "Youth Crime Gun Interdiction Initiative," announced by President Clinton in July 1996. The word "youth" in the title of the program served a purely public relations and marketing function. In truth, the initiative is a straightforward comprehensive gun tracing program. Under the program, cities send the ATF information about confiscated guns so the ATF can trace the guns from the point of manufacture or import to the point of first retail sale. The information obtained from gun tracing is useful in gathering intelligence about the flow of guns to illicit markets, about gun trafficking, and about which guns end up in the hands of criminals and how they get there. Gun tracing provides the intelligence necessary to develop supply-side intervention strategies. With much support from the Clinton administration during the late 1990s, the program expanded significantly, from sixteen participating cities in 1996 to about four dozen in 2002 (Cook and Braga 2003, 168). It is a policy that has had significant rewards, and it may well be one of the more promising gun control strategies in place (Cook and Braga 2003, 181–83). But clearly the program was not and is not "youth" oriented. "Youth" is so prominent in the name simply because youths are a good marketing device: it was easier to sell the program to the general public if it was perceived as oriented toward youth gun violence.

The other important factor, then, was a Republican platform that urged getting tough on crime, which put pressure on President Clinton to strongly support law enforcement initiatives. This produced some unexpected political alliances around youth gun intervention programs. A good illustration here was Project Exile, a federal gun-law enforcement policy that was developed under the administration of President Clinton but that received tremendous Republican support and became the main gun policy initiative of President George W. Bush. Project Exile was originally conceived in late 1996 and implemented in the Eastern District of Virginia U.S. Attorney's Office. It began as a collaborative effort between that office and the FBI, the ATF, the Virginia State Police, and the

Richmond police department. The idea was to target gun violence by prosecuting state and local gun arrests, whenever possible, in federal court under federal firearms statutes. Accordingly, suspects arrested in Richmond were screened by the ATF to see if a federal gun statute applied to their cases. If so, the cases were transferred from state to federal court for prosecution.

Under federal law, a convicted felon or a juvenile found in possession of a gun can be prosecuted, made subject to a stiffer federal sentence, and likely "exiled" in a distant federal penitentiary. In addition, once suspects are arrested and charged, the federal bail statute authorizes law enforcement to keep them in jail pending trial. According to the proponents of Project Exile, these acute federal consequences offered increased deterrence and broke the cycle of social influence between gun offenders and their communities. Coupled with the law enforcement effort was a media campaign and an education component. Ads on billboards, buses, and TV were designed to spread the word in high-crime neighborhoods that if you were caught with a gun, you would serve time in federal prison. In addition, elementary school children received gun safety training, sponsored in conjunction with the National Rifle Association and its "Eddie Eagle Gun Safety Program" (Richman 2001, 2003; Grier 2001).

Project Exile was implemented in February 1997, and within two weeks of announcing the program, the U.S. Attorney's office had true billed 59 indictments. Two years later that number had reached 438. Richmond's homicide rate fell from 140 in 1997 to 74 in 1999 (a 47 percent decrease), and the NRA credited the initiative with yielding a 65 percent drop in the city's overall crime rate. According to reports, the carry rate in Richmond—the number of individuals arrested who carry a weapon—also dropped dramatically (Richman 2001, 2003; Grier 2001). Subsequently these statistics and the overall effectiveness of Project Exile have been challenged (see Raphael and Ludwig 2003). But at the time, Project Exile was embraced as a winning gun strategy. The Democratic initiative was warmly received by Republican lawmakers and by all sides of the gun debates—from the NRA to Sarah Brady. In fact, Project Exile became the leading gun policy approach under the next presidential administration—that of George W. Bush—and was then extended nationwide under a slightly newer and more appealing rubric, "Project Safe Neighborhood." This spectacular bipartisan support for the program reflects well how a Democratic administration oriented to gun control, eager to find concrete crime fighting solutions, seized on the youth gun epidemic to develop gun policies in line with a future pro-gun Republican administration.

TABLE 12.1. *A genealogy of the field of youth gun studies*

Pre-1900		Émile Durkheim, *On the Division of Labor in Society* (1893)		Jeremy Bentham, *An Introduction to the Principles of Morals and Legislation* (1789) and the classical model	Cesare Lombroso, *Crime: Its Causes and Remedies* (1899), the Italian school, and scientific criminology
1910					
1920					
1930		Robert K. Merton, "Social Structure and Anomie" (1938)			
1940					
1950					
1960	Alvin W. Gouldner, "The Sociologist as Partisan" (1968) and radical theory	Oscar Lewis, *La Vida* (1966)	Daniel Patrick Moynihan, *The Negro Family* (1965) *In re Gault* (1967)	Gary Becker, "Crime and Punishment: An Economic Approach" (1968)	Edward C. Banfield, *The Unheavenly City* (1970)

1970				
1980		Civil liberties—defendant's rights (1980s)	William Julius Wilson, *The Truly Disadvantaged* (1987)	James Q. Wilson and Richard J. Herrnstein, *Crime and Human Nature* (1985)
1990	Travis Hirschi and Michael Gottfredson, *A General Theory of Crime* (1990)	Tom R. Tyler, *Why People Obey the Law* (1990)	William Julius Wilson, *When Work Disappears* (1996)	William J. Bennett, John J. DiIulio, and John P. Walters, *Body Count* (1996)
	Philippe Bourgois, *In Search of Respect* (1995)		Robert J. Sampson and Stephen W. Raudenbush, "Systematic Social Observation of Public Spaces" (1999)	Steven D. Levitt, "Juvenile Crime and Punishment" (1998)
	Ralph Cintron, *Angels' Town* (1997)			
2000				

At the same time, the Democratic strategy of focusing on youths and guns played into the moral poverty theories of William Bennett and John DiIulio and the notion of young "superpredators." The sustained attention to youths fueled the passage, in the vast majority of states, of transfer and waiver laws for juvenile gun offenders. These micropolitical forces helped construct the landscape of research on youth gun carrying—a field that is now organized primarily around six positions: moral poverty theories, the economic model of crime, new progressive approaches, due process liberalism, self-control theory, and a critical cultural approach. Their rich intellectual histories can be represented as shown in table 12.1.

13

THE LANDSCAPE OF LAW AND PUBLIC POLICY

The six positions at the bottom of the preceding genealogical map (table 12.1) define the space of youth gun studies and represent the leading alternatives in the related fields of law and public policy. Each position exemplifies a unique policy orientation and advances distinct recommendations for how to address youths' gun carrying. Each one is based on solid empirical evidence. Each is the product of significant social science research. The task here is to map these six positions onto the earlier methodological discussion in order to lay bare the assumptions about human behavior embedded in each. Let's begin, then, with moral poverty theory and proceed reading the last row, this time, from right to left.

THEORIES OF HUMAN NATURE AND MORAL POVERTY

This first approach focuses on the moral development of youths and attributes delinquency primarily to a human nature devoid of moral sentiment. Wilson and Herrnstein's treatise-sized *Crime and Human Nature* (1985), as well as Bennett, DiIulio, and Walters's *Body Count: Moral Poverty—and How to Win America's War against Crime and Drugs* (1996), exemplifies this first position.

In *Crime and Human Nature*, James Q. Wilson and Richard Herrnstein develop a comprehensive theory of crime that incorporates practically all known criminogenic factors—from genetic predisposition to education to social conflict—into the equivalent of a utility function. In some individuals this utility function produces a strong, practically irresistible disposition toward criminality. It reflects a complete lack of self-control, a kind of impulsiveness and present-orientedness that leads inexorably to delinquency. Other individuals evince a far greater ability to defer pleasure and to control desires and impulses.

From this perspective, the Catalina youths are not necessarily born bad—though some of them may have inherited criminogenic genes. But they develop into delinquent youths because of poor socialization, bad example, lack of parental or neighborhood supervision, and a host of other factors that result in moral poverty. Their utility function—one that prioritizes present and immediate pleasure—reflects a thick predisposition to commit crime. Their human nature, in essence, compels them to deviate. "The argument of this book," Wilson and Herrnstein emphasize, "is that there *is* a human nature that develops in intimate settings out of a complex interaction of constitutional and social factors, and that this nature affects how people choose between the consequences of crime and its alternatives" (1985, 508). By means of the concept of human nature, Wilson and Herrnstein incorporate earlier insights from sociology, biology, and psychology—in fact, the full range of social-level and individual-level explanations for crime—and place them within the framework of a utility function that then operates in the style of rational action theory. It is, though, a slightly distorted model of rationality: a paper-thin concept of rationality that blindly serves the deviate tendencies of the youths; a purely instrumental faculty that caters slavishly to their present-oriented desires.

The core assumption—that delinquent youths have a thick propensity to commit crime—is reflected in the idea of the young "superpredator," introduced earlier. William Bennett, John DiIulio, and John Walters describe this youth in *Body Count*:

America is now home to thickening ranks of juvenile "super-predators"— radically impulsive, brutally remorseless youngsters, including even more preteenage boys, who murder, assault, rape, rob, burglarize, deal deadly drugs, join gun-toting gangs, and create serious communal disorders. They do not fear the stigma of arrest, the pains of imprisonment, or the pangs of conscience. They perceive hardly any relationship between doing right (or wrong) now and being rewarded (or punished) for it later. To these mean-street youngsters, the words "right" and "wrong" have no fixed moral meaning. (Bennett, DiIulio, and Walters 1996, 27)

These "superpredators" are the product of moral decay—of the breakdown of civil society, the collapse of social norms, the loss of religious faith (Bennett, DiIulio, and Walters 1996, 14). They are conditioned to commit crime. Single-mindedly and impulsively, they seek out deviance. They do not even think about the risk of apprehension and thus cannot be deterred in the conventional manner. "Remember: most criminals don't expect to get caught, convicted, and locked away in the first place. Many felons think little about the risks of going to prison, and even less about likely conditions of confinement should they prove so 'unlucky'" (48). Their calculations are different, shaped by years of moral poverty:

The abject moral poverty that produces super-predators most often begins very early in life in settings where deep and abiding love is nowhere but unmerciful abuse is the norm. An extremely morally impoverished beginning early in life makes children vicious who are by nature merely aggressive, makes children remorseless who are disposed to be uncaring, and makes children radically impulsive who have difficulty sitting still, concentrating, and thinking ahead. In general, we believe, today's juvenile super-predators are children who, in order to be civilized and socialized into adulthood, would need a maximum dosage of moral tutelage from parents, teachers, coaches, clergy, and other responsible adults, but instead received either no such moral education, or were persistently exposed to its opposite by adults who severely abused and neglected them, encouraged them to act out, and rewarded their antisocial words and deeds. (Bennett, DiIulio, and Walters 1996, 57)

Bennett, DiIulio, and Walters do not dismiss out of hand the role of economic poverty. But, they emphasize, economic poverty does not *cause* crime. Some poor youths do *not* turn to crime. Others do. The real problem is not economic poverty, but poor socialization and lack of moral education. In this sense, the authors reject liberal root-cause explanations—the idea that poverty, inadequate welfare, or racism might cause crime. They also question some conservative catechisms; for instance, that more access to guns would bring about less crime, or that legal technicalities affect crime rates. It is, instead, the lack of moral upbringing that fuels alcohol and drug consumption, abuse, disorder, and, ultimately, crime. "What *is* the fundamental cause of predatory street crime?" they ask. "Moral poverty" (1996, 56).

Methodologically, then, theories of human nature and moral poverty are predominantly structuralist. The principal forces that condition and shape delinquent youths are the family and social structures that ultimately deprive them of moral education. Wilson and Herrnstein attempt to marry this structural perspective with rational action theory by expressing it in terms of a utility function. But the resulting union is terribly unbalanced. The structuralist forces do all the work. The concept of rationality is so extremely thin and instrumental that it merely facilitates the predisposition to commit crime. There is a slight role for scripts and practice theory, insofar as these youths mimic each other's behavior and are influenced by the deviate role models of their parents and peers. But overall, the theoretical framework turns principally on the idea that delinquent youths are molded by their environment—on a conception of human agency that assumes entrenched and deep-set predispositions.

A direct implication for law and public policy is that there is little if anything to be done for the Catalina youths. CMS-66, Jesús, Yusuf, Marc—these youths are beyond intervention. They are, in effect, *non récupérable*. And this is, naturally, a significant cost of believing theories of moral poverty. This is the price: there is practically no chance that we could successfully alter the utility functions of the Catalina youths, reorient their preferences, remake these youths. As Wilson and Herrnstein explain, it is "very hard for society to change, by plan, the subjective state of large numbers of persons" (1985, 377). For the Catalina youths, there is no hope. "After all is said and done, the most serious offenders are those boys who begin their delinquent careers at a very early age. The correlation between early age of onset and a high rate of offending is one of the best-established generalizations in all of criminology. As the twig is bent . . ." (Wilson and Herrnstein 1985, 509; final ellipsis in original).

From a policy perspective, reform must focus on the earliest ages. "The largest changes in crime rates over time, and the greatest differences in crime rates across cultures, are closely associated with changes in family processes" (1985, 526). Early family training of toddlers and young children, inculcating an ethic of self-control, cultivating character, and sharing religious faith are the policy recommendations of Wilson and Herrnstein (1985, 527–28). They urge promoting family through collective institutions that "uphold standards of right conduct" (528) and punishing offenders "as if crime were wholly the result of free choice" (529). In these tasks, society at large can play a significant role: "Society, by the institutions that it designs and the values it sustains, affects the extent to which families and communities are able and willing to lengthen the time horizon, inculcate a conscience, and instill a concern for others among the young in ways that make an orderly society possible" (508). Society at large can also help by cracking down on drugs and enforcing criminal sanctions.

"Where the drug and crime body count is concerned, the first two steps in the war on moral poverty—the immediate short-range effort—must be to stop revolving-door justice and to reinvest in anti-drug efforts" (Bennett, DiIulio, and Walters 1996, 81). With regard to crime, the authors recommend following initiatives like those of former police commissioner William Bratton in New York City and police chief Reuben Greenberg in Charleston, South Carolina: crack down on minor disorder, quality-of-life offenses, and minor crime as a way to target major crime. They also endorse severe sentences for offenders and eliminating good time and parole eligibility. The idea is to put an end, once and for all, to revolving-door justice. With regard to drugs, they recommend an array of initiatives focused primarily on teaching youths that drug use is wrong, cracking down on open-air drug markets, and sanctioning foreign countries that are the primary source of drugs.

"At this point, our views are clear enough," Bennett, DiIulio, and Walters declare: "Combatting moral poverty must include a full-scale, concentrated, intense effort at combatting drugs and crime. But the effort *cannot* be limited merely to the efforts of the criminal justice system; it must be prosecuted through any number of institutions—families, churches, schools, and the mass media, among others" (1996, 194). Churches play, in this sense, a pivotal role. For Bennett, DiIulio, and Walters, religious faith is crucial to the war on moral poverty. *Body Count* concludes precisely on this note:

> How do we restore these bonds? We believe the most obvious answer—and perhaps the only reliable answer—is a widespread renewal of religious faith and the strengthening of religious institutions. Many people have ignored or forgotten something that almost everybody once knew: *the good requires constant reinforcement and the bad needs only permission*. Religion is the best and most reliable means we have to reinforce the good. True religious faith enlarges the human heart; inspires us to revere and honor those things that are worthy objects of our attention; reminds people of their basic responsibilities and commitments; provides society with reliable moral and social guardrails; helps the impulse of compassion take on the name of action; and allows the "eyes of our heart" to see our fellow citizens not merely as distant body count statistics or as enemies or aliens or "other" but as moral and spiritual beings, as children of God.
>
> For that is, in fact, what they are. (1996, 208)

In sum, the central assumption underlying theories of human nature and moral poverty—the idea that certain youths develop a thick propensity to commit crime—leads to a policy orientation focused on early childhood development. For the very young and for future generations, the solution is moral and religious education with a premium on tough love and notions of individual responsibility that inculcate positive ethical values. For delinquent youths and mature criminal adults, in contrast, there is essentially no hope: incapacitation is the only viable alternative.

THE ECONOMIC MODEL OF CRIME

The second position builds on the classical model of criminology. The central insight is that the demand curve for crime—like most demand curves—slopes downward: as crime becomes more expensive, fewer and fewer people will want to engage in criminal conduct. The economic model posits that criminal behavior is, wholly or in significant part, influenced by rational calculation of the costs and benefits of committing crime. The model emphasizes marginal analysis. It focuses on changes in behavior associated with a marginal change in incentives.

The underlying assumptions of the economic model are in this sense egalitarian. The model does not assume that some individuals are by nature predisposed to crime. It does not embrace the notion of thick propensity. As Gary Becker suggests in "Crime and Punishment: An Economic Approach," the paper that launched the modern economic model, "A useful theory of criminal behavior can dispense with special theories of anomie, psychological inadequacies, or inheritance of special traits, and simply extend the economist's usual analysis of choice" (1968, 170). The model assumes only that the individual—any one of us—will engage in illegal activity as long as the benefits outweigh the costs. As long as the price is right.

The economic model has been extended to youths. Seminal in this regard is Steven Levitt's "Juvenile Crime and Punishment." Levitt argues there that juveniles, like adults, are deterred by more severe punishment—in essence, that youths are rational and respond to marginal increases in the cost of crime. In his paper, Levitt constructs and discusses three statistical tests and finds that the second validates his hypothesis. Levitt summarizes his findings as follows: "Juvenile crime is responsive to harsher sanctions" (1998, 1181).

As discussed earlier, there is a wide range of definitions and degrees of rationality within the larger rubric of rational action theories. The economic model of crime, for the most part, tends toward the thin side of the spectrum. The model is generally nonjudgmental in the sense that it does not treat a desire to kill, rape, or rob as irrational. Instead, the model presumes that much crime—especially property crime such as theft, fraud, or burglary, as well as some violent crime such as robbery—is financial in nature, and that other violent crimes such as rape or assault have value to the offender that can be quantified in financial terms. As Richard Posner explains in "An Economic Theory of the Criminal Law," "The major function of criminal law in a capitalist society is to prevent people from bypassing the system of voluntary, compensated exchange—the 'market,' explicit or implicit—in situations where, because transaction costs are low, the market is a more efficient method of allocating resources than forced exchange" (1985, 1195; see also Posner 1977, chap. 7; Cooter and Ullen 1997, 387–407).

As applied to the Catalina youths, the economic model would suggest that the youths engage in delinquent conduct because they perceive the benefits of crime to outweigh the costs. Yusuf, for example, took the Glock .45 semiautomatic handgun from his gangster cousin and went to the park to sell it because he expected to make $200, and that was more than the value he placed on the likelihood of being caught by the police and punished by the juvenile justice system. If the perceived cost to Yusuf had been marginally higher and exceeded the value of the gun—if, for example, Yusuf had a slightly higher expectation of being caught—he would have made a different calculation and avoided the criminal conduct. In this sense, the Catalina youths are not compelled by external forces or biological traits to commit crime. They *choose* to engage in delinquent activity because it appears profitable to them. And, like anyone else, the Catalina youths would respond rationally to an increase in the price of crime.

Methodologically, then, the economic model of crime is phenomenological: it focuses on the youths' deliberate decision making. There is evidence in the Catalina interviews to support this approach. Several of the youths stated that they would not carry guns specifically because of the risk of incarceration. One seventeen-year-old volunteered that "it's too much time to fuck with guns" (CMS-4, 4). He was one of a very few youths—four in all—who had never carried a gun. From the interview, it was apparent that he had made the calculation that the costs of carrying outweighed the possible benefits. Although he wanted a gun for protection and for the power, he was very concerned about doing time and as a result had decided not to get or to carry a gun (CMS-4, 16–17). Another seventeen-year-old who had carried a .22 when he was twelve years old made the decision not to bring his gun to school: "I'd always heard about the rumors, like, you can get in, like, deep shit and go to jail for bringing a gun to school so I decided not to, because I didn't want to get locked up" (CMS-25, 16). Yet another seventeen-year-old with a significant history of gun carrying volunteered that he once froze in a gunfight out of fear of going to prison. "I just froze up, and I was just 'Oh, man, please, God, please don't make me use this. I don't want to go to prison, really'" (CMS-66, 26).

On the other hand, several of the Catalina youths said they disregard the risk of incarceration. In their universe, the risk of death at the hands of rivals greatly outweighs the disadvantages of being sent to juvenile detention. Recall Marc, who carried a .38 for several months while he was on the run: "If I get caught and I go to jail, I'll still be alive. If I didn't have a gun, and someone held a gun to me . . . it's like, there goes my life" (CMS-17, 47). Similarly, a fifteen-year-old stated that he really didn't care about getting caught by the police when he was carrying. "I'd care, but I just didn't want to take the chance of getting shot" (CMS-70, 15). Arguably, these youths are also engaged in rational calculation. It's just that the cost of not carrying is prohibitive. But then, of course, there is Jesús, who intentionally did not think about the police when he was carrying so as not to jinx himself.

In any event, the methodological focus of the economic model of crime is on individual decision making—on the mental calculation of costs and benefits. As a result, a central policy is to raise the cost of gun carrying either by increasing the likelihood of detection or by lengthening the criminal sentence. The assumption of rationality favors policies oriented toward deterrence, with a premium on swift and certain punishment (see generally Cooter and Ullen 1997, 387–407). Increased punishment for juvenile offenders is generally viewed as a promising strategy to combat youth delinquency. As Steven Levitt suggests, "Taking juveniles into custody is an effective means of combating crime" (Levitt 1998, 1182).

Here too, though, the economic approach calls for cost-benefit analysis, and the cost of juvenile detention is not negligible. In the end, Steven Levitt is unwilling to endorse increased juvenile custody because of the financial burdens associated with such a policy:

> Any public policy recommendation must balance the benefits of reduced crime against the costs associated with holding juveniles, both in the short term and in the longer run. While it is difficult to make an absolute cost-benefit comparison, the relative short-run costs and benefits of locking up one juvenile versus one adult may be easier to evaluate . . . [T]otal spending per resident in public juvenile facilities was roughly $33,000 in 1990 . . . In comparison, . . . the average expenditure per state prisoner in fiscal 1992 was roughly $23,000. Thus there does not appear to be a clear gain in altering the relative concentration of juvenile and adult inmates at the present time. (Levitt 1998, 1182)

In the concluding paragraph of his paper, Levitt makes a passing reference to the potential benefits of treatment programs for juveniles in detention. But the bottom line remains: from a financial perspective, it makes more sense to simply incarcerate the delinquent youths when they reach majority.

Because of its traditional free-market orientation, the economic model of crime also tends toward policies that equate crime with work. Much economic research focuses on possible substitution effects between the two. Steven

Levitt and Sudhir Venkatesh's "An Economic Analysis of a Drug-Selling Gang's Finances" (1998) exemplifies this tendency. Their research explores the financial aspects of a local drug-dealing street gang. The authors find, for example, that the average wages of foot soldiers in the gang vary from a low of $130 per month during peaceful expansion periods before gang wars to a high of $540 during peaceful expansion periods immediately after gang warfare. The low returns to drug dealing for foot soldiers, Levitt and Venkatesh argue, suggest that legitimate work may be a good substitute for drug dealing. "One policy implication of this research is the potentially valuable role for job-market interventions for high-risk youths . . . To the extent that the attractiveness of legitimate sector jobs can be improved, either through increased wages or more attractive jobs, youths may reduce gang involvement" (1998, 31).

One policy initiative that accords well with the economic model is the "youth gun court," a specialized court for first-time juvenile gun offenders. The first youth gun court was launched in January 1995 by a family court administrator in Birmingham, Alabama (Storm 1996; Braun 2001), based on an earlier gun court experiment in Providence, Rhode Island (Daly 1995; Larrabee 1994; Cianci 2000). The youth gun court was premised on the idea that there should be swift and sure punishment for youths' gun offenses. The court has strict rules, which include a mandatory hold for youths arrested on gun offenses and a prohibition on diversion to other programs. Trials take place within ten days of the preliminary detention hearing, and the consequences are certain: all adjudicated youths are placed in a boot camp or committed to the Alabama Department of Youth Service. All are to suffer some type of incarceration. Preliminary studies, conducted after eighteen months of operation, revealed that 88 percent of adjudicated youths in fact received some form of incarceration. According to the youth gun court administrator, "In order for the principle to work, consequences must be sure and must be applied swiftly. The punishment must be appropriate and applied fairly. The Gun Court program and the action steps planned and taken are based on this simple idea" (Storm 1996). Like Project Exile, the youth gun court was warmly received by both the National Rifle Association and President Clinton's attorney general, Janet Reno (Braun 2001). Reno's Justice Department in fact listed the gun court as one of the nation's ten most promising crime reduction programs (Braun 2001).

Overall, then, the policy orientation favors swift deterrence and tends to shy away from moral or religious reeducation, treatment programs, or severe incapacitation. The model works only on the assumption of *marginal* deterrence: if minor crimes are punished with draconian sentences, "three strikes and you're out," or excessive mandatory minimums, there will be no incentive to abstain from more heinous crimes. Severe incapacitation, on this view, is likely to increase serious crime. The policy recommendations tend to focus instead on increased marginal deterrence and market substitutes for crime. With rare exceptions (see Dau-Schmidt 1990), most economic analyses focus on modifying incentives rather than shaping preferences.

A NEW PROGRESSIVE APPROACH

The third position represents a reaction against the first two as well as against earlier liberal, root-cause theories of crime. From the new progressive perspective, these other approaches fail to fully appreciate the structural obstacles to market participation in the inner city and the significant role of resulting neighborhood effects. On this view, the problem of crime and youth delinquency does not trace to moral impoverishment or a cultural deficit in the inner city—read *African American neighborhoods*. Nor does it trace simply to a free-flowing calculus of costs and benefits—a calculus that is so often oblivious to the symbolic dimensions of practices and behaviors. Nor, for that matter, does it trace simply to the larger problem of poverty and the lack of government welfare programs. Instead, crime and delinquency must be understood in the larger ecological context of the loss of jobs in the inner city and the resulting effect on the social relations and organic vitality of inner-city neighborhoods.

In *The Truly Disadvantaged* (1987) and his later work *When Work Disappears: The World of the New Urban Poor* (1996), William Julius Wilson launched the new progressive perspective by documenting the devastating effect that unemployment had on residents of the inner city. Robert Sampson's early research, especially "Urban Black Violence: The Effect of Male Joblessness and Family Disruption" (1987), also contributed to this new progressive perspective. In relation to crime and youth delinquency, though, it is Sampson's interdisciplinary research project on Chicago neighborhoods that is perhaps most important. This is the Project on Human Development in Chicago Neighborhoods (PHDCN), which Sampson has spearheaded in collaboration with Fenton Earls, Jeanne Brooks-Gunn, Stephen Raudenbush, and several others. The PHDCN builds on the new progressive tradition and focuses most directly on the impact of neighborhoods on crime.

Sampson and his colleagues in the PHDCN develop an approach that emphasizes the importance of neighborhood trust—what they call "collective efficacy." In "Systematic Social Observation of Public Spaces: A New Look at

Disorder in Urban Neighborhoods," Sampson and Raudenbush find that the "active ingredients in crime" trace back to "structural disadvantage and attenuated collective efficacy" (1999, 638). By collective efficacy, they mean the capacity of a social unit to regulate itself and realize collective goals. They define the term as "the linkage of cohesion and mutual trust with shared expectations of intervening in support of neighborhood social control" (1999, 612–13). To measure collective efficacy, Sampson and Raudenbush rely on survey data that address shared expectations for informal social control, social cohesion, and trust. Their structural constraint variable, "concentrated disadvantage," includes variables for poverty, public assistance, unemployment, and families headed by women.

Sampson and Raudenbush's theoretical framework bears a family resemblance to the earlier social disorganization theory of Clifford Shaw and Henry McKay. However, as Sampson and Raudenbush emphasize, their approach "diverges from a concern with the production of offenders . . . In the modern urban system, residents traverse the boundaries of multiple neighborhoods during the course of a day, a problematic scenario for neighborhood theories seeking to explain contextual effects on individual differences in offending." In contrast, they focus more on "how neighborhoods fare as units of control or guardianship over their own public spaces—regardless of where offenders may reside." For Sampson and Raudenbush, "the unit of analysis is thus the neighborhood, and our phenomenon of interest is the physical and social disorder within its purview" (1999, 613–14).

Methodologically, then, the new progressive position relies heavily on a structural approach that focuses on neighborhoods. There is little time or effort dedicated to the phenomenological—to exploring how collective efficacy would translate to the microlevel and enter individual mental processes and decision making. Insofar as collective efficacy affects nonresidents as well as residents, there is a role for practice theoretic insights and notions of scripts and social influence. But the unit of analysis is the neighborhood, not the individual. The idea of collective efficacy is strongly structural, as is the notion of concentrated disadvantage.

At the policy level, the new progressive approach has stimulated consideration of alternative policing strategies and punishments. Dan Kahan and Tracey Meares, in "Law and (Norms of) Order in the Inner City" (1998), build on the new progressive tradition to offer a concrete set of policies including antigang loitering ordinances and youth curfews. The policies they embrace tend to operate on the symbolic meaning of youth gun carrying. Loitering ordinances and youth curfews, for instance, are intended to change the perception among juveniles that peers value gang criminality by reducing the expressive function of the behavior: "Being out at night becomes a less potent means of displaying toughness because fewer of one's peers are around to witness such behavior" (Kahan and Meares 1998, 821). In addition, Tracey Meares, especially in "Place and Crime," focuses on neighborhood effects and social disorganization. Elsewhere she writes, "Socially organized or cohesive communities are better able to engage in informal social control . . . because such communities are able to realize common values, which can be continually reinforced in daily community life through conduct and discourse that centers on law abidingness" (Meares 1998a, 197; see also Meares 1998b, 675).

Kahan and Meares expressly position themselves in opposition to both the economic model of crime and moral poverty theories. Their intervention seeks to enrich the marginal deterrence model by incorporating social meaning into the study of rational choice in criminal law. As Dan Kahan explains,

> Economic analyses of criminal law that abstract from social meaning fail, on their own terms, because social meaning is something people value. As individuals, they take the meaning of their actions into account in responding to the incentives created by law; as communities, they structure the criminal law to promote the meanings they approve of and to suppress the ones they dislike or fear. Economic analyses that ignore these expressive evaluations produce unreliable predictions and uncompelling prescriptions. (Kahan 1998, 610)

At the same time, they explicitly reject moral poverty theory and the turn to incapacitation. The massive prison buildup, in their view, has only further undermined the social fabric of inner-city neighborhoods. Kahan and Meares affirmatively promote what they refer to as "milder public-order alternatives" like youth curfews, antigang loitering ordinances, and order-maintenance crackdowns (Kahan and Meares 1999b, 23). What makes these authors "new progressives" is precisely that they are offering concrete crime fighting alternatives to the draconian sentencing measures advocated by moral poverty theorists.

One initiative that fits well with the new progressive approach is the Boston Gun Project—a multifaceted youth gun initiative that includes order maintenance, targeted deterrence, curfew enforcement, and youth attitude modification. Several agencies—including the Boston Police Department, the ATF, federal and county prosecutors' offices, and departments of probation and parole as well as city-employed gang outreach and mediation specialists—teamed up in an attempt to decrease both the supply of and demand for guns among juveniles in Boston. The central strategy was to communicate directly with at-risk juveniles and to send a clear message that gun possession would not be tolerated. A team of officers and social workers would meet with gang members and at-risk youths and give them a choice: "Stop the flow of guns and stop the violence—or face rapid, focused, and comprehensive enforcement and corrections attention" (Kennedy 1997, 2). At the same time, law enforcement cracked down on minor disorderly conduct and monitored youths on probation to ensure compliance with curfews and court orders. The combined effect of the different prongs of the Boston Gun Project was to enhance informal mechanisms of social control in crime-ridden neighborhoods.[27]

The central tenets of the new progressive approach are that actions are socially influenced by the collective efficacy of a neighborhood, by structural disadvantage, including the lack of jobs in the inner city, and by the symbolic dimensions of practices and institutions. The approach rejects the central tenet of moral poverty theory—that delinquent youths have a thicker propensity to commit crime and, barring incapacitation, cannot be socially controlled. The resulting policy implications range widely, from creating jobs and fostering neighborhood trust in the inner city to order-maintenance policing, youth curfews, and antiloitering ordinances.

INSTITUTIONAL LEGITIMACY AND PROCEDURAL FAIRNESS

The fourth position on the genealogical map focuses on procedural justice and perceptions of institutional legitimacy. On this view, individuals respond to the perceived fairness of institutions and procedures: individual behavior reflects how each person feels about institutions of social control. When these institutions and practices are perceived as just, people are more likely to obey their command. Youths obey the law not so much out of fear of being apprehended or punished as out of respect for the institutions of justice. Tom Tyler's *Why People Obey the Law* (1990) and his later writings on procedural fairness and institutional legitimacy, including "Trust and Democratic Governance" (1998), helped launch this fourth position. It draws heavily on the logic of social capital, a conception made popular by Robert Putnam in *Bowling Alone*, as well as on the notion of collective efficacy from the work of Sampson and his colleagues. It bears a surprising family resemblance to earlier sociological theories of strain and conflict, but it has a more individual-level focus on decision making.

Tyler's theory rests on the assumption that individuals derive a strong sense of identity from their relationship with legal authority. When the relationship is positive and respectful, a form of social trust develops and promotes obedience to the law. "Social trust," Tyler contends, "is linked to creating a commitment and loyalty to the group and to group rules and institutions" (1998, 289). This commitment and loyalty to the group then translate into greater obedience to the law. Tyler's approach assumes no predisposition to commit crime and no differential propensity, nor does it assume different degrees of self-control or lack thereof. Like the economic model of crime, it is thoroughly egalitarian in its premises. Crime is the result not of inherent differences among individuals, or of human nature, but rather of differential perceptions of the legitimacy of authority that are formed, in large part, by the disparate treatment that individuals receive at the hands of authority. Crime may be higher in the urban ghetto, but not because of individual characteristics or personality traits of people in the area. It is instead negative perceptions of the police and law enforcement community within the inner city that may trigger higher levels of lawbreaking.

The approach is highly proceduralist. It is liberal legalist and places a strong emphasis on the rule of law. It builds, in this sense, on the due process revolution of the Warren Court. It assumes an authentic or direct link between being treated fairly and the *perception* of being treated fairly. At its core, the perception of legitimacy is based on the subject's actually believing that the criminal justice institutions and practices are themselves fair. This is very different from other types of legitimation theory. It could be, for instance, that perceptions of fairness are instead related to individual personality. On this view, some individuals might be deeply antiauthoritarian and thus skeptical of the legitimacy of governing institutions. Alternatively, it could be that perceptions of legitimacy are merely the internalizing of a dominant political ideology—along the lines of the legitimation theories developed by Antonio Gramsci and Georg Lukács. The proceduralist approach here, in sharp contrast, assumes a direct link between perception and actual treatment. What accounts for obedience to the law is one's treatment at the hands of law enforcement. As a result, the policy implications focus on *actual* treatment and not, for example, on brainwashing citizens to *believe* that law enforcement practices are fair or legitimate.

Methodologically, then, this position focuses on individual decision making. There is naturally a role for institutional structures insofar as the institutions and practices of the juvenile justice system are what trigger individual perceptions among youths. And there is also a role for practice theory insofar as youths may mimic, rehearse, and replay the reactions of their friends and other peers. But like the economic model of crime, this position is predominantly phenomenological in its approach.

Christopher Winship and Jenny Berrien, in their research on the Ten-Point Coalition in Boston, offer a vivid illustration of institutional legitimacy theory. In one prong of the Boston Gun Project discussed earlier, about forty ministers mobilized their religious communities to combat youth violence. In "Should We Have Faith in the Churches?" (2003), Winship and Berrien explore whether the Ten-Point Coalition had any effect on crime and ultimately conclude that, although there is little evidence of a direct link, the coalition may have influenced crime rates by transforming police-community relations and thus extending an umbrella of legitimacy over the police that significantly assisted them in fighting crime. "The key contribution of the Ten-Point Coalition and the efforts of other church-based groups," Winship and Berrien write, "lies perhaps not so much in their work with at-risk youth as in how they have changed the ways in which the police (and other elements of the criminal justice system) and Boston's inner-city community relate to each other. The coalition has done so by becoming an intermediary between the two parties" (2003, 224). By becoming intermediaries, the ministers were able to support appropriate police activity and restrain certain other practices, extending legitimacy in the eyes of the community:

> The [Ten-Point] coalition has created an umbrella of legitimacy for appropriate police activity. Activities carried out and decisions made under this umbrella are broadly seen by the community as being fair and just; those falling outside are brought to the attention of the media. Some youth have been sent to prison; others have been given second chances; and the vast majority are no longer being harassed on the street, or at least not as much as in the past. Because of the Ten-Point Coalition's involvement, the differential treatment of individual youth is more likely to be seen by the community as legitimate. Hard decisions are being made, but they are being made in a manner that is commonly viewed as fair and just. (Winship and Berrien 2003, 242)

In relation to the other approaches, the most fundamental assumption here is that youths can assess how they are being treated by the juvenile justice system and respond accordingly. Their behavior is not so much determined by fear of being arrested or by human nature or a thick propensity to commit crime. Instead, it is heavily determined by their relationship with authority figures and institutions. As a result, the approach does not tend toward deterrence or toward incapacitation as the primary method of dealing with youth delinquency. Instead, it proposes liberal democratic procedural solutions that emphasize making law enforcement more legitimate and procedures fairer—procedural mechanisms to enhance fair treatment of arrestees, respect for community leaders, cordial police-civilian encounters, and dignified courtroom practices. There are a number of specific policy initiatives that accord well with this approach, including proposals for "teen courts" in which youths act as jurors, judges, and attorneys in prosecutions of other youths, and "community conferencing," in which young offenders and their victims are placed in mediation with a trained arbitrator (see generally Scheff 1998; Harcourt 1998b). The policy orientation also focuses on maintaining the due process requirements and substantive practices of the juvenile court system, especially in the face of efforts to dismantle the courts, and on ensuring constitutional criminal procedure guarantees in police encounters with youths.

SELF-CONTROL THEORIES

Travis Hirschi and Michael Gottfredson's book *A General Theory of Crime* (1990) exemplifies the fifth position. It is the archetype of a reconstructed liberal approach: heavily influenced by early sociological theories, it consciously incorporates elements of the classical model and of the positivist tradition in an effort to produce a complete or general theory of crime that promotes liberal democratic values.

From the positivist tradition, Hirschi and Gottfredson borrow the concept of criminality, but they turn it on its head. In their view, the default is criminal conduct. It is not the *lack* of self-control that causes crime; it is instead the *presence* of self-control that produces obedience. "People naturally pursue their own interests and unless socialized to the contrary will use whatever means are available to them for such purposes," they declare (Hirschi and Gottfredson 1990, 117). Holding everything else constant, humans would all engage in criminal activity. It is self-control that limits criminality. "Low self-control is not produced by training, tutelage, or socialization . . . [T]he causes of low self-control are negative rather than positive; self-control is unlikely in the absence of effort, intended or unintended, to create it" (94–95).

From the classical model, Hirschi and Gottfredson retain a broad definition of crime. In their view, crime is not a special or distinct category of conduct. "Crime, like noncrime, satisfies universal human desires. It is, in terms of causation, indistinguishable from all other behavior" (1990, 10). This has significant implications for the way they approach the topic of crime:

> The idea that criminal acts are an expression of fundamental human tendencies has straightforward and profound implications. It tells us that crime is not unique with respect to the motives or desires it is intended to satisfy. It tells us that crime presupposes no particular skills or abilities, that it is within the reach of everyone without specialized learning. It tells us that all crimes are alike in that they satisfy ordinary and universal desires. It tells us that people behave rationally when they commit crimes and when they do not. It tells us that people are free to choose their course of conduct, whether it be legal or illegal. And it tells us that people think of and act first for themselves, that they are not naturally inclined to subordinate their interests to the interests of others. (Hirschi and Gottfredson 1990, 5)

Hirschi and Gottfredson thus share with Wilson and Herrnstein some affinity for the economic model. They too assume that criminals are rational—that "people behave rationally when they commit crimes and when they do not." But Hirschi and Gottfredson have a far more ecumenical attitude toward individuals. There is no sharp distinction between people who are present-oriented and those who are future-oriented. There is no sharp distinction between criminals and law-abiders. There are no thick preferences in utility functions. Rather than assuming these dichotomies, Hirschi and Gottfredson assume a spectrum of graded self-control. It is in this sense, they suggest, that crime is "within the reach of everyone without specialized learning."

Hirschi and Gottfredson locate the source of criminality in early childhood. The major determinant of self-control, they suggest, is child rearing. This key factor—self-control—is established very early in life, and according to the authors the differences in self-control between people are stable through adulthood. "In our view," Hirschi and Gottfredson write, "the origins of criminality of low self-control are to be found in the first six or eight years of life, during which time the child remains under the control and supervision of the family or a familial institution" (1990, 272).

Methodologically, this fifth position relies heavily on a structuralist approach: subjects are conditioned in early childhood by their family upbringing. There is an element of the phenomenological borrowed from the classical model of criminology—the idea that people do behave rationally—but again it is a very thin notion of rationality. Self-control does practically all the work. The focus on individual decision making is slight; the approach is predominantly structural. As a result, the major implications for public policy focus on early child rearing: promoting and enhancing family institutions in accordance with liberal democratic principles. Hirschi and Gottfredson reject incapacitation, deterrence, and policing reforms. Because of the stability of differences in self-control, they argue, modifications of the criminal justice system are not promising. Legal punishment, in their view, is not a lever that can be usefully adjusted: "The common expectation that short-term changes in the probabilities of punishment (such as arrest) or in the severity of punishment (such as length of sentence) will have a significant effect on the likelihood of criminal behavior misconstrues the nature of self-control" (1990, 255–56). Similarly, since many criminal acts have no larger purpose than immediate gratification, "Policies that seek to reduce crime by the satisfaction of theoretically derived wants (e.g., equality, adequate housing, good jobs, self-esteem) are likely to be unsuccessful" (1990, 256). Instead, they focus entirely on early childhood development: "Policies directed toward enhancement of the ability of familial institutions to socialize children are the only realistic long-term state policies with potential for substantial crime reduction" (1990, 272–73).

Hirschi and Gottfredson criticize the classical model—and by implication Wilson and Herrnstein as well—for its overemphasis on the criminal sanction and on political rather than social intervention. In their view, economic models result in too narrow a focus on state-sanctioned punishment. "The classical view," they argue, "presupposes the ready availability of draconian penalties inconsistent with the values of liberal democratic societies . . . and misapprehends the nature of people with high crime potential. As a result, the penalties available to the state are largely redundant, acting mainly on potential offenders already deterred by previous learning and social sanctions" (1990, 13). At the same time, Hirschi and Gottfredson are deeply skeptical of incapacitation and of policing reform. Selective incapacitation is prone to excessive "false positives"—predicted delinquents who turn out not to be delinquent (1990, 260). "We cannot predict relative criminal activity until the absolute likelihood of such activity has declined to the point that our prediction is of little practical value" (1990, 264–65). As for the police, the authors contend, they simply "are not a factor in the overwhelming number of robberies, burglaries, assaults, homicides, thefts, or drug deals . . . In the bulk of these offenses, the offender does not know or care about the probability of being observed by the police" (1990, 270). For similar reasons, Hirschi and Gottfredson also doubt the effectiveness of rehabilitation. Rehabilitation theory suffers from the same weakness as incapacitation theory: it is too difficult to identify the right population to "treat."

Franklin Zimring's extensive writings on youth gun violence concur with this approach. Instead of lack of self-control, though, Zimring uses terms like "irresponsibility," "immaturity," "diminished capacity," "impulsiveness," and "lack of mature judgment" (Zimring 1996). For him, lack of self-control is particular to youths—or at least more accentuated in youths than in adults. This is precisely what justifies the initial prohibition on youth gun possession. Teenagers are simply more immature and lack good judgment: "Kids that age [fifteen, sixteen, and seventeen years old] tend to have shorter monetary attention spans than adults, less monetary capital, and less regard for pieces of property as capital assets over a long term. Economic wants are many and the adolescent consumer can easily be distracted from one desired acquisition by the presence of alternative desired goods" (Zimring 1996, 33).

It is for just this reason that Zimring criticizes juvenile transfer laws that have increased the number of juvenile offenders treated as adults: "The same qualities of irresponsibility that justify laws that prohibit minors from acquiring weapons that are freely available to adults should also limit the amount of punishment that can be administered to those young offenders who violate the prohibition" (Zimring 1996, 26). Here Zimring is adamant. Since the conduct itself is the product of low self-control, our response should not be to treat delinquent youths as adults:

> Suppose the legislature finds that there is special danger in fourteen-year-olds possessing loaded handguns. Does that justify passing a law that treats any fourteen-year-old possessing a handgun as an adult in criminal court and imposing a mandatory ten-year prison term on conviction of the offense? The jurisprudential problem with such a law is that it depends on two inconsistent versions of the amoral and intellectual abilities of the fourteen-year-old. On the one hand, the legislature sees minors as possessing poor judgment and weak impulse controls. On the other hand, it seeks to treat a teenager who by violating the law has proved the legislative characterization correct as if he were now regarded as fully mature and responsible . . . When the juvenile targets of special age-related prohibitions turn out to be as immature as we feared, their diminished capacity should limit the extent of their penal liability. (Zimring 1996, 36)

Zimring endorses supply-side policies aimed at reducing the availability of guns among youths. These include making ammunition scarce, buying guns undercover to reduce the supply of guns to youths, talking to youths directly, and promoting treaties in which gangs renounce firearm use. The basic idea is to get guns out of the hands of youths—especially those with low self-control.

Another policy initiative that draws on this fifth approach is the Firearm Suppression Program implemented by the St. Louis, Missouri, police department. That program seeks to reduce the number of guns in the hands of juveniles by means of a voluntary search. When the police have reason to believe that a juvenile possesses a firearm, they go to the juvenile's home and request consent to search for and seize any guns found, in exchange for a promise not to prosecute the parents or the child (Rosenfeld and Decker 1996, 204–6). According to early reports, 402 firearms were confiscated in 1994, half of all the firearms seized by the police from juveniles. Police officers had a 90 percent compliance with their requests, and half of those searches netted firearms (209–10, 214–15).

Given that crime is the product of weak self-control and that criminal activity is fungible and nonspecialized, another approach is to make ordinary crime more difficult—to light dark areas, to add steering wheel locks, to install alarm systems in cars and homes, to place bars on windows. These policy proposals, generally referred to as "situational crime prevention," aim principally at making it harder to commit crimes (see generally Clarke 1995). The policy initiatives of the self-control approach focus, in sum, on promoting and supporting family institutions, reducing gun availability, and implementing situational crime prevention techniques. Although it shares with the moral poverty approach a focus on childhood development, it has radically different policy implications.

CRITICAL CULTURAL APPROACHES

The sixth position on the genealogical map draws on rich ethnographic accounts of youth deviance, on cultural production theory, cultural studies, and poststructuralism. It challenges the individualistic assumptions of the economic and institutional legitimacy theories and focuses instead on the social interactions, peer relations, and structural forces shaping youths in their risk environment. Its policy orientation tends toward deep structural reform of society. Philippe Bourgois's *In Search of Respect: Selling Crack in El Barrio* (1995) exemplifies this final approach.

In Search of Respect is a critical ethnographic, thick description of a crack den called the Game Room. Set in East Harlem, New York—known to many as El Barrio—this book explores the lives and relations of the youths and young men and women who live in and out of the Game Room, some managing and dealing crack, others buying and using it, and still others in complex relations with crack dealers and users. The title captures the core thesis—that the youths are trying to achieve a form of respect, though their attempts are often tragic.

Bourgois draws on cultural production theory, especially the work of Pierre Bourdieu, to understand how these youths ultimately destroy themselves. The central idea of cultural production theory is that these youths bring about their own demise: they resist the structural forces that constrain them—poverty or lack of education—by adopting practices that are ultimately self-defeating. "Street culture's resistance to social marginalization is the contradictory key to its destructive impetus," Bourgois contends. "Through cultural practices of opposition, individuals shape the oppression that larger forces impose upon them" (1995, 17). This allows Bourgois to circumvent earlier overly simplistic structuralist explanations of how poverty shapes inner-city residents—the culture of poverty theories—without giving up on the problem of poverty. Throughout, Bourgois is himself engaged in an act of intervention. "I have written this in the hope," he emphasizes, "that 'anthropological writing can be a site of resistance,' and with the conviction that social scientists should, and can, 'face power'" (1995, 18).

Youth delinquency is explained, then, by the combination of structural forces and cultural resistance. The structural forces consist of the increasing inequality and marginalization along class, ethnic, and gender lines associated with the restructuring of the world economy and the exhaustion of the welfare state. Another structural factor is the profitability of narcotics trafficking, which makes it an attractive nuisance. The moments of cultural resistance, in contrast, represent the scripts that the youths perform in and around the crack den—how they relate to each other, to the police, and to mainstream society. There is also significant space in Bourgois's theoretical framework for the performative. The youths are, at every moment, recreating their identities. They pose, but then they mock themselves. They confront each other, challenging each other's statements, identities, accomplishments, and failures. "Naah!" one of the youths, Primo, tells a thirteen-year-old. "You're going to be an idiot like me and Caesar. A no-good, good-for-nothing *desperdicia'o encicia'o* [vice-ridden, life-wasting man]" (1995, 265). They even challenge Bourgois himself and destabilize his efforts to capture them in his writing, to present them to the reader—to find a doer behind the deed. "Ooh, Felipe! You make us sound like such sensitive crack dealers" (1995, 318 [Caesar commenting on the manuscript]).

Ultimately in Bourgois's work, though, the structural seems to dominate. For most of the youths, there is really no way out. The structures compel criminal behavior. A good example is Ray, the owner of the Game Room and the leader of this drug-selling network. Ray is a successful dealer, but he wants to go straight and begin a legitimate business. So he buys a local club, but the obstacles are insurmountable. Ray does not have an identity card. He does not even have a driver's license. He cannot get the proper licenses to run the business. He turns to Bourgois to help him, but Bourgois is unwilling to get involved. Ultimately, Ray gives up. Clearly, this is not just a matter of self-destruction or counterproductive resistance. The structures of inequality are overpowering—in Bourgois's view. In the end, they give Ray no choice but to deal drugs. The profitability of the drug market and the hurdles of legitimate business compel these youths to deal.

Bourgois advocates decriminalizing drugs. "Street dealers would be forced out of business by the laws of neoclassical economics," he writes (1995, 321). But that is just the beginning:

> The psychological-reductionist and cultural-essentialist analyses of social marginalization that pass for common sense in the United States frame solutions to racism and poverty around short-term interventions that target the "bad attitude" of individuals . . . While these initiatives are not harmful, and might even help superficially on the margins, it is the institutionalized expression of racism—America's de facto apartheid and inner-city public sector breakdown—that government policy and private sector philanthropy need to address if anything is ever to change significantly in the long run. (1995, 323)

Katherine Beckett's *Making Crime Pay: Law and Order in Contemporary American Politics* (1997) also exemplifies this sixth position. Beckett argues that public concern with crime is an artifact of media attention and political initiative and is not primarily the consequence of crime rates. The crime "problem," Beckett suggests, serves a conservative political agenda aimed at replacing the welfare state with a penal state. Originally the focus on crime grew out of a southern conservative strategy of discrediting blacks during the civil rights movement. It has evolved, though, into a larger strategy to discredit welfare recipients in an effort to dismantle the welfare state. "In drawing attention to the problems of street crime, drug addiction, and delinquency, and by depicting these problems as examples of the immorality of the impoverished, conservatives promoted the latter image," Beckett contends. "The crimes of the poor were thus used as evocative symbols for their undeserving and dangerous nature. The racialized nature of this imagery has been a crucial resource for those attempting to promote this conception and policies that reflect it" (1997, 11).

On this view, criminology and crime policy are more political strategy than scientific theory. They serve concrete political ends and significantly affect social policy, especially economic distribution and racial segregation. They are, in this sense, discourses that influence politics. In terms of her own policy orientation, Beckett advocates infusing crime discourse with more of the "social cause" explanations as a way to displace the conservative discourses that have led to massive incarceration, marginalization, and segregation. Her policy orientation is toward structural reform through discourse. Beckett proposes alternative rhetoric as a way to promote the political goal of democratization—the underlying assumption being that rhetorical arguments can affect social policy and ultimately benefit the poor and underrepresented. Beckett concludes her book on the following note:

There is reason to believe that alternative crime frames might enjoy support from "experts" and the public alike. The view that crime has social causes and that certain kinds of rehabilitative programs are an effective means of responding to crime, for example, enjoys a significant degree of academic and popular support. The notion that "family life" is an important dimension of the crime problem is also widespread, but has served primarily as a resource for advocates of the "culture of welfare" explanation of "underclass" behavior. But this need not be the case: one potentially fruitful strategy for progressives would be to stress the ways in which structural forces such as unemployment, low wages, inadequate medical care, and limited access to child care diminish the capacity of parents to care for their young. Highlighting the impact of high rates of incarceration on individuals, families, and communities might also be a way of channeling concern about "social breakdown" in more progressive directions. The creation of a richer and more meaningful public discourse that includes these and other underrepresented perspectives is a first step toward the true democratization of crime and drug policy. This debate is not a peripheral one, but involves the very central question of whether state and social policy should emphasize and seek to promote inclusion or exclusion, reintegration or stigmatization. Nothing less than the true meaning of democracy is at stake. (Beckett 1997, 108–9)

MAPPING THE FIELD OF LAW AND PUBLIC POLICY

These six positions define the space of youth gun studies and at the same time delineate the leading orientations in law and public policy. Notice how the policy recommendations flow almost seamlessly from the social science research. In each case they draw on a well of scientific knowledge that infuses the policy discussion with legitimacy and certainty. Notice also how the policy orientations map neatly onto the underlying methodological approaches of the social science research. The earlier genealogy of the youth gun field exposed a number of useful dimensions that help define the different positions. One dimension aligned them along disciplinary lines—biology, sociology, and economics. Another aligned them along political lines—conservative or progressive. Useful, but somehow not as penetrating as the methodological dimension. Not as sharp or cutting. Only the methodological dimension seems to explain the policy outcomes so neatly.

The task here, then, is to map the six policy positions along the dimension of the methodological approaches using, again, correspondence analysis—to assign percentage distributions along the methodological dimension to the six policy positions,[28] and using those values, to conduct a correspondence analysis of the positions by their methodology. The resulting correspondence map is reproduced in figure 13.1.

As this correspondence map illustrates, the six positions cluster primarily around the structural and phenomenological approaches. From a methodological perspective, these are the dominant and most influential approaches in the youth gun policy arena. Along dimensions 1 and 2, the performative approach is the outlier. It is the least sympathetic to a policy orientation. Along with practice theory and the critical cultural approach, it helps define both dimensions along the lines of *prediction*. Particularly along dimension 2, the positions align from the most strongly predictive at the bottom of the map (structuralism, moral poverty, self-control), through the predictive though less powerfully so (phenomenology, economics, institutional legitimacy), to the least predictive approach of all (the performative).

What is equally striking from the map is that there is no clear political valence to the methodological mapping of the policies. There is no political right or political left on this particular correspondence map. Moral poverty theory—which is politically conservative—clusters close to self-control theory—a liberal democratic perspective—along both dimensions 1 and 2. This reflects the fact that they both trace criminality back to early stages of development and place great emphasis on family upbringing during the first six to

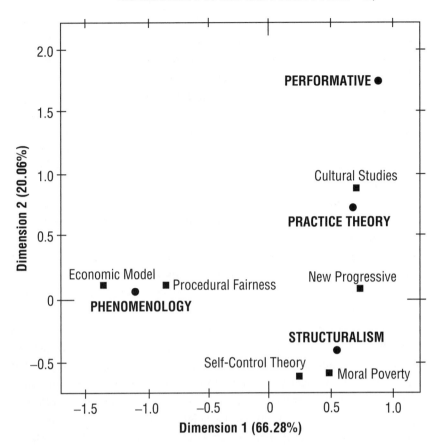

FIGURE 13.1. *Correspondence analysis of the policy orientations by social scientific methodological approach*

eight years of life. They are both strongly structuralist, though politically worlds apart. The same is true at the other end of dimension 1: along both dimensions 1 and 2, the economic model of crime—which, in its modern incarnation is more closely associated with a free-market, right-of-center orientation—maps closely to the institutional legitimacy approach, which is traditionally more liberal and left-of-center. As a result, the policy landscape reveals both conservative and progressive variations of similar methodological approaches. Methodology alone does not dictate political outcome and thus cannot be evaluated on political grounds.

In this sense, the methodological mapping also helps expose the political and ideological assumptions that the different policy orientations make.

If moral poverty and self-control theory share the same methodological approach and theoretical conclusion—that crime traces to early child rearing—then much of the policy analysis beyond those first few years of life is political in nature. Whether to incapacitate the Catalina youths or to aggressively implement situational crime prevention in Tucson neighborhoods is a political, social, and importantly *ethical* decision for both of these positions. It is not scientific; it is purely normative. It involves weighing the harms of future criminal conduct, the impact on the families of the Catalina youths and their victims, the costs and benefits of detention and of target hardening, among other things. The resulting policy orientation says a lot about politics and ethics but nothing about social science. *If* criminality traces to early child rearing, it is not a scientific choice—it is a political, social, and ethical choice.

But more important, the mapping exposes fundamental assumptions about human agency. The six positions map so neatly onto the methodological approaches because these four approaches shape policy orientation. Phenomenological approaches, because they locate the key to crime and deviance in the mental processes of individuals, produce a policy orientation that focuses predominantly on altering the individual decision-making calculus—whether it involves increasing the cost of gun carrying or improving the legitimacy of police authority and neighborhood leadership. Structural approaches, in contrast, because they focus on social or family institutions, tend to produce programs of structural reform—whether it involves enhancing family institutions to better socialize children, promoting neighborhood collective efficacy and trust, or eliminating racial apartheid in America. In this sense the correspondence map helps expose the assumptions that underlie the different policy positions. The economic and institutional legitimacy models, based as they are on a phenomenological approach, rest on assumptions about the decision-making capabilities of the Catalina youths. New progressive policies, in relying so heavily on scripts, practice theory, and the symbolic realm, assume, for instance, that a policy intervention can change the meaning of youth gun possession or gang membership—that a policy of encouraging snitching among juveniles could alter the meaning of youth gun carrying. Critical cultural approaches that embrace cultural production theory make important assumptions about the autonomy of individual choice in the face of oppressive societal structures. In each case, the key assumptions about human agency embedded in the policy proposals trace back to the methodological proclivities of the underlying social science research.

14

LEAPS OF FAITH IN LEVITT AND BOURGOIS

It is precisely along the dimensions of this correspondence map that the various policy positions in the youth gun field make critical assumptions about human agency. It is here that methodological sensibilities—preferences for the phenomenological, or structural, or practice-oriented, or performative—shape policy recommendations. This penultimate chapter puts the claim to an acid test. It explores in greater depth two of the most rigorous scientific positions, in opposite corners of the correspondence map, in order to determine whether they do in fact take that leap of faith. The first is a preeminent research paper from the field of economics, discussed earlier, Steven Levitt's "Juvenile Crime and Punishment" (1998). The second is a noted critical ethnographic monograph, also discussed earlier, Philippe Bourgois's *In Search of Respect: Selling Crack in El Barrio* (1995).

LEVITT AND JUVENILE CRIME

In "Juvenile Crime and Punishment," Levitt uses econometric modeling to demonstrate that changes in juvenile punishment affect juvenile criminal behavior. The starting point is the observation of a significant divergence in juvenile and adult violent crime rates between 1978 and 1993. During that period, arrests for violent crime increased three times faster for juveniles than for adults. During that same period, however, there were sharply different patterns of punitiveness between adult and juvenile populations: whereas the ratio of adult incarcerations in proportion to adult crimes (a proxy for punitiveness of the adult criminal justice system) increased by over 60 percent, the same ratio for juveniles decreased by about 20 percent. "Juvenile punishments, at least by this crude measure, were comparable to adult punishments in 1978, but were only about half as severe by 1993" (Levitt 1998, 1157).

Levitt hypothesizes that the divergence in juvenile and adult crime rates may be "a rational response to a change in the relative incentives for juveniles and adults to engage in criminal activities" (Levitt 1998, 1157). Levitt tests this hypothesis in a series of three analyses. First he tests the relation between juvenile crime and punitiveness. As the independent variable Levitt takes a measure of punitiveness using two methods: the first is the ratio of juveniles in custody to reported juvenile violent crime in the year (custody/crime); the second is the ratio of juveniles in custody to the juvenile population (custody/population). The dependent variable is juvenile crime rates. Levitt also holds constant an index of institutional, demographic, and economic variables that takes account of race, unemployment, and residence in metropolitan areas, among other factors.

In this first phase, Levitt finds a statistically significant relation between punitiveness and juvenile crime: the states that have a higher level of punitiveness (under either measure) have less juvenile crime. The statistical relation is significant at the .05 level. This is the key finding:

> The four specifications for violent crime yield an estimated reduction of between 0.49 and 0.66 violent crimes for each delinquent-year of custody. For property crime, the corresponding reduction is approximately three to four crimes. When one takes into account that these changes correspond only to the number of *reported* crimes rather than actual victimizations, the magnitude of the estimates is consistent with previous estimates of crime eliminated per incarcerated adult, both from prison surveys and from aggregate panel data studies. (Levitt 1998, 1167)

Levitt finds other connections as well. An increased black population is associated with *lower* juvenile crime rates. Moreover, "A one-percentage-point increase in the unemployment rate is associated with roughly a 1–2 percent increase in the number of juvenile crimes committed, with a larger impact on property crime" (Levitt 1998, 1168).

The problem with this first measure is that the result may simply be the product of incapacitation—an entirely different explanation of crime rates that does not assume rational action or any deliberation on the part of juveniles. The incapacitation explanation is simple: if a greater proportion of the juvenile population is incarcerated, there are fewer juveniles free to commit crimes. From the data and first analysis, however, there is no way to determine whether incarceration has a deterrent effect—the economic hypothesis—or an incapacitation effect. As Levitt explains, "It is impossible to differentiate between deterrence and incapacitation within the framework of the preceding section" (Levitt 1998, 1171).

Levitt's second analysis focuses on changes in juvenile behavior at the transition period from juvenile court to adult court. Levitt constructs a measure of the relative punitiveness of juvenile versus adult criminal justice systems in the various states. The idea is to place at one end of a spectrum states that have relatively lenient juvenile systems and strict adult systems and at the other end states that have relatively strict juvenile systems and lenient adult systems. The operating hypothesis here is that if juveniles are responding to punitive incentives—if they are acting rationally in response to punitiveness—then crime rates should decline more with the passage to majority in those states that have relatively lenient juvenile systems but strict adult systems.

Levitt calculates the relative punitiveness by computing the ratio of adult incarcerations per adult violent crime to juvenile incarcerations per juvenile violent crime. Levitt then analyzes the year-by-year changes in criminal behavior and compares the rates of increase/decrease, especially around the age of majority. Levitt finds that "in the states in which punishments increase the most with the adult court, violent crime rates fall by 3.8 percent for 18-year-olds. In contrast, where the transition to the adult court is most lenient, violent crime committed by 18-year-olds increases 23.1 percent. Where the rise in sanctions with adult court is intermediate, the rise in violent crime is also intermediate: 10.2 percent" (Levitt 1998, 1175).

Levitt concludes that the data support a deterrence interpretation: "Sharp drops in crime at the age of majority suggest that deterrence (and not merely incapacitation) plays an important role" (1998, 1156). "Evidence that a substantial fraction of the crime reduction results from deterrence (and not simply incapacitation) comes from analysis of changes in crime rates around the age of majority" (1998, 1159). The thrust of the article is that, based on the second analysis, juvenile punitiveness does *deter* juvenile crime.

Levitt conducts one further analysis, focusing on whether the severity of juvenile punishment has a lasting impact on later criminal involvement. In this third analysis, he runs a regression using as his dependent variable crimes committed by nineteen- to twenty-four-year-olds and as his independent variable the juvenile custody rate in the last year in which the cohort would have been subjected to the juvenile courts, holding constant the punitiveness of adult courts and other socioeconomic factors. The bottom line here is that "the severity of punishment in the last year as a juvenile has little apparent impact on adult criminal behavior. In none of the specifications is the coefficient statistically significant" (Levitt 1998, 1179). This suggests that "the punitiveness of juvenile sanctions does not have a first-order impact on later criminal involvement" (Levitt 1998, 1180).

In conclusion, Levitt finds that "the change in relative punishments for juveniles and adults can account for roughly 60 percent of the differential rate of change between juvenile and adult violent crime rates" (Levitt 1998, 1181). In the end, however, he does not endorse increased juvenile custody because, as I noted previously, the financial costs of such a policy, especially the high cost of incarcerating juveniles, may outweigh the benefits.

THE LEAP OF FAITH IN LEVITT'S RESEARCH

Levitt's study contains three analyses of the relation between punitiveness and crime. The first and third, he concedes, do not distinguish between incapacitation and deterrence. For Levitt, the key finding is the second, which focuses on changes in juvenile behavior at the transition period from juvenile court to adult court.

In introducing his second analysis, Levitt explains how the rate of change in criminal behavior at majority may give us some indication whether the effect is one of deterrence or incapacitation:

> In this section, a different identification strategy is used. In particular, changes in behavior immediately following the transition from the juvenile to the adult court are examined. This shift represents an abrupt change in punishments. If deterrence is at work, then one would expect an abrupt change in behavior associated with passage to adult status. If, on the other hand, incapacitation is the primary channel, then one would expect longer delays in the transition from the juvenile equilibrium to the adult equilibrium due to lags in the timing of arrest and sentencing, as well as the fact that juvenile records are sealed so that young adults initially receive relatively light sentences because of the absence of a criminal record. It seems likely that large immediate changes in behavior associated with the age of majority are likely to primarily reflect deterrence. (Levitt 1998, 1172)

The trouble with this analysis is that there is no good reason the deterrence effect would operate faster or slower than the incapacitation effect. There is no metric to test the speed of either mechanism alone, or to compare the speed of the two competing explanations. There is no way, a priori, to determine how long either effect would take—whether a month, two months, three months, six months, nine months, twelve months, eighteen months, two years, or more. As a result, there is no way to measure immediacy or lag.

A few preliminary points. First, there may be an omitted variable, since the model does not take account of the social norm associated with coming of age. States that have more punitive adult systems may also be states in which there is a more intense social responsibility message associated with becoming an adult. There may be another variable—the social meaning of majority—that has an effect on youth crime and on punitiveness. Second, correlations between punitiveness and crime rates may be subject to reverse causation: because the system is so much more punitive, it is overburdened and so can process fewer cases, thus sending a false signal that crime rates are relatively lower. Third, the claim that "juvenile records are sealed so that young adults initially receive relatively light sentences because of the absence of a criminal record" (Levitt 1998, 1172) is simply not correct. That juvenile records are "sealed" does not mean they are sealed *to sentencing judges*. Even records that are "expunged" are not always expunged from the view of sentencing judges.

In sentencing in adult court, almost all states allow consideration of prior juvenile adjudications, especially for serious offenses. An appendix lists and explains, for each state, the legal provisions regarding the consideration of juvenile records. About thirty-five states expressly allow for the use of juvenile records in presentencing investigations or in sentencing hearings. These states authorize the release of juvenile records to courts and court officials in determining sentences (including the preparation of presentencing reports): Alabama, Alaska, Arkansas, California, Colorado, Georgia, Illinois, Indiana, Kansas, Kentucky, Louisiana, Massachusetts, Minnesota, Mississippi, Missouri, Montana, Nebraska, New Jersey, New Mexico, New York, North Carolina, North Dakota, Ohio, Oregon, Pennsylvania, Rhode Island, South Dakota, Tennessee, Texas, Virginia, Vermont, Washington, West Virginia, Wisconsin, and Wyoming.

Most of the other states make juvenile records available to various parties, including probation officers preparing presentencing investigations and sentencing judges. They achieve this result either by preventing the juvenile court from sealing or expunging certain records (mostly of what would be violent felonies if committed by an adult), by requiring that juvenile records be shared with law enforcement and court administrators, or by declaring certain records public (mostly of offenses that would be violent felonies if committed by an adult). Five states (Arizona, Connecticut, Maine, Maryland, and Michigan) and the District of Columbia mandate sharing juvenile court records generally among state agencies charged with providing social services to delinquents and to law enforcement and the courts. Seven states (Delaware, Florida, Iowa, Nevada, New Hampshire, Oklahoma, and South Carolina) prohibit sealing, expunging, or destroying juvenile records that describe acts that if committed by an adult would lead to violent felony charges. Three states (Hawaii, Idaho, and Utah) declare that delinquent acts that would be charged as violent felonies are public.

While almost all states allow for the use of juvenile records in sentencing, there are of course subtle distinctions. Some states explicitly authorize the use of juvenile records in sentencing (for example, Massachusetts and Texas), while others mandate general information sharing or prohibit sealing or expunging certain records (for example, Colorado and Iowa) or declare certain juvenile records public (Idaho and Utah). In some states the burden is on the juvenile court to provide records (Arkansas, for example), while in others it is on the sentencing court to request them (Arizona, for example). Some states provide for certain age cutoffs, such as fourteen or sixteen years of age, when records can be disclosed (Hawaii, for example). Some states explicitly provide that juvenile records may be considered in enhancing sentences or qualifying an offender for a habitual offender program (California, for example), while other states prohibit the use of records for these purposes (Kentucky, for example). Several states, including Illinois, Nevada, and Arkansas, have recently amended their laws concerning the use of juvenile court records. These changes have exempted from sealing and expunging records that describe acts that would be charged as violent felonies if committed by an adult.

In sum, while the practices with regard to juvenile records vary from state to state, in most states sentencing judges may consider juvenile records in imposing criminal sentences on adults, particularly offenses that would have been charged as felonies if committed by an adult. Accordingly, it is incorrect to assume that first-time adult offenders will receive shorter sentences because their juvenile records are sealed. The records may be sealed to the public, but in most cases they are not sealed to the sentencing judge. As a result, the issue of juvenile records is unlikely to produce any time lag regarding incapacitation.

But putting this aside, the model itself cannot differentiate between the two competing explanations—deterrence and incapacitation. Most juveniles in custody are released when they reach their majority. As a result, the number of at-risk juveniles turned adults in the general population is, at that moment, significant. If the adult system is more punitive, especially in relation to the juvenile system, then there is likely to be a lot of detention and incarceration when those youths turned adults commit crimes upon their release. Those detentions and incarcerations are likely to have a significant incapacitating effect on crime, and there is no a priori reason that effect should be more or less immediate than the deterrent effect.

The model uses an *annual* measure of crime. Yet the incapacitation time lag—if there is one—may very well be shorter than that, which would then have little delayed effect on annual measures of crime. In fact, if true incapacitation theory is correct—the idea that about 6 percent of juveniles are responsible for about 50 percent of juvenile crime—one would expect that strict enforcement would have an immediate and sharp effect precisely at the moment when delinquent youths are released on attaining their majority. In other words, stringent arrest and detention policies—arrests on minor misdemeanors, "stop and frisks," and so on—should produce a significant incapacitation effect, *especially* if you believe in incapacitation theory.

In essence there is no measure, no metric, no standard against which we could declare that an effect on crime—deterrence or incapacitation—is abrupt or delayed. Nor is there any way to determine how the two effects would compare. We do not have a measure for the incapacitation effect and a separate one for the deterrence effect. We have just one number, and we have to guess whether it seems relatively immediate or relatively delayed. Since we do not know how long the incapacitation effect takes, there is no way of knowing from annual crime data whether the effect looks more immediate or more delayed—whether it is incapacitation or deterrence.

In the end, Levitt's study cannot make this distinction. As Levitt himself remarks regarding adult studies, "Few of these empirical studies have any power to distinguish deterrence from incapacitation and therefore provide only an indirect test of the economic model of crime" (Levitt 1998, 1158n2). And there is little else in the juvenile area to corroborate the purported deterrent effect. There have been no studies on this question since Levitt's, and there was remarkably little previous research:

> In contrast to the well-developed literature on deterrence and incapacitation effects of the adult criminal justice system, there is remarkably little previous academic research on the response of juvenile crime to sanctions. Although there are studies of the relative punitiveness of juvenile and adult criminal sanctions in a particular location at a given point in time, no attempt is made in these analyses to estimate whether differences in punishment affect relative crime rates . . . To the best of my knowledge, however, there are no previous systematic empirical analyses of the response of juvenile crime to sanctions. (Levitt 1998, 1158–59)

The result is that the associations between punitiveness and juvenile crime remain open to interpretation. The correlations may support a deterrence hypothesis but just as easily could support a theory of incapacitation. (In fact, the correlations are also consistent with other explanations.) How then should we interpret the data? How do we go about giving meaning to the correlation between punitiveness and crime?

There is no easy answer. The quantitative analysis does not speak for itself, and the Catalina youths speak in contradictory voices. On one hand, common sense suggests that some youths will be deterred by the threat of incarceration. On the other hand, strict logic tells us that incapacitation will reduce delinquency. In the end, the correlations remain open to different interpretations depending on our assumptions about human agency. And researchers very often project their disciplinary bias into the interpretation. That is what happened in Levitt's article. His empirical conclusions betray a penchant for rational action theory and project that sensibility onto a model that is in fact unable to differentiate between deterrence and incapacitation. It is here that Steven Levitt takes a leap of faith. But he is not alone.

BOURGOIS AND CRACK-DEALING YOUTHS

In his book *In Search of Respect* (1995), Philippe Bourgois is extremely sensitive to the interpretive dimensions of research and, as a result, does not jump to easy conclusions about the reasoning, drives, desires, emotions, and psychology of youths. Methodologically, Bourgois is keenly aware of the political difficulties and limitations of the ethnographic method. He draws in part on the postmodern critique of anthropology—of ethnographic authenticity and political neutrality—and he places his own research in the framework of critiques of the exoticizing of the "other" and of the self-indulgence of participant observation. "I guarded myself consciously in this work from a voyeuristic celebration of street dealers and inner-city street culture," Bourgois notes (1995, 15). He draws on postmodern sensibilities to address many of the shortcomings of the ethnographic method. As he remarks in his introduction, "The self-conscious reflexivity called for by postmodernists was especially necessary and useful in my case: I was an outsider from the larger society's dominant class, ethnicity, and gender categories who was attempting to study the experience of inner-city poverty among Puerto Ricans" (13).

Bourgois is highly self-reflexive about his own production of knowledge. He often interjects in his narrative discussion of his agonized decisions whether to reproduce text: "While editing thousands of pages of transcriptions I came to appreciate the deconstructionist cliché of 'culture as text.' I also became acutely aware of the contradictory collaborative nature of my research strategy. Although the literary quality and emotional force of this book depends entirely on the articulate words of the main characters, I have always had the final say in how—and if—they would be conveyed in the final product" (1995, 13).

When discussing acts of sexual violence perpetrated by his closest informants, Bourgois struggles with the reader over whether even to present the material and how to interpret it: "Rape is so taboo that I was tempted to omit this discussion, fearing that readers would become too disgusted and angry with the crack dealers and deny them a human face" (1995, 207). In this and other passages, Bourgois in fact places partial responsibility on readers: "I do not know if it is possible for me to present the story of my three and a half years of residence in El Barrio without falling prey to a pornography of violence, or a racist voyeurism—ultimately the problem and the responsibility is also in the eyes of the beholder" (18).

At the same time, Bourgois is explicitly disdainful of the "profoundly elitist tendencies of many postmodernist approaches" (1995, 14). He criticizes the closed discourse of postmodern academics, so far removed from the real world. "Postmodern debates titillate alienated, suburbanized intellectuals," he writes; "they are completely out of touch with the urgent social crises of the inner-city unemployed" (14). In contrast to this narcissism and elitism, Bourgois sets out to explore the real life of a crack den in East Harlem. He spends three and a half years participating, interviewing residents, and experiencing what life is like to the women and men inside and close to the Game Room. Bourgois steeps readers in the lives and experiences of his subjects. His text is a rich narrative—a fascinating and compelling account, with riveting stories of life in El Barrio.

In a short conclusion, Bourgois then sets out his policy agenda. American society, he suggests, lacks the political will to address the fundamental "dimensions of structural oppression in the United States" (1995, 318). He argues that the country needs to confront racial and class inequality. "We need to recognize and dismantle the class- and ethnic-based apartheids that riddle the U.S. landscape" (319). It is precisely the increasing inequality and marginalization along class, ethnic, and gender lines that constitute the structural roots of self-destructive behavior and drug use in the inner city.

Bourgois argues for decriminalizing drugs: "In terms of concrete, short-term public policy, the single cheapest and simplest way to wipe out the material basis for the most violent and criminal dimensions of street culture is to destroy the profitability of narcotic trafficking by decriminalizing drugs" (1995, 321). In addition, he argues for "aggressive political intervention . . . to promote economic opportunities for the marginal working class" (321).

This includes, for instance, eliminating "the hostile bureaucratic maze that punishes the poor for working legally" (322): we need to continue health, income, and in-kind benefits to those who leave public assistance and enter the working force and find other ways to make legitimate employment more attractive than drugs. He also urges redistribution of public services, which increasingly favor wealthy communities at the expense of the inner city.

Bourgois also emphasizes the need for a "politics of mutual respect" (1995, 324). The idea here is that inner-city youths are motivated not just by wealth maximization, but also by the search for respect and self-identity—hence the title, *In Search of Respect*. Boldly, Bourgois concludes his policy discussion on the following note:

> To draw on a classic metaphor from sports, the United States needs to level its playing field . . . Hundreds of short-term policy and legal reforms immediately jump to mind: from tax reform—namely, taxing the home mortgages of the upper middle class, and exempting the federal and state transfer benefits of the poor—to streamlining access to social welfare benefits and democratizing educational institutions—namely, universal affordable health care coverage, free day care, equalizing per capita funding for schools and universities, and so on. (1995, 323–24)

Bourgois acknowledges that his agenda is somewhat unrealistic. "Almost none of the policy recommendations I have made so far are politically feasible in the United States in the short or medium term" (1995, 325). Like Katherine Beckett's, though, his goal is to express these ideas and insert them into the public debate so that over time there may be an eventual shift in public discourse. These ideas might in some way, at some point, transform what he calls "the dead-end political debates between liberal politicians, who want to flood the inner city with psychiatric social workers or family therapists, and conservatives, who simply want to build bigger prisons, cut social welfare spending, and decrease taxes for big business and the wealthy" (325).

ANOTHER LEAP OF FAITH

Philippe Bourgois's ethnographic work is a masterpiece. But where, exactly, do these policy recommendations come from? How are they related to the rich narratives of his informant crack dealers? How can we know, from the ethnographic method, whether his informants would *change* their behavior if there were less inequality or racial apartheid in the United States? Bourgois's policy discussion sits uncomfortably on his brilliant ethnographic fieldwork.

It is presented as if it follows from his analysis, but there is no argument for a connection, no attempt to link the policies to any ethnographic findings. The policy discussion is presented as neutral, as if it did not inform the empirical analysis. But clearly that is not the case. Bourgois in fact started his project with these political intentions. When he first began his ethnographic work, he states, "I wanted to probe the Achilles heel of the richest industrialized nation in the world by documenting how it imposes racial segregation and economic marginalization on so many of its Latino/a and African-American citizens" (1995, 1). Bourgois writes in his introduction of the "political and ideological oppression" and of the "long-term colonial domination" that his informants and other Puerto Ricans experience (11). These are fighting words, and it is hard to believe they would not significantly shape the kind of policy analysis and interpretations that Bourgois would give to his research findings. Clearly they did.

Bourgois is deeply committed and politically engaged—much to his credit. But the interpretations he projects onto his ethnographic material merely reflect his assumptions about human behavior—about how his subjects are shaped by the economic conditions they experience and battered by their own self-destructive resistance. Bourgois simply assumes that they would lead different lives under different structural conditions. He projects his assumptions onto his policy analysis. The fact is, however, there is nothing in his data to tell us how his informants would act if there were less inequality or less racism in society. There is no reason to deduce from his data what would follow from radical political change. It requires a leap of faith.

In the end, there are gaps. Gaps between data and interpretation. Gaps between social science and policy. The only way we overcome these gaps is to take a leap of faith. In Levitt's case, the leap privileges deterrence, even though his model cannot rigorously adjudicate between the deterrence and the incapacitation explanations. In Bourgois's case, the leap privileges a structuralist and cultural account of poverty and delinquency, even though his model is not dynamic. Is it possible to avoid taking these leaps of faith? I do not believe it is. The gaps are inevitable. They are a by-product of human consciousness. And what they reveal, more than anything, is that ultimately the field of social science and law is not determined by science but must rest on ethical choice. In the end, we have no choice but to dirty our hands.

15

MAKING
ETHICAL
CHOICES IN
LAW AND
PUBLIC POLICY

In the very last moment of Jean-Paul Sartre's play *Les mains sales*, Hugo finally realizes the possibility of a new project—the possibility of vindicating his own politics and at the same time rehabilitating Hoederer. It is at that turning point, when he understands what it would mean to let himself be killed, that he exercises his full subjectivity with eyes wide open. That he finally *invents* himself. That he acts *in good faith*. And so, as his comrades return to gun him down, Hugo kicks the door open and screams at the top of his lungs, over Olga's pleas, "*Non récupérable.*"

I cannot say that for CMS-66. Or for Jesús, Yusuf, or Marc. Or for Paul, John, or the other Catalina youths. I cannot declare them *non récupérable*—beyond hope, beyond intervention, beyond help. That act, that decision, that *choice* would signify too much. It would *cost* too much. Here, then, is a first ethical choice: I will not take the leap of faith that would be required to believe with James Q. Wilson, Richard Herrnstein, and moral poverty theorists, or for that matter with Travis Hirschi, Michael Gottfredson, and self-control theorists, that human subjects are so fundamentally shaped in early childhood. I refuse to ignore the evidence that some of the Catalina youths *do* think about the legal consequences of gun carrying. I refuse to disregard the evidence that some of them reiterate and in the process slightly modify gun scripts in order to produce a safe result. I refuse to erase the evidence that some are genuinely torn between their life on the street and their desire to "stay clean." In sum, I refuse to take the leap of faith that would condemn these youths to a life of incapacitation or damage control.

At the same time, I simply cannot engage in the kind of abstract and callous cost-benefit calculation that is called for by a strictly economic view of the Catalina youths. Here I make a second ethical choice: I will not take the leap of faith that would be required to believe with Steven Levitt and the economic model of crime that juvenile and adult incarceration are in some sense fungible. Specifically, I refuse to take the leap necessary to embrace *this* mode of analysis: "Total spending per resident in public juvenile facilities was roughly $33,000 in 1990. In comparison, the average expenditure per state prisoner in fiscal 1992 was roughly $23,000. Thus there does not appear to be a clear gain in altering the relative concentration of juvenile and adult inmates at the present time" (Levitt 1998, 1182). If the theory of deterrence is correct and these youths do in fact need to be in an institutional setting for a year in order to avoid engaging in crime as adults—in order to avoid being incarcerated in an Arizona penitentiary when they reach majority—then I am unwilling to treat the remedy on a par with later punishment. I refuse to sacrifice their future.

At the other extreme of the methodological map, I also cannot accept the idea that the Catalina youths' resistance to admittedly oppressive structures of society—to racial hierarchy, to economic poverty, to the lack of employment opportunities—leads unidirectionally to self-destructive behavior. Here, then, is a third ethical choice: I will not take the leap of faith that would be required to believe, with cultural production and critical culture theorists, that resistance to oppression is predominantly harmful to the Catalina youths—that "street culture's resistance to social marginalization is the contradictory key to its destructive impetus" or that "through cultural practices of opposition, individuals shape the oppression that larger forces impose upon them" (Bourgois 1995, 17). I choose to read into these apparently self-destructive behaviors not just the negative, but also the positive. Not all acts in good faith are wise; they may nevertheless have value. There is more to the Catalina youths' resistance than self-destruction alone. There are also positive constitutive aspects to their resistance—even when resistance leads to gun carrying. When John pulls out his 9-mm at the Rillito River wash and taunts his rival—"You know both you and me aren't gonna pull the trigger, so why don't you shut up and leave?"— he has created a valuable script. To be sure, a script with a gun. A dangerous script. But a valuable script nonetheless.

Encompassing these specific choices is a larger ethical sensibility and project: to understand the Catalina youths the way I would try to understand my own children. To listen to them as I would listen to my children. To model their behavior the way I would try to model my own children's behavior. To extend to the Catalina youths the same respect and dignity. Notice, I have not said to *treat* them the same way I treat my own children. I do not pretend to be so righteous—nor would it necessarily be a good idea for a parent qua parent to become policy maker, judge, or advocate. But to *try to understand* the Catalina youths the way I try to understand my own children, yes, that is possible, and it is my larger ethical project. Ultimately, that is how I choose to place myself on the policy map of youth gun studies. It is, in the end, an ethical question.

Listening carefully to the Catalina youths, then, I discern in their voices elements of a common language of guns. This language is shared among them. They are familiar with it. They know the terms well—"straps," "protection," "dogging," "talking shit," "tight." They can play the next measure of the script, changing it ever so slightly, regenerating it. This language of guns represents a backdrop against which they seem to strategize, adopting some of the meanings, rejecting others, mocking them, rebelling. "Anybody can fight with a gun, anybody can pull a trigger. It takes somebody, like a real man, to fight somebody." Now he doesn't need a gun. He doesn't want a gun. These youths do not seem to be giving meaning to guns in an autonomous way, independently, on their own, outside the webs of meanings. They are not the "signifiers." Instead, they seem to come to the social space and interact with it. They develop their relation to guns *through* this medium. There is, in this sense, a dynamic interaction between any one Catalina youth and the web of primary meanings of guns. And the language of guns seems to influence some of their behaviors. To be sure, it does not *control* or *constrain* their behavior in any real way. But it offers them a way in some cases to resist gun carrying and in others to embrace guns. "They're exciting. I mean, what the hell. You feel powerful when you have a gun. You get respect."

The robust connection between the registers of gun talk and the contexts of gun carrying and gang membership suggests that instead of thinking about these Catalina youths through the lens of traditional categories of race or class or juvenile records, it may make sense to think about them *through the lens of the symbolic meanings*. There is a clear association between the registers of gun talk and carrying status. The action/protection cluster of meanings—the symbolic realm of protection, danger, attraction, power, jail, action, belonging, and death—is most closely associated with extensive carrying. The other clusters of meaning—recreation/respect and commodity/dislike—are more closely associated with low or no carrying. In trying to understand these Catalina youths, it may make sense to think through these clusters of meaning.

This could translate, at the policy level, into taking several approaches to target the different Catalina youths. The correspondence maps reveal that nongang youths associate guns more with exchange value (the commodity cluster), and that gang members associate them more with use value (the action/protection cluster). This might suggest that nongang youths may be more likely to relate to the exchange value of guns in an economic sense and therefore may be more likely to respond to traditional rational choice approaches. In contrast, gang members may be relatively immune to rational choice approaches and may need different appeals, such as practice-based alternatives (orienting them to alternative practices that encourage belonging and other sorts of meaningful action). Since the first set of youths are far less likely to be carrying guns, it may be a waste of resources to target recreational uses of guns or even commodity exchanges (selling, buying, and trading). It may be wiser to confiscate guns from youths who are selling or playing with them, rather than to prosecute them. As for the second set of youths—those who are more closely associated with the action/protection cluster—rational choice approaches are unlikely to succeed. For these youths, the risks of death associated with guns may far outweigh the cost of incarceration. When we add to this the deep sensual and moral attraction to guns, it becomes clear that adjudicative responses are unlikely to succeed. Instead, it may be more productive to find substitutes for guns and to reduce, as much as possible, the availability of guns among youths.[29]

If we listen closely to the Catalina youths, we may also acquire different vantage points on the policy of incarcerating youths for gun violations. Some of the youths sound deterred by the threat of jail time, but others seem to ignore the risk. On one hand, the correspondence maps suggest that guns are far more attractive to youths who have *not* been charged and detained on a gun charge. Youths who have never been incarcerated on gun charges are also more likely to view guns as offering a sense of belonging. In addition, incarceration on a gun charge seems to accentuate the danger associated with guns—not just the risk of getting caught and sent to prison (the jail meaning), but also the risk of harming yourself or others (the danger meaning itself). To be sure, the causal arrows are not entirely clear; but these factors suggest that incarceration may have a chilling effect on the attraction of guns.

On the other hand, a number of other signals caution against the use of incarceration. What remains constant and robust in the correspondence maps is the close association between gun carrying, gang membership, and the need for protection in an aggressive, preemptive way. Incarceration does not alter the centrality of the protection meaning among gun-carrying youths. In other words, the policy of gun detention does not seem to shake loose the protection meaning—the one meaning with the greatest frequency of gun carrying. The central symbol of gun carrying and gang membership is simply not affected by the policy of incarcerating youths who carry guns. In addition, again based on the correspondence maps, youth incarceration seems to increase the danger associated with guns, in turn accentuating the need for guns to gain protection from other youths, to exercise control, or to inflict or avoid death. That is, incarceration underscores how dangerous the world is and how necessary guns are and in this way may reinforce the central symbolic meaning of guns—aggressive protection.

The centrality of action/protection to gun carrying, to gang membership, and also to the youths who are incarcerated on gun infractions suggests the need to target the idea that guns afford protection. This may translate into a number of policies, including a focus on youth conflict resolution, parental and school supervision, safety monitoring in schools and public areas, architectural redesign of schools, practice-based alternatives, and counseling. It may also mean finding ways to help the Catalina youths discover how to express an identity that does not center on aggressive self-protection or involve life-threatening weapons—alternative ways for these youths to achieve respect for themselves and to create their own identity. This may be labor intensive. It may mean rethinking how to intellectually stimulate the Catalina youths. It may entail creating job training and valuable job opportunities. It may mean redesigning our educational system.

Regardless of the specific intervention, though, the idea would be to target, by every means possible, the felt need for protection that action/protection youths associate with guns: to engage in a concerted effort to confiscate guns through consensual search policies and supervision; to implement practice-based alternatives to gun carrying; to make youths' environments feel safer. And to investigate every means possible to *reduce youths' access to guns*. That, in turn, may entail a combination of legal strategies, including holding gun owners legally accountable for their guns, requiring safe storage of guns in homes and automobiles, confiscating guns from youths through policies like the St. Louis police department's "consent to search and seize" program (Rosenfeld and Decker 1996), and otherwise continually targeting gun sources as they emerge (see, e.g., Ash et al. 1996, 1758; Sherman et al. 1998). It might even include a system of annual inspection and registration of guns modeled on automobile regulation. All in all, it is essential from a policy perspective to treat guns for what they are to the most susceptible youths: seductively dangerous.

The multiplicity of meanings, resistance, and contexts in a setting like the Catalina Mountain School in Tucson, Arizona, suggests that there is no quick fix, no silver bullet for youths' gun possession. There is no single meaning that we could reengineer to change these youths' behaviors. There is no one perception that we could leverage to alter their gun carrying. From a policy perspective, we need to develop an eclectic approach that is tailored to the different meanings, contexts, and preferences—especially the action/protection cluster. Given that guns are so seductive to these adjudicated youths and that so many of them feel a compelling need to arm themselves for protection, the emphasis will have to be on developing local interventions specifically tailored to their local meaning structures. I emphasize here *local* meaning structures. The registers of gun talk from these Catalina interviews reflect only local meanings—meanings particular to the Catalina school, embedded as it is in the Southwest and so close to the Mexican border.[30]

"Do you think you can govern innocently?" Hoederer asks. In the field of law and public policy, many turn to the social sciences in order to answer yes. Yes, we can model behavior and choose outcomes that offer the greatest benefit to the most people. Here I throw in my lot with Michael Walzer: "My own answer is no, I don't think I could govern innocently. But this does not mean that it isn't possible to do the right thing while governing" (1973, 161). In the end, the choice of a methodological approach in social science research is not dictated by science, and the implications we draw for our laws and public policies are not entirely scientific. When we adopt a social science method, we make a decision about the way in which we are going to shape the human subject. And in the process, we dirty our hands. We have made an ethical choice.

ACKNOWLEDGMENTS

Over the past few years, as this project took shape, I had the enormous good fortune of being surrounded by a supportive, critical, and engaged group of colleagues, friends, and family and the great pleasure of spending time at several universities, each of which contributed in special ways to the ultimate production of this book. I am particularly grateful to Ronald Breiger for encouraging me to explore correspondence analysis and to Andrew Abbott, Jeffrey Fagan, David Garland, Ted Gerber, Michael Gottfredson, Calvin Morrill, Norval Morris, Robert Sampson, and Franklin Zimring for innumerable and always fascinating discussions of social science methodologies and research. I also owe special gratitude to Seyla Benhabib, Janet Halley, Duncan Kennedy, Frank Michelman, Martha Minow, Carol Steiker, Richard Tuck, and Iris Marion Young for innumerable and always penetrating discussions of social theory and jurisprudence.

In writing this book and making the manuscript final, I benefited greatly from dialogue, guidance, comments, and criticisms from (and I am immensely grateful to) Al Alschuler, David Barron, Gary Becker, Anthony Braga, Philip Cook, Suzanne Dovi, Chris Eisgruber, Philip Heymann, Travis Hirschi, Jim Jacobs, Dan Kahan, David Kennedy, Randall Kennedy, David Kopel, Jens Ludwig, Toni Massaro, Tracey Meares, Martha Nussbaum, Richard Posner, Dan Richman, Gerald Rosenberg, Henry Ruth, Mia Ruyter, Steve Schulhofer, Jerry Skolnick, Alan Stone, Bill Stuntz, Cass Sunstein, and Chris Winship. Leonard Post read and criticized every page of the manuscript, and for that, Leonard, I owe you. Portions of this book were presented at workshops at Princeton University, Harvard University, the University of Chicago, the University of California at Berkeley, and the University of Michigan, and I appreciate the comments and reactions I received there.

Many outstanding students helped me with this project. I am deeply grateful to Craig LaChance and Timothy Jafek at the University of Arizona, who helped me design the project and lay its foundation. For extraordinary research assistance, I am also extremely indebted to Jamie Watson, Imraan Mir, Cytheria Jernigan, David Tang, and Leo Wise at Harvard Law School; Bryn Dodge and Sarah Nolan at New York University; and Ranjit Hakim, Kate Levine, Jennifer Miller, and Ward Penfold at the University of Chicago. Special thanks go to Dan Montgomery and Sam Lim at the Illinois Mathematics and

Science Academy for help at the last stages. I also thank, for outstanding librarian assistance, Maureen Garmon at the University of Arizona, Maura Kelley at Harvard Law School, and Margaret Schilt and Greg Nimmo at the University of Chicago.

This book benefited greatly from many intense and insightful conversations with J. Alex Schwartz, my editor at the University of Chicago Press, and for that and for his encouragement and support, I am profoundly thankful. I also thank Catherine E. Beebe for outstanding assistance at every juncture of the editorial process and Alice Bennett for copyediting the manuscript. This project required funding and was launched thanks to a grant from the University of Arizona. I owe a great debt to my deans, who generously supported this research—Toni Massaro at the University of Arizona, Saul Levmore at the University of Chicago, Robert Clark at Harvard Law School, and John Sexton at New York University.

For me this project is tied, more than anything, to many deep, rich, and inspiring conversations with my best and most critical reader, the source of so much inspiration, especially over the course of these past few years of struggle—my mother, Renée Harcourt. Mia Ruyter and our children, Isadora and Léonard, and my sister, Caroline Harcourt, and her family participated in so much of this and gave constant support and encouragement. I dedicate this book to you, The Mutz.

APPENDIX

Treatment of Juvenile Records in State Sentencing

STATE	TREATMENT	DETAILS
Alabama	Consider in sentencing	AL ST § 12-15-72: Disposition of a child shall not be admissible in any other court except in sentencing proceedings after conviction of a crime
Alaska	Consider in sentencing	AK ST § 47-12-300: A person may not used sealed records for any purpose except under court order by an officer of the court in making a presentencing report
Arizona	Disclose to law enforcement and courts	AZ ST § 8-208: On a request of an adult probation officer or state or local prosecutor, the juvenile court shall release all information in its possession concerning a person who is charged with a criminal offense
Arkansas	Consider in sentencing	AR ST § 9-27-309: Records of delinquency adjudications for which a juvenile could have been tried as an adult shall be made available to prosecuting attorneys for use at sentencing
California	Consider in sentencing	CA PENAL § 667: Juvenile records may qualify adult offender for sentence enhancement and/or habitual offender program
Colorado	Consider in sentencing	CO ST § 19-1-306: Expunged records shall be available to any judge and the probation department for use in any future juvenile or adult sentencing hearing
Connecticut	Disclose to law enforcement and court	CT ST § 54-76l: Records of any youthful offender on or after October 1, 1995, may be disclosed between state agencies providing services to the youth, law enforcement, state and federal prosecutorial officials, and court officials

STATE	TREATMENT	DETAILS
Delaware	No expunging for serious offense	DE ST § 10-1001: Adjudications involving murder, arson, and burglary may not be destroyed according to expunging procedure applicable to juvenile records generally
District of Columbia	Disclose to court	DC CODE § 16-2332: Inspection of juvenile records shall be permitted to judges and professional staff of the Superior Court (the trial court in DC)
Florida	No expunging for violent felonies	FL ST § 985.04: Records of child found to have committed a delinquent act that if committed by an adult would be a violent felony may not be destroyed pursuant to program for destruction of juvenile records, generally
Georgia	Consider in felony sentencing	GA ST § 15-11-79.1: Disposition of a child may not be used against a child in any proceeding in any other court except for establishing conditions of bail, plea negotiations, and sentencing in felony offenses; in such cases juvenile records shall be treated like adult records
Hawaii	Public records for violent felonies	HI ST § 571-84.6: Records of minor adjudged a delinquent for an act that would be a violent felony that is more than fourteen years old will be public
Idaho	Public records for violent felonies for juveniles fourteen years old and older	ID ST § 20-525: Records of juvenile charged with an offense that would be a felony if committed by an adult are public
Illinois	Consider in sentencing	IL ST CH 705 § 405/5-150: Evidence and adjudications in delinquency proceedings shall be admissible in criminal proceedings to determine bail, fitness of the defendant, or in sentencing
Indiana	Consider in sentencing	IN ST § 31-39-2-4: Juvenile records available without court order for use in pre-sentencing report
Iowa	No sealing for violent felonies	IA ST § 232.150: Records of juveniles who commit offenses that would be felonies may not be sealed according to procedure generally applicable to juvenile records

STATE	TREATMENT	DETAILS
Kansas	Consider in sentencing	KS ST § 21-4724: The department of corrections shall have access to juvenile records for use in determining the person's criminal history classification, upon which the sentencing court shall rely
Kentucky	Consider in sentencing	KY ST § 610 – 320: Juvenile records may be used during sentencing phase of a criminal trial; they may not be used in finding the child to be a persistent felony offender based on that adjudication
Louisiana	Consider in sentencing	LA Ch.C Art. 414: Upon written request, reports and records concerning juvenile court proceedings shall be released to sentencing judge for sentencing and to district attorney for charging an individual as a habitual offender
Maine	Information shared with court	ME ST T. 15 § 3308: Nothing in this section precludes information sharing among law enforcement agencies or the courts for the administration of criminal justice
Maryland	Information shared with law enforcement	MD CTS & JUD PRO § 3-828: This section does not prohibit access in an investigation and prosecution by a law enforcement agency
Massachusetts	Consider in sentencing	MA ST RCRP Rule 28: The probation officer shall inquire into the nature of every criminal case or juvenile complaint and report to the court
Michigan	Information shared	MI ST 791-228: The department of social services shall furnish to the department of corrections information, on request, concerning any individual having a previous record as a juvenile probationer who comes within the jurisdiction of the department
Minnesota	Consider in sentencing	MN ST § 260B-171: The juvenile court shall keep records of proceedings until person they concern reaches the age of twenty-eight and shall release these records on request to adult court for the

STATE	TREATMENT	DETAILS
		purposes of sentencing; if the juvenile commits a felony as an adult the court shall retain the juvenile records for as long as the records would be maintained if the offender had been an adult when the offense was committed
Mississippi	Consider in sentencing	MS ST 43-21-261: Juvenile records may be disclosed to the judges of circuit and county courts and presentencing investigators for the circuit courts
Missouri	Consider violent felonies	MO ST 211-321: List of certain juvenile offenses furnished for presentencing report
Montana	Consider in sentencing	MT ST 41-5-215: Youth court and department records open to any court and its probation staff when considering what sentence to be imposed on the party
Nebraska	Consider in sentencing	NE ST § 29-2261: The presentencing investigation report shall include history of delinquency or criminality
Nevada	No automatic seal for violent felonies	NV LEGIS 285 (2001): Nevada recently changed its law on juvenile records (juvenile records covering acts that would be charged as sexual offenses, and violent felonies if committed by an adult may not be automatically sealed when child reaches twenty-one years of age)
New Hampshire	Share information with law enforcement for investigation and prosecution	NH ST § 169-B-35: Once a delinquent reaches twenty-one years of age, records shall be closed and placed in inactive files; police officers and prosecutors may use these records in the investigation and prosecution of criminal acts and if a prosecutor has reason to believe the individual may be a witness to a criminal case
New Jersey	Consider in sentencing	NJ ST 2A-4A-48: Disposition of a juvenile's case shall not be admissible in any criminal or penal case except for consideration in sentencing

STATE	TREATMENT	DETAILS
New Mexico	Included in presentencing report	NS ST § 32A-2-18: A judgment on a petitioner under the Delinquency Act shall not be deemed a conviction of a crime and shall not be admissible as evidence against a child in any case or proceeding except in sentencing after conviction of a felony and then only for purposes of the presentencing report
New York	Consider in sentencing	NY FAM CT § 381-2: Another court, in imposing sentence on an adult for a conviction, may receive and consider the records and information on file with the family court
North Carolina	Consider in sentencing as an aggravating circumstance	NC ST § 7B-3000: The juvenile record of an adjudication for an offense that would be a violent felony may be used in subsequent criminal proceeding against the juvenile or to prove an aggravating factor in sentencing
North Dakota	Consider in sentencing	ND ST 27-20-51: Juvenile court records may be inspected by any court and its probation and other officials and the attorney for defendant in preparing a presentencing report
Ohio	Consider in sentencing	OH ST § 2151-358: Sealing procedure for juvenile delinquent does not apply to delinquent that committed acts that would be charged as violent felonies if committed by an adult; disposition of a child in a delinquency proceeding may be considered in imposing a sentence
Oklahoma	No confidentiality for violent felony	OK ST T. 10 § 7307-1.2: Confidentiality requirements shall not apply for juvenile court records and law enforcement records upon the charging of a violent felony
Oregon	Consider in sentencing	OR ST § 419A.255: Juvenile records privileged except in connection with presentencing investigation

STATE	TREATMENT	DETAILS
Pennsylvania	Consider in sentencing	PA ST 42 Pa.C.S.A. § 6308: Law enforcement records concerning a child may be inspected pursuant to drafting a presentencing report
Rhode Island	Consider felonies at sentencing	RI ST § 14-1-40: Any finding of delinquency based on acts that would constitute a felony if committed by an adult shall be available to the attorney general for use in its recommendation to any court in sentencing
South Carolina	No expunging for violent felonies	SC ST § 20-7-1335: Under no circumstances is a person allowed to expunge from his record an adjudication for having committed a violent crime
South Dakota	Consider in sentencing	SD ST § 26-7A-120: Juvenile records are confidential but may be inspected or disclosed to justices, judges, magistrates, and employees of the judicial system in the course of their duties
Tennessee	Consider serious offenses in sentencing as enhancement factor	TN ST § 40-35-114: Enhancement factors may include a juvenile adjudication if the offense would have constituted a felony if committed by an adult
Texas	Consider in sentencing	TX-ST-ANN § 51.13: An order of adjudication or disposition under the Juvenile Justice Code may be used in sentencing proceedings in criminal court
Utah	Public for violent felonies	UT ST J ADMIN Rule 4.202.02: Record of juvenile act that if committed by an adult would be charged as a violent felony shall be public
Vermont	Consider in sentencing	VT ST T. 33 § 5536: Inspection of juvenile court records is not prohibited by court imposing a sentence
Virginia	Consider in sentencing	VA-ST-ANN § 16.1-306: A copy of the court order of disposition in a delinquency case shall be provided to a probation officer or attorney of the Commonwealth, when requested, for the purpose of calculating sentencing guidelines

STATE	TREATMENT	DETAILS
Washington	Consider in sentencing	WA ST 13.50.050. The juvenile offense record of any adult convicted of a crime and placed under the supervision of the adult correction system shall be released upon request to the adult corrections system
West Virginia	Consider in sentencing	WV ST § 49-5-17: Upon written petition and pursuant to a written order, the circuit court may permit disclosure of juvenile records to a court exercising criminal jurisdiction over the juvenile that requests such records for the purpose of a presentencing report or disposition proceeding; records of a juvenile describing an act that would be a violent felony if committed by an adult may not be sealed
Wisconsin	Consider in sentencing	WI ST 938.78: Confidentiality requirement of juvenile records does not prohibit disclosure for a presentencing investigation
Wyoming	Consider in sentencing	WY ST § 14-3-437: Juvenile records shall be sealed and the court shall not release them except to an agency preparing a presentencing report for another court

NOTES

1. I deliberately chose to speak with male rather than female youths for a number of reasons, although I fully realize that it injects tremendous gender bias into my research—
and to that I must, uncomfortably and unhappily, plead guilty. I wanted to speak with
youths who had firsthand experience with guns, and those rates are highest among
male incarcerated youths. But even more important, I wanted to conduct most of the
interviewing myself, and I felt more comfortable doing same-sex interviews, especially with adolescents who are incarcerated. The interviews were conducted in private, in a conference room in the administration building, and it was important for the
success of the research to create a closed, intimate environment where the youths felt
safe talking about things that could incriminate them. I thought it would be more convenient and less dangerous to create this environment with male youths. Given the
highly sexual nature of the attraction to guns and the sexual-symbolic dimensions of
guns and gun carrying, I can only hope that future researchers will focus on female
youths as well.

2. I personally conducted twenty-two of the interviews, and my assistant Craig
LaChance, a second-year law student with a master's degree in philosophy, conducted
eight. Before he interviewed any youths, I instructed LaChance on the interview protocol and techniques and had him review in detail both a written transcript of an interview I had conducted and an audiotape of another interview I had conducted. I also
reviewed the audiotape of LaChance's first interview and gave him comments and
direction regarding his interview techniques.

3. There are, naturally, drawbacks to interviewing *incarcerated* youths, especially the
possible bias introduced by interviewing within the prison system (see Wright and
Decker 1994, 5). However, the likelihood of getting a large sample of youths who had
firsthand experience with guns, given the high rates of past gun carrying among male
youths in detention, is a distinct advantage. And as Wright and Decker note, "There is
little hard evidence available on which to judge whether active offenders really do
think and act differently than their incarcerated counterparts" (Wright and Decker
1994, 6).

4. Replicability is, of course, a critical concern. The best way to validate the results
I obtained is to perform an internal audit (Morrill et al. 2000, 535).

5. In their study, Sheley and Wright report that their respondents' desire to arm themselves is motivated primarily by a perceived need for protection (1995, 64–65, 67, 115).
In the Ash study conducted in Atlanta, Georgia, forty-seven, or approximately 89 percent, of the fifty-three juvenile offenders who had carried guns responded that the
most important reason to carry a gun was "for protection" (Ash et al. 1996, 1755; see
also Ash et al. 1996, 1757n5, 1757n14; May 1999, 101; Page and Hammermeister 1997,
507; Goldberg and Schwabe 1999, 19; "Kids and Guns" 2000, 7; Decker, Pennell, and

Caldwell 1997, 4). David Hemenway and his colleagues administered a survey to more than one thousand seventh-through tenth-graders at twelve inner-city schools in two large cities in the Northeast and Midwest and also found that the overwhelming reason youths gave for carrying guns was self-protection (Hemenway et al. 1996).

6. I have been focusing here on primary associations. There was, of course, much talk about peers and their feelings about guns, which I coded as tertiary associations, and these too were mixed. CMS-6, for example, explains that his friends "didn't really want me around them" when he was carrying a gun (CMS-6, 24). CMS-46 explains that his friends—with the exception of one who carries a .45 semiautomatic all the time—would try to talk him out of carrying. "They'd probably just, you know, question me, why, why do I carry the gun. You know, it's gonna cause me more problems. And just they'll be questioning me about it" (CMS-46, 22). On the other hand, although these youths may not think guns are cool, they are likely to say that their friends would probably think that carrying a gun was cool. CMS-53, who himself thinks that guns are "dumb," stated that his friends "probably think it was cool" (CMS-53, 17). Similarly, CMS-69, who believes that guns are "stupid," believes his friends think guns are "cool" (CMS-69, 6).

7. There is, possibly, a fourth cluster that associates the "kill" meaning with "revenge." These two meanings are slightly outside the action/protection cluster. They are not that far out, but a bit off, a bit farther to the extreme. In the subsequent analysis it will become clear that this cluster merges into the action/protection cluster and plays a rather insignificant role in the analysis. Accordingly, I will note this cluster here but not emphasize it.

8. When using the SAS program, the scores on Dimension 1 in figures 5.1 and 5.2 are inverted. Since it is the relational features of correspondence analysis that are definitive, and not which end of the axis is put on the left or right of the graph, it is possible to flip a dimension without affecting its meaning. In other words, one can multiply all scores on any axis by minus one without changing the correspondence analysis results. In this case I have done just that. I have multiplied the scores for the gang analysis by minus one, in order to preserve symmetry with figure 5.1.

9. A beer run is when a youth enters a convenience store, grabs a six-pack, and runs. The thrill is to make it out without getting caught by the attendant.

10. "Faites-vous une distinction entre signification et signifié?"

11. "Oui, pour moi le signifié c'est l'objet. Je définis mon langage qui n'est pas nécessairement celui des linguistes: cette '*chaise*,' c'est l'objet, donc c'est le signifié; ensuite, il y a la signification, c'est l'ensemble logique qui sera constitué par des mots, la signification d'une phrase. Si je dis 'Cette table est devant la fenêtre,' je vise un signifié qui est la table par des significations qui sont l'ensemble des phrases qui sont constituées, et *je me considère moi-même comme le signifiant*. La signification, c'est le noème, le corrélat de l'ensemble des éléments vocaux proférés" (emphasis added).

12. The act of negation—of rejecting our condition—occurs when the individual pursues a project, goes after a goal, acts intentionally. And it is through this act of negating the present that the individual is free. Freedom is precisely the ability to negate a present

condition. "Freedom is the human being placing his past off-sides, and secreting his own nothingness" (1943, 64). This is, for Sartre, a moment of great anxiety—an anxiety that makes us conscious of our freedom. "It is through anxiety," Sartre holds, "that man becomes conscious of his freedom" (1943, 64).

13. For Sartre, central to any analysis is discovering the subject's fundamental project, the one that integrates all other projects, and exploring how it changes as the person is faced with new situations. This is the goal of "existential psychoanalysis," which Sartre developed and applied in his existential biographies such as *Saint Genet*. And there is a strong parallel here with the idea of hope or faith: the idea that youths are stuck in their situations because they lack hope, they lack a vision of a better world, they lack the tools to even imagine a better world. It is unclear, in Sartre's work, how the subject steps back, what it is that promotes this move, what triggers the negation. But what is clear is that it is central to acting freely, to getting into a position to change one's situation. And this makes every one of us responsible for our own situation.

14. Here Sartre develops a really radical conception of freedom. As he emphasizes, "I am condemned to exist for ever beyond . . . the motives and motivations of my act: I am condemned to be free" (1943, 494). Or as Sartre writes in another passage of *L'être et le néant*: "I emerge alone and in anxiety, faced with the unique and first project that constitutes my being. All barriers, all restraints fall, negated by the conscience of my freedom: I do not have, nor can I have, any recourse to any value against the fact that it is me that keeps values alive; nothing can save me from myself, cut off from the world and from my essence by this nothingness that I *am*. I have to realize the meaning of the world and of my essence: I decide, alone, unjustifiably and without excuse" (Sartre 1943, 75).

15. Incidentally, Hugo is not alone. Hoederer himself also gave meaning to Hugo's act. In his final gasp, Hoederer saves Hugo from the bodyguard, telling the bodyguard that he had been sleeping with Hugo's wife—a complete fabrication meant only to redefine Hugo's act and save him from immediate execution. Sartre himself placed great importance on Hoederer's final act, suggesting that Hoederer was trying to avoid further internal strife in the party—that Hoederer's act reflected a deep commitment to the party (Sartre 1976, 217–20). (Another reading is that it reflected Hoederer's love for Hugo.)

16. Mostly for historical reasons, there were no direct points of contact between Sartre and Lévi-Strauss during the early formative period of existentialism. Lévi-Strauss spent most of the war in the United States, as well as the next several years serving as a cultural attaché, and was not well versed in the early existentialist writings (Lévi-Strauss and Éribon 1988, 70). Lévi-Strauss had only a passing acquaintance with the early existentialism and, as we will see, was at odds with it methodologically (Lévi-Strauss 1955, 61). Surprisingly, one of the only indirect points of contact in this period was a review by Simone de Beauvoir of Lévi-Strauss's first book, *Les structures élémentaires de la parenté*, that appeared in Beauvoir and Sartre's journal, *Les Temps Modernes* (Beauvoir 1949). So what we have to do here is creatively imagine the conversation that would have occurred—a conversation that Lévi-Strauss himself,

perhaps, would not have contemplated (see Lévi-Strauss and Éribon 1988, 101: "Le terme [structuraliste] a été galvaudé, on en a fait des applications illégitimes, parfois même ridicules. Je n'y peux rien").

17. Alternatively, drawing on Lévi-Strauss's writings on kinship, we could try to decipher recurring sociocultural patterns of relations between the Catalina youths and their peers, parents, or parole officers. Here again, we would need to place the youths' narratives within the larger framework of kinship relations in their time and place, but the resulting structural analysis would allow us to better understand how the relations interact with each other. One idea, for instance, would be to try to treat these four relations as a kinship structure, as a unit of kinship, and to locate patterns in the set of oppositions between these paternal, maternal, spousal, and mentor relations. We could code these for whether they are "free and familiar relations" or characterized "by hostility, antagonism, or reserve" (Lévi-Strauss 1967a, 43) and then try to identify recurring oppositions between these relations. Applying this method to some of Malinowski's findings, Lévi-Strauss explained: "When we consider societies of the Cherkess [Caucasus] and Trobriand [Melanesia] types it is not enough to study the correlation of attitudes between *father/son* and *uncle/sister's son*. This correlation is only one aspect of a global system containing four types of relationships which are organically linked, namely: *brother/sister*, *husband/wife*, *father/son*, and *mother's brother/sister's son*. The two groups in our example illustrate a law which can be formulated as follows: In both groups, the relation between maternal uncle and nephew is to the relation between brother and sister as the relation between father and son is to that between husband and wife. Thus, if we know one pair of relations, it is always possible to infer the other" (Lévi-Strauss 1967a, 40).

This would represent yet another way to approach the dynamics within the Catalina interviews. In effect, the idea would be to try to decipher the youths' social relationships *in relation* to oppositions between other kinship relations.

18. Lévi-Strauss's tendency toward binarism is reflected well, for instance, in the following passage from *The Savage Mind*: "All the levels of classification in fact have a common characteristic: whichever, in the society under consideration, is put first it must authorize—or even imply—possible recourse to other levels, formally analogous to the favoured one and differing from it only in their relative position within a whole system of reference which operates by means of a pair of contrasts: between general and particular on the one hand, and nature and culture on the other" (Lévi-Strauss 1966, 135; see also 217).

19. It is in this context that Lévi-Strauss famously describes the processes of the "untamed mind" as resembling *bricolage*—the art or craft of salvaging elements from previous uses and recycling them to create new objects and accomplish new projects. Lévi-Strauss compares this form of scientific thought to Western scientific approaches— what he refers to as *engineering*. The engineer, in contrast to the *bricoleur*, privileges raw materials and specifically designs tools and mechanisms for the completion of the project (Lévi-Strauss 1962, 26–33).

A central tenet of Lévi-Strauss's work, naturally, was that the two modes of thought do not in fact differ as much as one would expect. The difference between the two, he observes, is "less absolute than it might appear": the engineer, it turns out, just like the *bricoleur*, "has to begin by making a catalogue of a previously determined set consisting of theoretical and practical knowledge, of technical means, which restrict the possible solutions" (Lévi-Strauss 1966, 19 [1962, 29]). His point is that native thought processes do not in fact differ from modern ones. This point he made much earlier, in 1955, in "The Structural Study of Myth," where he wrote: "Prevalent attempts to explain alleged differences between the so-called primitive mind and scientific thought have resorted to qualitative differences between the working processes of the mind in both cases . . . If our interpretation is correct, we are led toward a completely different view—namely, that the kind of logic in mythical thought is as rigorous as that of modern science, and that the difference lies, not in the quality of the intellectual process, but in the nature of the things to which it is applied . . . [T]he same logical processes operate in myth as in science, and . . . man has always been thinking equally well; the improvement lies, not in an alleged progress of man's mind, but in the discovery of new areas to which it may apply its unchanged and unchanging powers" (Lévi-Strauss 1967d, 227).

20. Similarly, in *Tristes tropiques*, Lévi-Strauss described the existentialist approach as "completely illegitimate by reason of its complacency regarding the illusion of subjectivity. Its tendency to promote personal preoccupations to the level of philosophical problems threatens to lead to a sort of vulgar metaphysics, excusable as a didactic measure but very dangerous if it interferes with the mission of philosophy (a mission given to philosophy until such time as science becomes strong enough to replace it), which is to understand Being in relation to itself, and not in relation to myself. Instead of abolishing metaphysics, phenomenology and existentialism introduce its alibi" (Lévi-Strauss 1955, 61).

21. Sartre's attempted reconciliation of existentialism and Marxism in the *Critique* rests primarily on two key concepts: scarcity and seriality. The notion of scarcity stands for the uneven distribution and short supply of goods necessary to satisfy our basic needs. In essence, Sartre argues in the *Critique* that the present condition of scarcity is not inevitable and will be overcome when men and women dismantle the social structures, namely the class structures, that have emerged in response to scarcity. In his view, the impediments to the more equal distribution of goods are of people's own making and will be resolved when groups of individuals take on the type of projects that are more familiar to us from Sartre's earlier existentialist writings. The notion of seriality represents the initial stage of group formation, and the key to resolving collective action problems. Seriality, in contrast to the already formed group, occurs when a cluster of people are brought together by contingencies and begin to see that they have something in common. Sartre's famous illustration is people waiting at a bus stop and beginning to form alliances when the bus does not arrive on time. According to Sartre, these "groups in fusion" offer the potential for radical action because they have not yet become bureaucratized (for an interesting contemporary

discussion of seriality, see Young 1997). Sartre's *Critique* thus offers both a historical analysis of our present condition and a historical account of potential future action that attempts to incorporate both his earlier notion of the individual's radical freedom and a theory of dialectical materialism.

22. In addition, for many young leftists in France during the 1960s, the structuralism of Lévi-Strauss offered a theoretical avenue that valued other cultures, especially non-Western cultures. Not only did Lévi-Strauss's work explicitly reject the idea that primitive societies were in any sense inferior, it also offered a critique of the universalizing tendencies in Western thought that seemed to serve only imperialist goals. As Mark Lilla explains, "Lévi-Strauss' structuralism cast doubt on the universality of any political rights or values, and also raised suspicions about the 'man' who claimed them. Weren't these concepts simply a cover for the West's ethnocentrism, colonialism, and genocide, as Lévi-Strauss charged? And wasn't Sartre's Marxism polluted by the same ideas?" (Lilla 2001, 167). By studying non-Western cultures and praising them, Lévi-Strauss was offering a living example of the value of the other. "And though Lévi-Strauss may not have intended it, his writings would soon feed the suspicion among the New Left that grew up in the Sixties that all the universal ideas to which Europe claimed allegiance—reason, science, progress, liberal democracy—were culturally specific weapons fashioned to rob the non-European Other of his difference" (Lilla 2001, 168).

23. A number of American sociologists, especially Ronald Breiger and John Mohr, are pushing the frontiers of practice theory and focusing precisely on "the duality of culture and practice" (Mohr and Duquenne 1997; see also Mohr 1998, 2000; Breiger 2000). The central argument of these practice theorists, as Ronald Breiger explains, "is that the material world (the world of action) and the cultural world (the world of symbols) interpenetrate, and are built up through the immediate association of each with the other" (Breiger 2000, 92). As a result, they argue, the best way to understand social institutions and institutional practices is to explore the interrelationship between the web of meanings surrounding particular categories of actors and the web of practices that the institutions engage in. Much of this work also draws on the innovative research of Roger Friedland and Robert Alford and is in this sense closely connected to the new institutionalism approach in sociology (Friedland and Alford 1991; see generally Powell and DiMaggio 1991).

24. Calvin Morrill and Michael Musheno, in their research on youth conflict, have developed the idea of youth "action tales," by which they mean narratives of youth encounters that rest on taken-for-granted assumptions about roles, identities, and relationships between youths. Action tales, they suggest, are made up of prescripted, ingrained reactions and behaviors that are triggered by certain identifiable stimuli like a bump, a shove, or a stare. They represent a type of "interpersonal path dependency" that is structured by unstated cognitive expectations (Morrill et al. 2000, 17). "There is a preconscious, semi-automatic nature to the reasoning in an action tale that suggests practical action, rather than calculative or explicitly rule-based behavior . . . The authors of action tales emphasize 'the way things are' (especially personal

relationships and peer conflict) and the way 'conflict is to be handled' among peers. In their stories, conflict is a core mechanism by which assumptions about interpersonal relations are constituted, enacted, and sometimes tacitly challenged" (Morrill et al. 2000, 25). Morrill and Musheno locate their notion of "action tales" in the tradition of theories of practical action, more specifically in the work of cognitive sociologists and new institutional theorists (Morrill et al. 2000, 25, referring specifically to Cicourel 1974 and Powell and DiMaggio 1991).

25. "Poststructuralism" is a deeply contested term. For present purposes, I would locate the poststructuralist break with the linguistic structuralism of Claude Lévi-Strauss in the work of Michel Foucault. In relation to the four basic tenets of structuralism discussed in chapter 8, poststructuralism builds on the first three tenets but rejects the fourth—the idea that we could discover general laws. It builds on the notion that meanings are derived from relations of difference, that these are largely subconscious, and that they form a structure. But it emphasizes the gaps and ambiguities in the structure of meanings. Recall Lévi-Strauss's statement that "starting from ethnographic experience, I have always aimed at drawing up an inventory of mental patterns, to reduce apparently arbitrary data to some kind of order, and to attain a level at which a kind of necessity becomes apparent, underlying the illusions of liberty" (Lévi-Strauss [1964] 1970, 10). Poststructuralism does not subscribe to this. There are fluidities and slippages, and these help bring about shifts and changes in meaning and structure. In this sense, poststructuralism rejects the fourth tenet: structures of meanings are not universal and do not reflect ontological truths about humans or society. They have their own histories. They have developed over time and are shaped in part by the subject. Poststructuralists tend to historicize the structure of meaning, excavating the layers, exposing the contingency of the system and also showing how it shapes and is shaped by the subject. Note that Judith Butler locates the poststructuralist break principally in the work of Jacques Derrida (see Butler 1990, 158n6) and defines it as the rejection of "the claims of totality and universality and the presumption of binary structural oppositions that implicitly operate to quell the insistent ambiguity and openness of linguistic and cultural signification" (40). Whereas for Butler structuralists recognize the arbitrariness of the sign, they nevertheless tend to focus more on the completeness of the linguistic system at the expense of the moment of difference between the signifier and the signified. In contrast, Butler posits, poststructuralists focus on this moment of difference. "As a result, the discrepancy between signifier and signified becomes the operative and limitless *différance* of language, rendering all referentiality into a potentially limitless displacement" (40).

26. Youth firearm violence decreased significantly during the mid- to late 1990s. According to the Office of Juvenile Justice and Delinquency Prevention, there has been a sharp decline in homicides by juveniles between 1994 and 1997, and this drop is attributable entirely to a decline in firearm homicides (Snyder and Sickmund 2000, 54). Moreover, with regard to trends in weapons use by juveniles (including firearms, knives, or any other weapon type), the Office of Juvenile Justice and Delinquency Program notes that the arrest rate of juveniles for transgressions against weapons laws

doubled between 1987 and 1993. After 1993, the rates began declining and had dropped by 63 percent from 1994 to 1999 (Snyder 2000). The trend in juvenile gun homicides is vividly represented in figure 12.2 (adapted from Snyder and Sickmund 2000, 54).

Despite the downward decline, though, youth gun homicides have remained relatively high, proportionally, during this period. There is, in the words of Philip Cook and John Laub, "a hangover from this binge of violence" (Cook and Laub 2001, 4): "First, the relative importance of youths in the national violence picture, which increased greatly during the epidemic, has remained relatively high by historical standards; killers under age 25 account for 60 percent of homicides in 1998, compared to 43 percent in 1982 (before the epidemic began). Second, the relative involvement of blacks in homicide, which increased during the epidemic, has remained high during the downturn. Third, while gun homicides accounted for all of the youth homicide increase, they have shared the decline with non-gun homicides; the result is that the gun percentage in youth killings was almost as high in 1998 as in 1993, and much higher than in 1985" (Cook and Laub 2001, 4).

Cook and Laub explore a range of plausible explanations to make sense of these data, including cohort effects (especially the controversial abortion thesis) and period or environmental effects (especially the Blumstein drug market–firearm diffusion hypothesis). Although they exclude cohort effects, they do not offer a consensus explanation other than to observe that youths may be "responding to the same environmental factors associated with law enforcement, the economy, cultural change, routine activities, drug and gun markets, and so forth as are older adults" (2001, 22). In the end, though, it is still true, as Cook and Laub suggest, that "the drop in youth violence has been something of a mystery, just as was the prior increase" (2001, 4). The result, though, is that "the high concentration among minorities and males, and the prevalence of guns, may be long-lasting hangovers from the epidemic" (2001, 21).

27. Another initiative that resonates with the new progressive approach was launched by a judge in Detroit and involves an educational program for youthful gun offenders. The Handgun Intervention Program is intended to foster attitudinal and behavioral changes among young offenders who have been arrested for carrying a concealed weapon. As a condition of pretrial release these youths are diverted to "a class in which they would learn the negative consequences of gun use and be challenged to take personal responsibility for reducing those consequences" (Roth 1998, 1). Since the program began in 1993, more than six thousand youths have participated. The four-hour class is conducted on Saturday in a courtroom. "It attempts to awaken the participants to issues of personal choice, individual responsibility, and the role of non-violence in African-American history" (Roth 1998, 1). Apparently more than 90 percent of the participants are African American.

28. I assigned values to each of the six positions based on the analysis in the previous sections of this chapter. The assigned values are reflected in the following table (in percentages).

APPROACH	PHENOMENOLOGICAL	STRUCTURAL	PRACTICE THEORY	PERFORMATIVE
Moral poverty theory	10	85	5	0
Economic model	100	0	0	0
New progressivism	0	60	40	0
Procedural fairness	75	15	10	0
Self-control theory	20	80	0	0
Critical cultural studies	5	40	35	20

29. Moreover, as a way to target the action/protection cluster, a comparison of the correspondence maps strongly suggests that our policies should focus on gangs and gang membership. Given the strong association of attraction to guns—and more generally of the meanings of danger, protection, action, power, and belonging—to both gun carrying *and* gang membership, the analysis here suggests that antigang strategies are likely to be an effective way to address youths' gun carrying. The point here is that the symbolism of the gun that is connected to gun carrying also seems to be closely tied to the institution of gangs. Reducing gang practices may be an important way to get at the action/protection cluster.

30. Before extending the findings and analysis of this book beyond the narrow setting of the Catalina Mountain School, it would of course be necessary to listen to the voices of more youths, especially youths at the site of any planned intervention. There are reasons to believe that some of the responses of the Catalina youths may be similar to those of youths in other parts of the United States. Jeffrey Fagan and Deanna Wilkinson have conducted interview research in New York City among males sixteen to twenty-four, and they discovered many similar associations with guns (Fagan and Wilkinson 1998, 2000). Nevertheless, it is important to emphasize that this is a very localized study and that it would be absolutely necessary to conduct further research before extending these findings to other youths.

REFERENCES

Abbott, Andrew. 1997. "Seven Types of Ambiguity." *Theory and Society* 26:357–91.

Abel, Lionel. 1970. "Sartre vs. Lévi-Strauss." In *Claude Lévi-Strauss: The Anthropologist as Hero*, ed. E. Nelson Hayes and Tanya Hayes, 235–46. Cambridge: MIT Press.

Anderson, Elijah. 1999. *Code of the Street: Decency, Violence, and the Moral Life of the Inner City*. New York: Norton.

Ash, Peter, Arthur Kellermann, Dawna Fuqua-Whitley, and Amri Johnson. 1996. "Gun Acquisition and Use by Juvenile Offenders." *Journal of the American Medical Association* 275 (22): 1754–58.

Baker, Al. 2001. "Steep Rise in Gun Sales Reflects Post-attack Fears." *New York Times*, December 16.

Banfield, Edward C. 1958. *The Moral Basis of a Backward Society*. New York: Free Press.

————. 1970. *The Unheavenly City: The Nature and Future of Our Urban Crisis*. Boston: Little, Brown.

————. 1974. *The Unheavenly City Revisited*. Boston: Little, Brown.

————. 1991. *Here the People Rule: Selected Essays*, 2nd ed. Washington, DC: American Enterprise Institute.

Beauvoir, Simone de. 1949. *"Les structures élémentaires de la parenté*, par Claude Lévi-Strauss." *Les Temps Modernes* 49:943–49.

————. 1963. *La force des choses*. Paris: Gallimard.

Becker, Gary S. 1968. "Crime and Punishment: An Economic Approach." *Journal of Political Economy* 76 (March–April): 169–217.

Becker, Howard S. 1963. *Outsiders: Studies in the Sociology of Deviance*. New York: Free Press.

Beckett, Katherine. 1997. *Making Crime Pay: Law and Order in Contemporary American Politics*. New York: Oxford University Press.

Bennett, William J., John J. DiIulio, and John P. Walters. 1996. *Body Count: Moral Poverty—and How to Win America's War against Crime and Drugs*. New York: Simon and Schuster.

Bentham, Jeremy. 1789. *An Introduction to the Principles of Morals and Legislation*. London: T. Payne.

Beresford, Lisa S. 2000. "Is Lowering the Age at Which Juveniles Can Be Transferred to Adult Criminal Court the Answer to Juvenile Crime? A State-by-State Assessment." *San Diego Law Review* 37:783–851.

Bernard, Harvey Russell. 1995. *Research Methods in Anthropology: Qualitative and Quantitative Approaches*. Thousand Oaks, CA: Sage.

Berrien, Jenny, and Christopher Winship. 2003. "Should We Have Faith in the Churches? The Ten-Point Coalition's Effect on Boston's Youth Violence." In *Guns, Crime, and Punishment in America*, ed. Bernard E. Harcourt, 222–48. New York: New York University Press.

Black, Donald. 1983. "Crime as Social Control." *American Sociological Review* 48:34–45.

Blasius, Jörg. 1994. "Correspondence Analysis in Social Science Research." In *Correspondence Analysis in the Social Sciences: Recent Developments and Applications*, ed. Michael Greenacre and Jörg Blasius, 23–52. San Diego, CA: Academic Press.

Blasius, Jörg, and Michael Greenacre. 1994. "Computation of Correspondence Analysis." In *Correspondence Analysis in the Social Sciences: Recent Developments and Applications*, ed. Michael Greenacre and Jörg Blasius, 53–78. San Diego, CA: Academic Press.

———, eds. 1998. *Visualization of Categorical Data*. San Diego, CA: Academic Press.

Blumstein, Alfred. 1995. "Youth Violence, Guns, and the Illicit-Drug Industry." *Journal of Criminal Law and Criminology* 86:10–36.

———. 1998. "Violence Certainly Is the Problem—And Especially with Handguns." *University of Colorado Law Review* 69 (4): 945–67.

Blumstein, Alfred, and Daniel Cork. 1996. "Linking Gun Availability to Youth Gun Violence." *Law and Contemporary Problems* 59:5–19.

Blumstein, Alfred, and Richard Rosenfeld. 1998. "Explaining Recent Trends in U.S. Homicide Rates." *Journal of Criminal Law and Criminology* 88:1175–1216.

Bourdieu, Pierre. 1977. *Outline of a Theory of Practice*. Trans. Richard Nice. Cambridge: Cambridge University Press.

———. [1979] 1984. *Distinction: A Social Critique of the Judgement of Taste*. Trans. Richard Nice. Cambridge, MA: Harvard University Press.

———. [1984] 1988. *Homo Academicus*. Trans. Peter Collier. Stanford, CA: Stanford University Press.

———. 1990. *In Other Words: Essays towards a Reflexive Sociology*. Trans. Matthew Adamson. Stanford, CA: Stanford University Press.

———. 2000. *Pascalian Meditations*. Trans. Richard Nice. Cambridge: Polity Press.

Bourdieu, Pierre, and Loïc J. D. Wacquant. 1992. *An Invitation to Reflexive Sociology*. Chicago: University of Chicago Press.

Bourgois, Philippe. 1995. *In Search of Respect: Selling Crack in El Barrio*. Cambridge: Cambridge University Press.

Braun, Stephen. 2001. "The Young Guns of Alabama." *Los Angeles Times,* January 16. Available on *Westlaw* at 2001 WL 2452554.

Breiger, Ronald L. 1974. "The Duality of Persons and Groups." *Social Forces* 53:181–90.

———. 2000. "A Tool Kit for Practice Theory." *Poetics* 27:91–115.

Brown, Richard H. 1978. "Dialectic and Structure in Jean-Paul Sartre and Claude Lévi-Strauss." *Dialectica* 32 (2): 165–84.

Buchan, Bruce A. 1996. "Situated Consciousness or Consciousness of Situation? Autonomy and Antagonism in Jean-Paul Sartre's *Being and Nothingness*." *History of European Ideas* 22 (3): 193–215.

Butler, Judith. 1990. *Gender Trouble: Feminism and the Subversion of Identity*. New York: Routledge.

———. 1997. *Excitable Speech: A Politics of the Performative*. New York: Routledge.

Butterfield, Fox. 1999. "Overview: America under the Gun." *New York Times*, September 16. Available at http://www.nytimes.com/library/national/091699guns-overview.html.

Carley, Kathleen. 1993. "Coding Choices for Textual Analysis: A Comparison of Content Analysis and Map Analysis." *Sociological Methodology* 23:75–126.

Caws, Peter. 1988. *Structuralism: The Art of the Intelligible*. Atlantic Highlands, NJ: Humanities Press International.

———. 1992. "Sartrean Structuralism?" In *The Cambridge Companion to Sartre*, ed. Christina Howells, 293–317. Cambridge: Cambridge University Press.

Cianci, Vincent. 2000. "R.I.'s Capital City Is Still on a Big Roll." *Providence Journal*, June 27, 2000. Available on Westlaw at 2000 WL 21735931.

Cicourel, Aaron V. 1974. *Cognitive Sociology: Language and Meaning in Social Interaction*. New York: Free Press.

Cintron, Ralph. 1997. *Angels' Town: Chero Ways, Gang Life, and Rhetorics of the Everyday*. Boston: Beacon Press.

Clarke, Ronald. 1995. "Situational Crime Prevention." In *Building a Safer Society: Strategic Approaches to Crime Prevention*, ed. M. Tonry and D. Farrington, 91–150. Chicago: University of Chicago Press.

Clarke, Ronald V., and Pat Mayhew. 1988. "The British Gas Suicide Story and Its Criminological Implications." In *Crime and Justice: A Review of Research*, ed. Michael Tonry and Norval Morris, 10:107. Chicago: University of Chicago Press.

Cohen, Albert K. 1955. *Delinquency Boys: The Culture of the Gang*. New York: Free Press.

Cohen, Dov. 1996. "Law, Social Policy, and Violence: The Impact of Regional Cultures." *Journal of Personality and Social Psychology* 70 (5): 961–78.

———. 1998. "Culture, Social Organization, and Patterns of Violence." *Journal of Personality and Social Psychology* 75 (2): 408–19.

Cohen, Dov, and Joe Vandello. 1998. "Meanings of Violence." *Journal of Legal Studies* 27 (2, part 2): 567–84.

Cook, Philip J., and Anthony A. Braga. 2003. "New Law Enforcement Uses for Comprehensive Firearms Trace Data." In *Guns, Crime, and Punishment in America*, ed. Bernard E. Harcourt, 163–87. New York: New York University Press.

Cook, Philip J., and John H. Laub. 2001. "After the Epidemic: Recent Trends in Youth Violence in the United States." National Bureau of Economic Research, Working Paper 8571. Available at http://www.nber.org/papers/w8571.

Cooter, Robert D., and Thomas S. Ullen. 1997. *Law and Economics*, 2nd ed. Chicago: Scott, Foresman.

Cork, Daniel. 1999. "Examining Space-Time Interaction in City-Level Homicide Data: Crack Markets and the Diffusion of Guns among Youth." *Journal of Quantitative Criminology* 15:379–406.

Corzine, Jay, Lin Huff-Corzine, and Hugh P. Whitt. 1999. "Cultural and Subcultural Theories of Homicide." In *Homicide: A Sourcebook of Social Research*, ed. Dwayne M. Smith and Margaret A. Zahn, 42–57. Thousand Oaks, CA: Sage.

Daly, Christopher B. 1995. "Judge Draws a Powerful Weapon: Special Rhode Island 'Gun Court' Takes Aim at Firearms-Related Crime." *Washington Post,* February 24. Available on *Westlaw* at 1995 WL 2080119.

Dau-Schmidt, Kenneth G. 1990. "An Economic Analysis of the Criminal Law as a Preference-Shaping Policy." *Duke Law Journal* 1990:1.

Decker, Scott H., Susan Pennell, and Ami Caldwell. 1997. "Illegal Firearms: Access and Use by Arrestees." *National Institute of Justice Research in Brief*, January 1997.

Delacampagne, Christian, and Bernard Traimond. 1997. "La polémique Sartre/Lévi-Strauss revisitée: Aux sources des sciences sociales d'aujourd'hui." *Les Temps Modernes* 596:10–31.

Descombes, Vincent. 1979. *Le même et l'autre: Quarante-cinq ans de philosophie française (1933–1978)*. Paris: Éditions de Minuit.

———. 1980. *Modern French Philosophy*. Trans. L. Scott-Fox and J. M. Harding. Cambridge: Cambridge University Press.

Donohue, John, and Steven Levitt. 2001. "The Impact of Legalized Abortion on Crime." *Quarterly Journal of Economics* 116 (2): 379–420.

Dovi, Suzanne. 2005. "Guilt and the Problem of Dirty Hands." *Constellations* 12 (1): 128–46.

Drug Enforcement Administration. 1999. U.S. Department of Justice, Drug Enforcement Administration, "Drugs of Concern." Available at http://www.usdoj. gov/dea/concern.

Durkheim, Émile. [1893] 1984. *On the Division of Labor in Society*. New York: Free Press.

———. 1901. "Deux lois de l'évolution pénale." *Année Sociologique* 1899–1900.

———. 1995. *The Elementary Forms of Religious Life*. New York: Free Press.

Elster, John. 1983. *Sour Grapes: Studies in the Subversion of Rationality*. Cambridge: Cambridge University Press.

———. 1989. *The Cement of Society: A Study of Social Order*. Cambridge: Cambridge University Press.

Emerson, Robert M., Rachel I. Fretz, and Linda L. Shaw. 1995. *Writing Ethnographic Fieldnotes*. Chicago: University of Chicago Press.

Fagan, Jeffrey. 1999a. "Context and Culpability in Adolescent Crime." *Virginia Journal of Social Policy and the Law* 6:507–81.

———. 1999b. "Social Contagion of Violence." Paper presented at the Fortunoff Colloquium Series, Center for Research on Crime and Justice, New York University Law School, April 19.

Fagan, Jeffrey, and Deanna Wilkinson. 1998. "Guns, Youth Violence, and Social Identity in Inner Cities." In *Crime and Justice: A Review of Research*, no. 24, ed. Michael Tonry et al., 105–88. Chicago: University of Chicago Press.

———. 2000. *Situational Contexts of Gun Use by Young Males, Final Report, January 2000*. Report submitted to National Science Foundation, National Institute of Justice, and U.S. Department of Health and Human Services.

Fagan, Jeffrey, and Franklin Zimring. 2000a. "Editors' Introduction." In *The Changing Borders of Juvenile Justice: Transfer of Adolescents to the Criminal Court*, ed. Jeffrey Fagan and Franklin Zimring, 1–10. Chicago: University of Chicago Press.

———, eds. 2000b. *The Changing Borders of Juvenile Justice: Transfer of Adolescents to the Criminal Court*. Chicago: University of Chicago Press.

Fagan, Jeffrey, Franklin E. Zimring, and June Kim. 1998. "Declining Homicide in New York City: A Tale of Two Trends." *Journal of Criminal Law and Criminology* 88:1277–1324.

Fan, D. 1988. *Predictions of Public Opinion from the Mass Media: Computer Content Analysis and Mathematical Modeling*. New York: Greenwood Press.

Flyvbjerg, Bent. 1998. *Rationality and Power: Democracy in Practice*. Chicago: University of Chicago Press.

———. 2001. *Making Social Science Matter: Why Social Inquiry Fails and How It Can Succeed Again*. Cambridge: Cambridge University Press.

Ford, Richard T. 2002. "Beyond 'Difference': A Reluctant Critique of Legal Identity Politics." Paper delivered to the Spring 2002 Faculty Workshop Series at Harvard Law School, May 1.

Foucault, Michel. 1966. *Les mots et les choses*. Paris: Gallimard.

———. 1975. *Surveiller et punir*. Paris: Gallimard.

———. 1979. *Discipline and Punish*. Trans. A. Sheridan. New York: Vintage Books.

———. 1983. "Structuralisme et poststructuralisme." In *Dits et écrits 1954–1988*, vol. 4, *1980–1988*, 431–57. Paris: Éditions Gallimard.

Fox, James Alan. 1999. Uniform Crime Reports [United States]: Supplementary Homicide Reports, 1976–1994. ICPSR 6754. Ann Arbor, MI: Inter-University Consortium for Political and Social Research.

Friedland, Roger, and Robert R. Alford. 1991. "Bringing Society Back In: Symbols, Practices and Institutional Contradictions." In *The New Institutionalism in Organizational Analysis*, ed. Walter W. Powell and Paul DiMaggio, 232–63. Chicago: University of Chicago Press.

Garland, David. 1990. *Punishment and Modern Society*. Chicago: University of Chicago Press.

———. 2001. *The Culture of Control*. Chicago: University of Chicago Press.

Gastil, Raymond D. 1971. "Homicide and a Regional Culture of Violence." *American Sociological Review* 36:412–27.

Geertz, Clifford. 1967. "The Cerebral Savage: On the Work of Claude Lévi-Strauss." *Encounter* 48 (4): 25–32.

Geis, Gilbert. 2000. "On the Absence of Self-Control as the Basis for a General Theory of Crime: A Critique." *Theoretical Criminology* 4 (1): 35–53.

Gest, Ted. 1997. "A Taxpayer's Guide to Crime and Punishment: A New Study Shows What Strategies Work." *U.S. News and World Report*, April 21. Available on Westlaw at 1997 WL 8331912.

Gest, Ted, and Dorian Friedman. 1994. "The New Crime Wave: A Teen Boom Will Fuel More Violence No Matter What Washington Does." *U.S. News and World Report*, August 29. Available on Westlaw at 1994 WL 11127447.

Goldberg, Julie H., and William Schwabe. 1999. *How Youthful Offenders Perceive Gun Violence*. Washington, DC.: RAND.

Golub, Andrew Lang, and Bruce D. Johnson. 1997. "Crack's Decline: Some Surprises across U.S. Cities." *National Institute of Justice, Research in Brief*, July 1997.

Goodman, Leo A. 1996. "A Single General Method for the Analysis of Cross-Classified Data: Reconciliation and Synthesis of Some Methods of Pearson, Yule, and Fisher, and Also Some Methods of Correspondence Analysis and Association Analysis." *Journal of the American Statistical Association* 91:408–28.

———. 1997. "Statistical Methods, Graphical Displays, and Tukey's Ladder of Re-expression in the Analysis of Nonindependence in Contingency Tables: Correspondence Analysis, Association Analysis, and the Midway View of Nonindependence." In *The Practice of Data Analysis: Essays in Honor of John W. Tukey*, ed. D. R. Brillinger, L. T. Fernholz, and S. Morgenthaler, 101–32. Princeton, NJ: Princeton University Press.

Gouldner, Alvin W. 1968. "The Sociologist as Partisan: Sociology and the Welfare State." *American Sociologist* 3:103–16.

———. 1970. *The Coming Crisis of Western Sociology*. New York: Basic Books.

Greenacre, Michael J. 1993. *Correspondence Analysis in Practice*. London: Academic Press.

———. 1994. "Correspondence Analysis and Its Interpretation." In *Correspondence Analysis in the Social Sciences: Recent Developments and Applications*, ed. Michael Greenacre and Jörg Blasius, 3–22. San Diego, CA: Academic Press.

Greenacre, Michael, and Jörg Blasius, eds. 1994. *Correspondence Analysis in the Social Sciences: Recent Developments and Applications*. San Diego, CA: Academic Press.

Grier, Chris. 2001. "Many Tout Gun Law's Success, but Not Everyone; Experts Debate Gun Law's Effects: Project Exile Hasn't Been Proven to Cut State Crime Some Say." *Virginia Pilot*, February 5, 2001. Available on Westlaw at 2001 WL 9709893.

Grogger, Jeffrey, and Michael Willis. 2000. "The Emergence of Crack Cocaine and the Rise of Urban Crime Rates." *Review of Economics and Statistics* 82:519–29.

Harcourt, Bernard. 1998a. "Reflecting on the Subject: A Critique of the Social Influence Conception of Deterrence, the Broken Windows Theory, and Order-Maintenance Policing New York Style." *Michigan Law Review* 97:291–389.

———. 1998b. "Placing Shame in Context: A Response to Thomas Scheff on Community Conferences and Therapeutic Jurisprudence." *Revista Juridica U.P.R.* 67:627–34.

———. 2001. *Illusion of Order: The False Promise of Broken Windows Policing*. Cambridge, MA: Harvard University Press.

———, ed. 2003. *Guns, Crime, and Punishment in America*. New York: New York University Press.

———. 2006. *Against Prediction: Sentencing, Policing, and Punishing in an Actuarial Age*. Chicago: University of Chicago Press. Forthcoming.

Hartmann, Klaus. 1971. "Lévi-Strauss and Sartre." *Journal of the British Society for Phenomenology* 2 (3): 37–45.

Haussler, Alexa. 1995. "Guns, Gangs, Drugs Raise Toll of Dead Teens." *Arizona Daily Star*, July 23.

Hemenway, David. 2004. *Private Guns, Public Health*. Ann Arbor: University of Michigan Press.

Hemenway, David, Deborah Prothrow-Stith, Jack M. Bergstein, Roseanna Ander, and Bruce P. Kennedy. 1996. "Gun Carrying among Adolescents." *Law and Contemporary Problems* 59:39–53.

Hirschi, Travis, and Michael Gottfredson. 1990. *A General Theory of Crime*. Stanford, CA: Stanford University Press.

———. 2000. "In Defense of Self-Control." *Theoretical Criminology* 4 (1): 55–69.

Hollway, Wendy, and Tony Jefferson. 2000. *Doing Qualitative Research Differently: Free Association, Narrative and the Interview Method*. London: Sage.

Huizinga, David, and Delbert S. Elliott. 1986. "Reassessing the Reliability and Validity of Self-Report Delinquency Measures." *Journal of Quantitative Criminology* 2 (4): 293–327.

Jacobs, James B. 2002. *Can Gun Control Work?* New York: Oxford University Press.

Jeanson, Francis. 1955. *Sartre par lui-même*. Paris: Éditions du Seuil.

Jolls, Christine, Cass R. Sunstein, and Richard Thaler. 1998. "A Behavioral Approach to Law and Economics." *Stanford Law Review* 50:1471–1550.

Kahan, Dan M. 1998. "Social Meaning and the Economic Analysis of Crime." *Journal of Legal Studies* 27:609–22.

Kahan, Dan M., and Tracey L. Meares. 1998. "Law and (Norms of) Order in the Inner City." *Law and Society Review* 32:805–38.

———. 1999a. "When Rights Are Wrong." *Boston Review* 24 (2): 4–8.

———. 1999b. "Meares and Kahan Respond." *Boston Review* 24 (2): 22–23.

Katz, Jack. 1988. *Seductions of Crime: Moral and Sensual Attractions in Evil Doing*. New York: Basic Books.

Kaufmann, Walter. 1971. "Sartre as a Playwright: *The Flies* and *Dirty Hands*." In *Sartre: A Collection of Critical Essays*, ed. Mary Warnock, 244–59. Garden City, NY: Anchor Books.

Kennedy, David M. 1997. "Juvenile Gun Violence and Gun Markets in Boston." *NIJ Research Preview*, March 1997.

———. 1998. "Pulling Levers: Getting Deterrence Right." *National Institute of Justice Journal* 236 (July): 2–8.

Kennedy, Duncan. 1994. "A Semiotics of Legal Argument." In *Collected Courses of the Academy of European Law*, vol. 3, bk. 2, 309–65. Netherlands: Kluwer Academic.

"Kids and Guns." 2000. *Juvenile Justice Bulletin*. U.S. Department of Justice, Office of Justice Programs, Office of Juvenile Justice and Delinquency Prevention, March.

Kilborn, Peter T. 1992. "The Gun Culture: Fun as Well as Life and Death." *New York Times*, March 9, 1992.

Kiser, Edgar. 1997. "Comment: Evaluating Qualitative Methodologies." *Sociological Methodology* 27:151–58.

Kris, Anton O. 1982. *Free Association: Method and Process*. New Haven, CT: Yale University Press.

Larrabee, John. 1994. "'You're Going to Jail Fast' in Nation's First Gun Court." *USA Today,* December 19. Available on *Westlaw* at 1994 WL 11077134.

LeDuff, Charlie. 2001. "A Perilous 4,000-Mile Passage to Work." *New York Times*, May 29, 2001.

Lévi-Strauss, Claude. 1955. *Tristes tropiques*. Paris: Librairie Plon.

———. 1962. *La pensée sauvage*. Paris: Librairie Plon.

———. [1964] 1969. *The Raw and the Cooked: Introduction to a Science of Mythology*. Trans. John Weightman and Doreen Weightman. New York: Harper and Row.

———. 1966. *The Savage Mind*. Trans. John Weightman and Doreen Weightman. Chicago: University of Chicago Press.

———. 1967a. "Structural Analysis." In *Structural Anthropology*, ed. Claire Jacobson and Brooke Grundfest Schoepf, 29–53. Garden City, NY: Doubleday.

———. 1967b. "Language and the Analysis of Social Laws." In *Structural Anthropology*, ed. Claire Jacobson and Brooke Grundfest Schoepf, 54–65. Garden City, NY: Doubleday.

———. 1967c. "The Sorcerer and His Magic." In *Structural Anthropology*, ed. Claire Jacobson and Brooke Grundfest Schoepf, 161–80. Garden City, NY: Doubleday.

———. 1967d. "The Structural Study of Myth." In *Structural Anthropology*, ed. Claire Jacobson and Brooke Grundfest Schoepf, 202–28. Garden City, NY: Doubleday.

Lévi-Strauss, Claude, and Didier Éribon. 1988. *De près et de loin*. Paris: Éditions Odile Jacob.

Levitt, Steven D. 1998. "Juvenile Crime and Punishment." *Journal of Political Economy* 106 (6): 1156–85.

Levitt, Steven D., and Sudhir Alladi Venkatesh. 1998. "An Economic Analysis of a Drug-Selling Gang's Finances." National Bureau of Economic Research Working Paper, June 1998.

Lewis, Oscar. 1966. *La Vida: A Puerto Rican Family in the Culture of Poverty—San Juan and New York*. New York: Vintage Books.

Lilla, Mark. 2001. *The Reckless Mind: Intellectuals in Politics*. New York: New York Review Books.

Lombroso, Cesare. [1899] 1912. *Crime: Its Causes and Remedies*. Trans. Henry P. Horton. Boston: Little, Brown.

Lott, John R. 1998. *More Guns, Less Crime*. Chicago: University of Chicago Press.

Lott, John R., and John E. Whitley. 2000. "Safe Storage Gun Laws: Accidental Deaths, Suicides, and Crime." SSRN Paper Collection at http://papers.ssrn.com/sol3/papers.cfm?abstract_id=228534, revised March 29, 2000.

Ludwig, Jens, and Philip J. Cook, eds. 2003. *Evaluating Gun Policy*. Washington, DC: Brookings Institution.

May, David C. 1999. "Scared Kids, Unattached Kids, or Peer Pressure: Why Do Students Carry Firearms to School?" *Youth and Society* 31 (1): 100–127.

McCall, Dorothy. 1969. *The Theatre of Jean-Paul Sartre*. New York: Columbia University Press.

Meares, Tracey L. 1997. "It's a Question of Connections." *Valparaiso University Law Review* 31:579–96.

———. 1998a. "Social Organization and Drug Law Enforcement." *American Criminal Law Review* 35:191–227.

———. 1998b. "Place and Crime." *Chicago-Kent Law Review* 73:669–705.

Mears, Daniel P. 2000. "Assessing the Effectiveness of Juvenile Justice Reforms: A Closer Look at the Criteria and the Impacts on Diverse Stakeholders." *Law and Policy* 22 (2): 175–202.

Mednick, Sarnoff S., Terrie E. Moffitt, and Susan A. Stack, eds. 1987. *The Causes of Crime: New Biological Approaches.* Cambridge: Cambridge University Press.

Merton, Robert K. 1938. "Social Structure and Anomie." *American Sociological Review* 3:672–82.

Mishler, Elliot G. 1986. *Research Interviewing: Context and Narrative.* Cambridge, MA: Harvard University Press.

Mohr, John W. 1998. "Measuring Meaning Structures." *Annual Review of Sociology* 24:345–70.

———. 2000. "Introduction: Structures, Institutions, and Cultural Analysis." *Poetics* 27:57–68.

Mohr, John W., and Vincent Duquenne. 1997. "The Duality of Culture and Practice: Poverty Relief in New York City, 1888–1917." *Theory and Society* 26:305–56.

Morrill, Calvin, Christine Yalda, Madelaine Adelman, Michael Musheno, and Cindy Bejarano. 2000. "Telling Tales in School: Youth Culture and Conflict Narratives." *Law and Society Review* 34:521–66.

Moynihan, Daniel Patrick. 1965. *The Negro Family: The Case for National Action.* Washington, DC: U.S. Government Printing Office.

Murtha, Lynn, and Suzanne L. Smith. 1994. "'An Ounce of Prevention . . .': Restriction versus Proaction in American Gun Violence Policies." *St. John's Journal of Legal Commentary* 10:205–35.

Myers, David L. 1999. "Excluding Violent Youths from Juvenile Court: The Effectiveness of Legislative Waiver." PhD diss. Available at http://www.preventingcrime.org/r2/index.html.

Myers, Gail P., Gene A. McGrady, Clementine Marrow, and Charles W. Mueller. 1997. "Weapon Carrying among Black Adolescents: A Social Network Perspective." *American Journal of Public Health* 87 (6): 1038–40.

Page, Randy M., and Jon Hammermeister. 1997. "Weapon-Carrying and Youth Violence." *Adolescence* 32 (127): 505–14.

Park, Robert E., and Ernest W. Burgess. [1921] 1970. *Introduction to the Science of Sociology.* Chicago: University of Chicago Press.

Pettit, Philip. 1975. *The Concept of Structuralism: A Critical Analysis.* Dublin: Gill and Macmillan.

Posner, Richard A. 1977. *Economic Analysis of Law*, 2nd ed. Boston: Little, Brown.

———. 1985. "An Economic Theory of the Criminal Law." *Columbia Law Review* 85:1193–1231.

———. 1998a. "Rational Choice, Behavioral Economics, and the Law." *Stanford Law Review* 50:1551–75.

———. 1998b. "Social Norms, Social Meaning, and Economic Analysis of Law: A Comment." *Journal of Legal Studies* 27:553–65.

Pouillon, Jean. 1965. "Sartre et Lévi-Strauss." *L'ARC* 26:60–65.

Powell, Walter W., and Paul DiMaggio, eds. 1991. *The New Institutionalism in Organizational Analysis*. Chicago: University of Chicago Press.

Putnam, Robert D. 2000. *Bowling Alone: The Collapse and Revival of American Community*. New York: Simon and Schuster.

Raphael, Steven, and Jens Ludwig. 2003. "Do Prison Sentence Enhancements Reduce Gun Crime? The Case of Project Exile." In *Evaluating Gun Policy*, ed. Jens Ludwig and Philip J. Cook, 251–86. Washington, DC: Brookings Institution.

Reno, Janet. 2000. "Promising Strategies to Reduce Gun Violence." Publication of the Office of Juvenile Justice and Delinquency Prevention, U.S. Department of Justice. Available at http://www.ojjdp.ncjrs.org/pubs/gun_violence/contents.html.

Richman, Daniel C. 2001. "'Project Exile' and the Allocation of Federal Law Enforcement Authority." *Arizona Law Review* 43:369.

———. 2003. "'Project Exile' and the Allocation of Federal Law Enforcement Authority." In *Guns, Crime, and Punishment in America*, ed. Bernard E. Harcourt, 321–42. New York: New York University Press.

Riley, K. Jack. 1999. "1998 Annual Report on Drug Use among Adult and Juvenile Arrestees." National Institute of Justice Arrestee Drug Abuse Monitoring Program.

Roberts, C. W. 1989. "Other Than Counting Words: A Linguistic Approach to Content Analysis." *Social Forces* 68:147–77.

Roberts, Dorothy E. 1993. "Crime, Race, and Reproduction." *Tulane Law Review* 67:1945–77.

———. 1999. "Foreword: Race, Vagueness, and the Social Meaning of Order-Maintenance Policing." *Journal of Criminal Law and Criminology* 89:775–836.

Rosen, Lawrence. 1971. "Language, History, and the Logic of Inquiry in Lévi-Strauss and Sartre." *History and Theory* 10 (3): 269–94.

Rosenfeld, Richard, and Scott H. Decker. 1996. "Consent to Search and Seize: Evaluating an Innovative Youth Firearm Suppression Program." *Law and Contemporary Problems* 59:197–220.

Roth, Jeffrey. 1998. "The Detroit Handgun Intervention Program: A Court-Based Program for Youthful Handgun Offenders." *NIJ Research Preview*, November.

Sampson, Robert J. 1987. "Urban Black Violence: The Effect of Male Joblessness and Family Disruption." *American Journal of Sociology* 93:348–82.

Sampson, Robert J., and Stephen W. Raudenbush. 1999. "Systematic Social Observation of Public Spaces: A New Look at Disorder in Urban Neighborhoods." *American Journal of Sociology* 105 (3): 603–51.

Sartre, Jean-Paul. 1943. *L'être et le néant*. Paris: Gallimard.

———. 1948. *Les mains sales*. Paris: Gallimard.

———. 1958. *L'existentialisme est un humanisme*. Paris: Éditions Nagel.

———. 1965. "L'écrivain et sa langue" (interview with Pierre Verstraeten). *Revue d'Esthétique* 3–4:306–34.

———. 1966. "Jean-Paul Sartre répond" (interview with Bernard Pingaud). *L'ARC*, 30:87–96.

———. 1976. *Sartre on Theater*. Ed. Michel Contat and Michel Rybalka. New York: Pantheon.

Saussure, Ferdinand de. 1989. *Course in General Linguistics*. La Salle, IL: Open Court.

Scheff, Thomas. 1998. *Community Conferences and Therapeutic Jurisprudence*. Revista Juridica U.P.R. 67:95–120.

Schulhofer, Stephen J. 1997. "Youth Crime—And What *Not* to Do about It." *Valparaiso University Law Review* 31:435–84.

Schwartz, Gary. 1972. *Youth Culture: An Anthropological Approach*. Addison-Wesley Modular Publications, module 17, 17-1-17-47. Boston: Addison-Wesley.

Schwinn, Elizabeth. 1995. "House GOP Takes Aim at Crime Bill. Midnight Basketball Would Vie for Funds Available to Add Police." *Pittsburgh Post-Gazette*, February 2. Available on Westlaw at 1995 WL 3359140.

"Second Chances: Giving Kids a Chance to Make a Better Choice." 2000. *Juvenile Justice Bulletin*. U.S. Department of Justice, Office of Justice Programs, Office of Juvenile Justice and Delinquency Prevention, May.

Shaw, Clifford R., and Henry D. McKay. 1942. *Juvenile Delinquency and Urban Areas: A Study of Rates of Delinquents in relation to Differential Characteristics of Local Communities in American Cities*. Chicago: University of Chicago Press.

Sheley, Joseph F., and James D. Wright. 1995. *In the Line of Fire: Youths, Guns, and Violence in Urban America*. New York: Aldine de Gruyter.

Sherman, Lawrence W., Denise C. Gottfredson, Doris L. MacKenzie, John Eck, Peter Reuter, and Shawn D. Bushway. 1998. "Preventing Crime: What Works, What Doesn't, What's Promising." *National Institute of Justice Research in Brief*, July.

Silverman, Hugh J. 1978. "Sartre and the Structuralists." *International Philosophical Quarterly* 18 (3): 341–58.

Snow, David A., Louis A. Zurcher, and Gideon Sjoberg. 1982. "Interviewing by Comment: An Adjunct to the Direct Question." *Qualitative Sociology* 5 (4): 285–311.

Snyder, H. 2000. *Juvenile Arrests 1999*. Washington, DC: Office of Juvenile Justice and Delinquency Prevention. Available at http://ojjdp.ncjrs. org/ojstatbb/html/ qa268.html.

Snyder, H., and M. Sickmund. 2000. *Juvenile Offenders and Victims: 1999 National Report*, Office of Juvenile Justice and Delinquency Prevention, Washington, DC. Available at http://ojjdp.ncjrs.org/ojstatbb/html/qa139.html.

Stansky, Lisa. 1996. "Age of Innocence." *A.B.A. Journal*, November, 60–61.

Steiker, Carol. 1997. "Punishment and Procedure: Punishment Theory and the Criminal-Civil Procedural Divide." *Georgetown Law Journal* 85:775–819.

———. 1999. "More Wrong Than Rights." *Boston Review* 24 (2): 13–14.

Steiker, Carol, and Jordan Steiker. 1995. "Sober Second Thoughts: Reflection on Two Decades of Constitutional Regulation of Capital Punishment." *Harvard Law Review* 109:355–438.

Sterngold, James. 2001. "Devastating Picture of Immigrants Dead in Arizona Desert." *New York Times*, May 25, 2001.

Storm, Sandra. 1996. "Juvenile Crime Issues." Congressional Testimony of Judge Sandra Storm, June 27, 1996, Federal Document Clearing House. Available on Westlaw at 1996 WL 10829545.

Stuntz, William. 1998. "Race, Class, and Drugs." *Columbia law Review* 98:1795–1842.

Suffredini, Brian R. 1994. "Juvenile Gunslingers: A Place for Punitive Philosophy in Rehabilitative Juvenile Justice." *Boston College Law Review* 35:885.

Thompson, E. P. 1991. "The Moral Economy of the English Crowd in the Eighteenth Century." In *Customs in Common*, 185–258. New York: Penguin Books.

Tonry, Michael. 1996. *Sentencing Matters*. New York: Oxford University Press.

Traver, Daniel E. 2000. "The Wrong Answer to a Serious Problem: A Story of School Shootings, Politics and Automatic Transfer." *Loyola University Chicago Law Journal* 31:281–315.

Tyler, Tom R. 1990. *Why People Obey the Law*. New Haven, CT: Yale University Press.

———. 1998. "Trust and Democratic Governance." In *Trust and Governance*, ed. Valerie Braithwaite and Margaret Levi, 269–94. New York: Russell Sage Foundation.

U.S. Department of Justice, Bureau of Justice Statistics. 2004. "Homicide Trends in the U.S.: Weapons Used." http://www.ojp.usdoj.gov/bjs/homicide/weapons.htm.

van Meter, Karl, Marie-Ange Schiltz, Philippe Cibois, and Lise Mounier. 1994. "Correspondence Analysis: A History and French Sociological Perspective." In *Correspondence Analysis in the Social Sciences: Recent Developments and Applications*, ed. Michael Greenacre and Jörg Blasius, 128–37. San Diego, CA: Academic Press.

Wacquant, Loïc. 1998. "L'ascension de l'état pénal en Amérique." *Actes de la Recherche en Sciences Sociales* 124:7–26.

———. 1999. *Les prisons de la misère*. Paris: Raisons d'Agir.

Wagoner, Jay J. 1977. *Early Arizona: Prehistory to Civil War*. Tucson: University of Arizona Press.

Walzer, Michael. 1973. "Political Action: The Problem of Dirty Hands." *Philosophy and Public Affairs* 2 (2): 160–80.

Weber, R. 1984. "Computer-Aided Content Analysis: A Short Primer." *Qualitative Sociology* 7:126–47.

Weller, Susan C., and A. Kimball Romney. 1990. *Metric Scaling: Blasius Correspondence Analysis*. Newbury Park, CA: Sage.

Wilbon, Michael. 1994. "Midnight Basketball Is a Success." *Chicago Sun-Times,* August 21. Available on *Westlaw* at 1994 WL 5530865.

Wilson, James Q. 1975. *Thinking about Crime*. New York: Basic Books.

Wilson, James Q., and Richard J. Herrnstein. 1985. *Crime and Human Nature*. New York: Simon and Schuster.

Wilson, William Julius. 1987. *The Truly Disadvantaged*. Chicago: University of Chicago Press.

———. 1996. *When Work Disappears: The World of the New Urban Poor*. New York: Knopf.

Winship, Christopher, and Jenny Berrien. 2003. "Should We Have Faith in the Churches? The Ten-Point Coalition's Effect on Boston's Youth Violence." In *Guns, Crime, and Punishment in America*, ed. Bernard E. Harcourt, 222–48. New York: New York University Press.

Witkin, Gordon. 1998. "Anti-violence Efforts Show Few Results: School Crime." *U.S. News and World Report*, April 6. Available on Westlaw at 1998 WL 8126554.

Wright, Richard T., and Scott Decker. 1994. *Burglars on the Job: Streetlife and Residential Break-Ins*. Boston: Northeastern University Press.

Young, Iris Marion. 1997. "Gender as Seriality." In *Intersecting Voices: Dilemmas of Gender, Political Philosophy, and Policy*. Princeton, NJ: Princeton University Press.

Zimring, Franklin E. 1996. "Kids, Guns, and Homicide: Policy Notes on an Age-Specific Epidemic." *Law and Contemporary Problems* 59:25–37.

Zimring, Franklin E., and Gordon Hawkins. 1997. *Crime Is Not the Problem: Lethal Violence in America*. New York: Oxford University Press.

INDEX

Abbott, Andrew, 237, 257
Abel, Lionel, 144
ACLU, 181
action meaning, 48–49; definition, 55; frequency, 56
Adam, Karen, 19
Alford, Robert, 252n23
Alschuler, Al, 237
American Civil Liberties Union (ACLU), 181
American Handgunner magazine, 4, 6, 20
Anderson, Elijah, 138
Angels' Town: Chero *Ways, Gang Life, and Rhetorics of the Everyday* (Cintron), 182, 191
archetypes, 61–72, 118–19, 122, 230
archetypes, primary: Jesús, 61–65, 118, 119; Marc, 67–72, 118, 119; Yusuf, 65–67, 118, 119–20
archetypes, secondary: CMS-8 (John), 130–32; CMS-40 (Paul), 129–30; CMS-66, 3–7, 106–10 passim, 118–19
Arizona Department of Juvenile Corrections, 3, 16
Aron, Raymond, 135
Ash, Peter, 13, 74, 234
attraction meaning, 8, 37–40, 55, 56, 232

bad faith, 117, 120. *See also* phenomenological approach, subjects as signifiers; structuralist methodology, bad faith and
Banfield, Edward C., 181, 190
Barron, David, 237
Barthes, Roland, 110
Beauvoir, Simone de, 123, 160, 249
Beccaria, Cesare, 180
Becker, Gary, 180, 182, 198, 237

Becker, Howard, 181
Beckett, Katherine, 182, 214, 215, 228
behavioral law and economics, 109, 168
belonging meaning, 51–53; definition, 55; frequency, 56
Benhabib, Seyla, 237
Bennett, William, 183, 192, 193, 194, 195, 196
Bentham, Jeremy, 180, 190
Benzécri, Jean-Paul, 27
Berrien, Jenny, 207
betrayal (as structural element), 126, 127, 132. *See also* structuralist methodology
binarism (as structural element), 134, 160, 168, 250n18
biological determinism, 181
Black, Donald, 97
Blasius, Jörg, 26, 27, 28, 29
Blumstein, Alfred, 185, 186, 187
Bourdieu, Pierre, 27, 28, 29, 110, 145–56, 213; *Distinction: A Social Critique of the Judgment of Taste*, 27; habitus, 151–52, 157; *Homo Academicus*, 27; Kabyle house, 153–56; *Outline of a Theory of Practice*, 145. *See also* practice theory
Bourgois, Philippe, 100, 178, 182, 212, 214, 219, 231; critique of, 228–29; discussion of rape, 227; *In Search of Respect: Selling Crack in El Barrio*, 219, 226–29; postmodern critique, 226, 227. *See also* leaps of faith
Brady, Sarah, 189
Braga, Anthony, 188, 237
Bratton, William, 196
Breiger, Ronald, 28, 29, 30, 156, 237, 252n23
Brooks-Gunn, Jeanne, 202